From the Collection of
Dr. Glenn Loney
3 East 71st St.
New York, N.Y. 10021

The
Theatre Workshop
Story

To most people Theatre Workshop means *Oh What A Lovely War, Fings Ain't Wot They Used T'Be, Mrs Wilson's Diary* and a string of other hits directed by Joan Littlewood. But they were only the culmination of a story that goes back to the Depression years when the Salford Red Megaphones were founded to play to the dole queues. Theatre Workshop itself sputtered into life in 1945, rehearsing over a room in the Conservative Club in Kendal and touring one-night stands to remote Welsh villages.

Often reduced to penury, the Company only slowly gained recognition for their remarkable style and their ambitious repertoire, from *Volpone* to *The Good Soldier Schweik,* from Molière to Brendan Behan. They were more honoured abroad than at home until the move to Stratford, East London, and the succession of hits which brought as many problems as rewards.

Howard Goorney was himself a member of the Company for over 30 years, and many other Theatre Workshop 'graduates' have participated in the book, which also includes extracts from early plays and manifestos, and a complete chronology of productions 1945–1973.

The cutting on the front cover comes from the *Westmorland Gazette* in August 1945. The photo on the back cover appeared in *The Guardian* in January 1974 and is by courtesy of the Press Association.

HOWARD GOORNEY

The
Theatre Workshop
Story

EYRE METHUEN · LONDON

First published in Great Britain in 1981
in simultaneous hardback and paperback editions by
Eyre Methuen Ltd,
11 New Fetter Lane, London EC4P 4EE

Copyright © 1981 by Howard Goorney

ISBN 0 413 47610 3 (Hardback)
ISBN 0 413 48760 1 (Paperback)

*The author acknowledges assistance
from the Arts Council of Great Britain*

Typeset by Computacomp (UK) Ltd,
Fort William, Scotland.
Printed in Great Britain by
Richard Clay (The Chaucer Press) Ltd,
Bungay, Suffolk

To Stella, Alice and Matthew

Contents

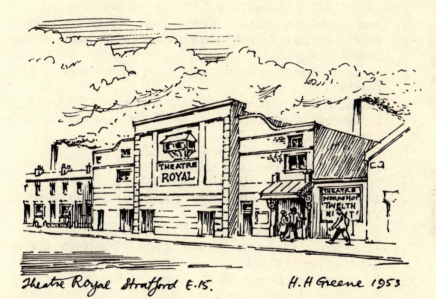

Theatre Royal Stratford E.15.   H.H Greene 1953

Illustrations and Sources

The line drawings are by Harry (Howard) Greene and are taken from sketches he made while a member of Theatre Workshop.

Preface

The writing of this book had its origins in a relatively modest project I had undertaken for the North West Arts Association in 1977 dealing with the origins of Theatre Workshop in Manchester in the pre-war years and its subsequent connections with that city. It was while I was researching this project that Ewan MacColl suggested I attempt something more ambitious and write the history of Theatre Workshop. As an idea, it was exciting, but I was far from convinced that I could tackle it, and it was only after a great deal of prodding and encouragement from friends that I reluctantly took the first positive step. I prepared a synopsis and Tony Adams, a publisher friend, applied for a grant to the Arts Council on my behalf. I was offered little hope that the Literature Finance Committee would be able to help me. Their task was to encourage literature, and my project hardly came into that category, but to everyone's surprise I was offered a grant. I received the news with mixed feelings, grateful for the encouragement, but awed by the confidence placed in me. I was also aware that having accepted financial help, there was no turning back and that I was now under a clear moral obligation to proceed without further delay.

In no time at all I realised that my original doubts and hesitations had been well founded, and that the task was even more formidable than I had imagined. How to present a factual picture of forty crowded years without becoming too dull and academic; how to make the story interesting without turning it into a 'coffee table book'? Two things were clear from the outset. Firstly, though I had been personally involved for most of the time, it could not take the form of an autobiography. My own recollection of events was insufficiently clear. I had been away from the Company from time to time, and in any case, a subjective account of my own life in Theatre Workshop, while not without interest, could hardly be described as a *history* of the whole Company. Secondly, though the name of Joan Littlewood is, in most people's minds, synonymous with that of Theatre Workshop and she would naturally feature prominently in any book on the subject, it was not her biography I was writing. My aim all along has been to try and concentrate on the group rather than on the individual contribution. All who worked in Theatre Workshop are a part of the history while they were there. What happened to them after they left, whether they fell by the wayside or went on to become household names is irrelevant to the story.

As to the form the book was to take, Ewan MacColl suggested it should be approached as a piece of oral history. By interviewing on tape a cross section of those involved at different periods, I was able to draw on a collective memory of events, and divergent views and opinions. By using these tapes as a source of verbatim quotation rather than as research material, and thereby retaining the differing idioms of speech, I hope something of the atmosphere of the events has been created in addition to an account of the events themselves. No one person has total recall, but by putting the pieces together, as in a jigsaw, hopefully the picture emerges. The facts relating to plays, places and so on were, of course, my responsibility, and I have done my best to ensure their accuracy.

It was only possible to interview a small proportion of the many people who have been involved, directly or indirectly, over the years, and the choice of whom to talk to was, to some extent, an arbitrary one. There is no-one who could not have contributed something of value and interest. The obvious choices were those with specialised knowledge; John Bury on lighting and design, Harry Greene on the building of sets and props, Jean Newlove on the Laban theories of movement, and so on. All I could do then was to try and make my choice as representative as possible, making sure that I covered every aspect and period of the work. I was aware that this left a great number of people who had worked in Theatre Workshop not mentioned at all in the text, but I could see no way of avoiding this. To have included everybody, over three hundred names, was clearly impractical, and for obvious reasons, I was not prepared to 'select' those who should be included. So the names that do crop up are in no way predetermined and occur spontaneously in the context of the events. I did also try to compile as complete a 'cast list' as possible giving the names of everyone who was ever a member of Theatre Workshop. This list appears in the appendix and I hope it goes some way to make amends for omissions of names in the text.

The Arts Council grant was the starting point for this long task and in my criticism of the Arts Council I am aware that I have bitten the hand that fed me. But, short of suppressing the facts, there seemed no alternative. The relationship between Theatre Workshop and the Arts Council was never a happy one, and the table in the appendix showing grants over the years speaks for itself. A company must prove its worth, of course, before it can expect substantial grants of public money, but twenty-six years of deliberation would seem to be carrying caution to excess.

My natural modesty prompts a word of explanation on the selection of the photographs. As I captioned them, I became more and more aware of the number of times I was writing my own name. This bothered me, and I raised the matter with my editor. He dismissed my qualms, pointing out that, as I had in fact played leading parts in a large number of the plays, particularly in the early days, it was natural that I should appear in the photographs. He reminded me also that they had been chosen for the particular insight they gave into each production and for no other reason.

The death in France of Gerry Raffles on 11 April 1975, after nearly forty years' work both in Theatre Workshop and before the war in Theatre Union, was a great loss to the many friends he had made in that time. I trust the value and extent of that work emerges clearly in this book. I had known Gerry for the greater part of my life – we were at elementary school together in Manchester in the thirties. We sometimes disagreed profoundly on matters of policy or in the handling of individuals, but I would not wish these differences to detract from my tribute to his memory, or from the sadness I share with others at his death.

Finally, I would like to thank all those who put their thoughts down on tape so freely, allowing me to make whatever use of it I thought appropriate; to Ewan MacColl for starting me off on this venture and for his help since; to Clive Barker for his wise counsel and for introducing me and my project to Nick Hern of Eyre Methuen; to Bill Bryden and Sebastian Graham Jones for their help and encouragement and for allowing me space in their office to write while I was working at the National Theatre as an actor; to Doris Thorpe; to Nina Lawton for her researches at the Theatre Royal, Stratford; to Simon Guttmann and Report for their help with the photographs; and to the late Frank Norman who gave permission, shortly before his sad death in December 1980, to quote from his book, *Why Fings Went West*.

There seems to be included in nearly all lists of acknowledgements, thanks from the writer to their wife/husband for her/his patience, encouragement, understanding etc. I'm going to do the same but it's no mere formality. My sincere thanks to my wife, Stella, for the many hours of hard typing she put in, having learned to type from a do-it-yourself book. Also for the many helpful suggestions she made. Her assistance was invaluable.

One

Drama, singing and music has played a part in the cultural life of the socialist movement since the turn of the century. But in the late twenties, as an aftermath of the General Strike, there was an upsurge of theatrical activity, and groups sprang up all over the country, under the banner of the Workers' Theatre Movement. They were openly revolutionary and agitational and concerned with the day to day issues of the class struggle, rather than more general political and social questions. Though they won support from a broad spectrum of the Labour Movement, they tended to be identified with the Communist Party and its policies. The W.T.M. groups rejected naturalism in the theatre on the grounds that it revealed only the surface of things, and not the realities of the capitalist system that lie underneath. They were committed to using theatre as a weapon in the class struggle, performing short sketches and satires, often in the open air. This style of playing became known as 'Agit-prop' – agitational and propaganda – a term that was to become international, linking together similar groups all over the world.

The origin of Theatre Workshop lies in one of these groups. Ewan MacColl, then Jimmy Miller, had joined the Clarion Players in Salford in 1929 as a young teenager to play in Upton Sinclair's *Singing Jailbirds* – a play in the repertory of a number of groups at that time. But Ewan soon decided that this was not for him. The play was too pessimistic in outlook and was being played mainly to the converted. To a youngster full of revolutionary fervour, the place to be was out in the streets where the workers gathered to protest against their conditions of living and where the day to day struggles were being fought. So in 1931 Ewan and a few others formed a new, young group, taking the name 'The Red Megaphones' from a famous German street theatre group, adopting later the slogan of the London groups – 'A Propertyless Theatre for the Propertyless Class.'

Salford, in the early thirties, relied on basic industries, and these had been hard hit by the economic crisis, so unemployment in that town was particularly high. The Group performed short sketches against the hated Means Test to dole queues outside Labour Exchanges, sometimes to sixty or seventy people. To keep pace with an ever changing situation, they developed a form of instant theatre; sketches written in the morning were performed to the afternoon dole queues. As the National Unemployed Workers Movement gathered momentum, it exploded into large and often violent political meetings and demonstrations, and the Red Megaphones were there, exposing in simple and direct terms, the Capitalist system. To an audience that was on the dole, no subtlety was required to pin-point the Boss-class as the villain of the piece ... Though the Group were in their early teens and lacking in theatrical experience and skills, their own backgrounds made them very aware of the problems that faced working people at that time.

A strict censorship administered by the Lord Chamberlain's office ensured that the established theatre in Britain was cut off from the political and social realities that were part and parcel of Ewan's own life:

> The West End theatre, or the formal theatre of that time, was not concerned with the lives of ordinary folk, and it had become stultified as a result. Its language was artificial. It was the language of the cocktail bar rather than the workshop, and the settings of the plays reflected this, in the sense that you almost felt lost if there wasn't a french window or a Tudor fireplace. We felt that the heroes of the theatre had to change, that conflict had to be brought back. That the theatre had to reflect what was happening immediately around us, and the problems of a society in the throes of a world economic crisis, with a third of the working population unemployed.

However the Red Megaphones had no illusions that their work was going to change the shape of British theatre. Their immediate political task was to forge themselves into a useful weapon in the class struggle, learning as they went along, for there was no-one to teach them.

The essence of street theatre lay in its simplicity and directness. The actors who represented types rather than individual characters were of the same class and background as the audience, so there was no gap between them. The directness of the approach made the onlooker feel part of the performance rather than simply a passive spectator.

Props and costumes were minimal. The three actors in 'Rent, Interest and Profit' all wore identical clothes – bib and brace overalls and top hats with 'R. I.' and 'P.' on them. The worker, identified by the cloth cap he was wearing, starts out as a victim but ends up the victor.

In 1930–32 there erupted all over Lancashire the strikes of the cotton workers against the introduction of eight-loom working in the mills, and the Group involved itself completely in this widespread movement of protest. Many of the looms were now over a hundred years old, and handling four was difficult enough. Coping with eight would be well-nigh impossible apart from the further unemployment that would be created.

Because of the craft nature of the cotton industry it was impossible to organise a general strike. There were numerous craft unions, varying in size from less than a hundred members to many thousands. To complicate the situation still further, different textiles were manufactured in different towns, velvets in one, poplins in another and so on. So the problems varied from town to town, and even from mill to mill. The Group had to be adaptable and do what they could to help bring about some measure of unity amongst the mill workers. They were back to instant theatre; arriving at a mill where a strike decision was about to be made, collecting the facts during the morning tea-break, writing a sketch and performing during the lunch-break. The aim was to link up the struggle from mill to mill and, by bringing in news from other areas, to try and reduce the feeling of isolation.

As the cotton strikes spread over North Lancashire, the Group would travel, by public transport, from town to town, covering a wide area, dramatising the day-to-day issues, and joining in the marches and demonstrations. The police kept them on the move. In Wigan, for example, on a Saturday afternoon they played a sketch, written on the journey up, to an audience of football supporters coming from a match, followed by ten minutes at the market place, a few satirical songs on the steps of the Public Baths and a short play outside a factory gate. They collected money for the strikers, going from door to door with a barrel organ. Ewan recalled:

It was deadly serious, we believed we were helping to change the course of history, and we'd begun to believe we were changing the course of theatrical history.

Ewan, with the help of two girls in the Group who had worked in the mills, and so had the benefit of first-hand experience, wrote the scripts, and also directed. This mainly consisted of drilling the chorus moves and lines and speeding up the cues. Rehearsals were held in the evenings in the cellar of the Workers' Arts club, which stood behind the Gasworks on a croft in Salford. It was used for boxing, snooker and Saturday night hops, and was awaiting demolition. The gas lighting didn't extend to the basement so torches had to be used.

Though the political alignment of the Group was close to the Communist Party, there was no direct link, only two of the Group being members of the Young Communist League. The Party was small, and the political tasks it set itself were many and varied. The emphasis was on the day-to-day struggle; 'cultural' activity, which included work in the theatre, was given a low priority. Those few Party members who were active in agit-prop groups were criticised for 'wasting time', an attitude which modified as the political value of their work became more apparent.

In 1933 an International Olympiad of Workers' Theatres was held in Moscow attended by twenty members from several groups, and it was clear from reports that came through that, technically, the British groups were lagging far behind and that the German groups, in particular, were very advanced. They were composed of professionally trained actors, dancers and singers, often politically committed, and sponsored by trade unions and political parties. They would travel to housing estates, factories and meeting places in large pantechnicons, which could be quickly converted into open air stages. The German groups started off with an advantage. Their theatre, generally, was much more advanced than that of this country; and the influence of Expressionism, with its use of montage and its reaction against bourgeois art forms, made for a more ready acceptance of theatre as political weapon. The British groups had none of these advantages or resources, as Ewan recalled:

> Our groups were pitiful when I look back, and in our area anyway we were all youngsters without even a knowledge of amateur theatre. We had no knowledge of the skills that were needed to work in the theatre, just a desire to speak for the people we believed we were representing. So we decided that we needed all the vitality of the street theatre and some of the acting technique of the legitimate theatre, developed and made much more flexible. Our actors must be able to dance, sing, play musical instruments and act! It was necessary to train from the very beginning and look at the concept of theatre in a completely new way. To draw on the experiences that were common in any working-class community, particularly in Lancashire in the thirties – the theatrical experiences of childhood, the street performers – escapologists, singers, tumblers – coming round the streets, creating a very lively kind of theatre.

Ewan was now convinced of the absolute necessity for training, and this view was strongly supported by another member of the Group, Alf Armitt. Alf was a lens grinder, and as a skilled worker himself, he realised the importance of skills and techniques in putting over the message in the best possible way. It was not sufficient to know what to say, they had to know how to say it efficiently. Speech and movement had to be disciplined and choreographed, and more time was needed for rehearsal and preparation of scripts.

By the end of 1933 it was clear that, with the rise of Hitler to power in Germany, and the spread of International Fascism, the dangers facing the working class were very grave indeed. The Unemployed Workers' Movement was less active, and the fight against the eight looms had been lost. The Group felt that the broader political issues that now had to be faced could not be encompassed within the limitations of street theatre, and that if the necessary technical advances were to be made, they must move indoors. From the purely practical point of view, most people were not prepared to stand in the cold for any length of time, thus making it impossible to develop any argument properly. Also, as it got dark in the evenings around 3.30 in the North of England, it was only possible to play during the day, which meant limiting the audience to the unemployed.

Some form of lighting was now needed, and having no knowledge of the subject, Ewan and Alf went to the local library, where they discovered the theories of Adolphe Appia, the Swiss scenic designer, on the nature and function of stage lighting. The implications of this discovery were to be far reaching, and they influenced the whole approach to all future work.

Appia believed in a comprehensive artistic unity on the stage; a bringing together of dance, music, lighting and painting, a synthesis of all the arts. He rejected the flatness of painted scenery in favour of three dimensional settings for a three dimensional actor, and a form of lighting which would emphasise, by its use of shading, the stability of the human form: 'Stage decoration is regulated by the presence of the living body of the actor.' He saw light behaving on the stage with all the flexibility of natural light, and as the visual counterpart to music. Rather than being used simply to illuminate a flat setting, it would combine with the three dimensional or architectural type of setting, and actually arouse an emotional response in the audience. This flexible form of lighting, which could be varied in intensity, colour and direction, was in use in many Continental theatres at that time, and has now become the basis of all modern dramatic lighting. Apart from a few amateur experimental theatres like The Unnamed Society in Manchester, Rochdale Curtain Theatre and Terence Gray's Festival Theatre of Cambridge, the British theatre still used light simply to illuminate settings composed of painted canvas flats.

To Ewan and Alf, Appia's theories came as an exciting revelation, resolving and clarifying many of their own half-formulated ideas. They made clear the whole relationship of the actor to the space in which he works, and to music, light and all the elements which went to make up the flexible theatre they were seeking. This was the beginning of a period of transition from a theatre which had been using, of necessity, crude forms for direct political action, to a theatre which was to fulfil Appia's concept of a synthesis of all the arts.

Playing on a rostrum, the steps of a Public Baths, and on the back of a lorry were clearly forms of three dimensional settings, so the use of steps and rostra in a hall followed naturally enough from this, but lighting had to be bought and there was no money. However, there was no lack of ingenuity, and the Group made do with what was available. Alf Armitt went out and 'acquired' a number of bullseye lanterns – the type used on roadworks and, using hundred watt bulbs, converted them into red, green and yellow spotlights. There was no means of fading them, of course, but it was a start, and they were first used, switched on and off at the suitable dramatic moment, at a declamation of Funarov's revolutionary poem 'The Fire Bearers' at the Socialist Sunday School in Hyde in 1934.

In the same year, the Group adopted the name 'Theatre of Action' and issued its manifesto (see pages 12–13). A period of rapid development now began, owing in the main to the arrival in Manchester of Joan Littlewood; but the richness of the political and cultural life in the city at this time also provided an important and quite unique stimulus. The strangulation of the cotton trade and the resulting depression and high level of unemployment had led to the rise of a relatively strong Communist movement and, at the other extreme, Mosley's British Union of Fascists. Clashes between the two were frequent at street corner meetings, particularly when held in Jewish areas, and at the large meetings held in the Free Trade Hall, uniformed Fascists beat up their opponents and threw out hecklers.

In terms of material prosperity, the gap between North and South was a great deal wider than it is today. Culturally, Manchester was the Second City, a position she has maintained to this day. The first Repertory Theatre in Britain had been opened in 1908 by Miss Horniman in the Gaiety Theatre. Many realistic plays of provincial life were produced there including several by the 'Manchester School' of Stanley Houghton, Harold Brighouse and others. Though the Gaiety had become a cinema in 1921, its influence on the cultural life of the city was still evident in the 1930's. There were pre-West End openings at three theatres, strong progressive amateur drama groups like the Unnamed Society and Rochdale Curtain Theatre, and in 1933, Walter Greenwood had written *Love on the Dole* (dramatised in 1934), based on his experiences in various unskilled jobs and in unemployment. The Hallè orchestra was flourishing; L. S. Lowry, Emmanuel Levy and Eric Newton were painting, and The Manchester Guardian boasted contributors like Malcolm Muggeridge, Neville Cardus and Donald Boyd. Socially committed producers like Archie Harding and writers like D. G. Bridson were experimenting in the B.B.C. studios in Manchester with new radio techniques and dramatised documentaries like *March of the '45*, *Coal* and *Tunnel* were classic examples of the imaginative use of sound.

It was unorthodox casting by Archie Harding that gave Jimmy Miller – he had not yet adopted the name Ewan MacColl – his first opportunity to use his talents on radio. The son of an unemployed steel worker, who had moved to Salford in the 1920s in search of work, Ewan had left school at fourteen and proceeded to educate himself. He completely lacked the conventional background or qualifications of an actor of that time. He was heard busking folk songs outside a theatre, and was advised to contact Archie Harding who, appreciating the potential of Ewan's 'unactorish' working class voice and accent, asked him to read a poem in a programme, and this led to further acting, reading and singing on radio. This enabled him to work in the Group while making some sort of living, and, while rehearsing *Tunnel*, he first met Joan Littlewood, who was also taking part. Joan had previously been a student at the Royal Academy of Dramatic Art, and, reacting against all she was being taught there and against the West End theatre generally, she left before the end of the course and went to France, hoping to find work with Gaston Baty. It was the time of the Stavisky affair, and fears of a Fascist coup had led to the closing of the theatres, so she was forced to return to England. While she had been at R.A.D.A. Archie Harding had presented her with a medal for radio technique. So, on being offered a part in *Tunnel*, she walked and hitched her way to Manchester. Joan was now very clear as to the sort of theatre she didn't want, and it was natural that Ewan's research and experiments in Theatre of Action should appeal to her. A long and fruitful period of collaboration began. To earn a living, Joan was working in the Rusholme Repertory theatre in the Hulme district of Manchester, not playing leading parts – she was still only in her late teens – but, according to Ewan, always stealing the show. When in 1935 Ernst Toller, the German Expressionist playwright, came to the Repertory Theatre to produce his own play *Draw the Fires*, which dealt with the revolt of the German Navy in 1917, he needed actors to play stokers, stripped to the waist, shovelling coal into boilers. The actors in the Company were totally unconvincing. Toller was in despair, and Joan suggested he use Ewan and his friends, who were quite used to handling a shovel and making themselves heard above the noise of machinery. This was Ewan's first experience of commercial theatre, and though the play was a good deal more interesting theatrically and in terms of its social comment than the usual run of repertory plays, the direction (by Toller and Dominic Roche), which confined itself to where they should stand and where they should move, confirmed for him all the limitations of this way of working.

Joan had collaborated with Ewan the previous year, 1934, on the Theatre of Action production of 'Newsboy' (see pages 14–17), originally produced in New York by the Workers' Laboratory Theatre. The plight of the Unemployed is enacted against a background of world events. Using symbolic figures, stylised movements, orchestrated chorus speaking, it moved at great speed. The conflicts were brought out by precise timing and continuous action, and lighting alone was used as a means of splitting up the acting area.

Ideally, trained dancers were needed, and these, of course, the Group lacked; but they fortunately did have someone who had a natural feeling for movement, Bunny Bowen, who earned his living in a steel works, and he was able to play the part of the Newsboy. Techniques had to be invented as they went along, and in solving the problems by experiment, they began to lay the foundations for future work. They evolved a training programme and read all they could about the great theatres of the past and present. Always their premise was a rejection of the conventional theatre of the time, its plays, its techniques and its method of training actors. They were searching for an aesthetic, a philosophy of theatre, and gradually it began to emerge, basing itself on:

(1)   An awareness of the social issues of the time, and in that sense, a political theatre;

(2)   A theatrical language that working people could understand, but that was capable of reflecting, when necessary, ideas, either simple or involved, in a poetic form;

(3)   An expressive and flexible form of movement, and a high standard of skill and technique in acting;

(4)   A high level of technical expertise capable of integrating sound and light into the production.

In 1934, Joan and Ewan attended a conference of Left Wing theatre groups held in London. They soon found themselves quite out of sympathy with the other delegates, who stressed always the content of plays and neglected the importance of form. Experiment in form was eschewed because 'the workers wouldn't understand it'. Straight propaganda plays, a form of Socialist Realism, were advocated, which Joan and Ewan now understood could only result in sectarianism and a preaching to the converted. The need to move indoors was perhaps the only point of agreement, and, in 1935, Unity Theatre was formed, committed to direct political theatre. It became obvious that, though they all shared the same political beliefs, when it came to expressing those beliefs in terms of theatre they had little in common, and Joan and Ewan, from this time, went their own way. Leon Moussinac's book, *The New Movement in the Theatre*, published in English in 1931, was an exciting introduction to modern staging and inspired them to find out all they could about the techniques of advanced Continental theatre. Direct results of this line of research were the production in 1938 of *The Good Soldier Schweik* and an early acquaintance with the work of Rudolf Laban. Scripts, too, were now being exchanged between Workers' Theatre Groups all over the world, and they could also keep in touch with each other through a magazine printed in Moscow by the International Union of Revolutionary Theatre.

Joan and Ewan now set about completely re-adapting a naturalistic anti-war play called *Hammer* which had been performed at the conference. They used no naturalistic dialogue at all, a constructivist set on three levels and a very disciplined, stylised production in which speech, movement and lighting were very precisely synchronised. It was retitled *John Bullion – a Ballet with Words* and the following extract shows how fully the action was choreographed:

THE SECOND MOVEMENT

– Which lasts for ten seconds. During the black-out two desks are brought on and placed down right and down left. During this movement typing is heard off-stage keeping time to the rhythm of the music. Lights flash up. Stylised TYPIST *discovered in an insouciant attitude on desk down left.*

1 . 2 . 3. TYPIST *takes imaginary powder puff* (1). *flicks it* (2). *powders her nose* (3).

1 . 2. MISS BANKS *enters* (1). *takes one step and is shocked* (2).

3 . 4. TYPIST *shrugs shoulders* (3). *plants hands on hips* (4).

1 . 2 . 3 . 4. MISS BANKS *takes four determined and offended steps which land her down centre. on* (4) *she turns and faces the* TYPIST *grimly.*
I / used / to be / his secre – tri – /

> *The words are spoken by a hyper-pathetic voice coming from off-stage.* MISS BANKS *makes four movements expressing the sense of the phrase. The voice off-stage repeats:* I / used / to be / his secre – tri – / *in the same rhythm. This time the* TYPIST *responds with four movements, then:*

1 . 2 . 3 . 4. MISS BANKS *moves to desk right, puts down imaginary papers.*

1 . 2. MISS BANKS *turns* (1). *sniffs* (2).

3 . 4. TYPIST *flourishes puff* (3). *makes contemptuous hand movement* (4).
He'll turn / you over / to the Junior / Director.

> *This is spoken by an ultra-unpleasant voice coming from off-stage.* MISS BANKS *acts it in four vicious movements.*

He'll turn / you over / to the Junior / Director.

> *Repeated by off-stage voice on a slightly higher note.* MISS BANKS *and* TYPIST *freeze. The back plane is faded up to reveal a replica of* BIRTHRIGHT (*right*) *and the* JUNIOR DIRECTOR (*left*). *On* He'll turn / you over BIRTHRIGHT *makes a scornful movement of throwing something over on to the* JUNIOR DIRECTOR. *the* J.D. *comes to life* (to the), *looks down his nose at* MISS B. (Junior), *cocks his thumb down disparagingly* (Director).

The characters were deliberately two dimensional bearing the names Sir

W. Birthright, Lord Winmore, Mister Fortune; and various theatrical
devices were employed. For example, a clergyman is delivering a pious
speech on the virtues of peace, which is taken up by a double standing
behind him. As this happens, he leans round the side of the pulpit and
talks of investing Church money in Vickers arms shares.

In the final scene, the mutograph, an electric newspaper which has been
projecting pro-capitalist headlines on the upstage wall, is taken over by the
workers.

> *Sirens are heard off-stage. The Internationale is heard faintly. It grows as
> the lights come up, and the sound and light drown the mutograph. The
> Internationale is taken up in several different languages. Workers march
> onto the stage from all sides. The two munition workers march forward to
> join them. The Internationale floods the stage, the typists are lost amongst
> the workers. The four DIRECTORS and PYE collapse like deflated
> balloons in a heap down-centre. The Internationale reaches a peak. The
> lights fade down to darkness and the voices are heard dying away as if
> marching into the distance.*

It was a far cry from the earlier agit-prop shows, and though the
conception was largely Joan's, she and Ewan, working together in the
production, were beginning to evolve a creative partnership which was to
develop over the years. Manchester Guardian critic Teddy Thompson
described Theatre of Action as 'The nearest thing any British Theatre has
got to Meyerhold'. Praise indeed. But not everyone was so appreciative.
Some Communist Party members took the familiar line that plays should
be simple, direct propaganda for the Cause. Others went even further and
accused Joan and Ewan of using their work in the theatre as a means of
avoiding day to day political work, of placing themselves above Party
discipline, and of behaving like prima donnas. They were actually told that
'Art and Politics don't mix', a misconception that still lingers on, even
today, and, after a series of bitter meetings, they were expelled from the
Party by the casting vote of the Chairman.

They had been offered scholarships at the Moscow Union of Cinema and
Theatre Schools, and, tired of the running battle with the Party, they
decided to go to London while waiting for their visas. They raised enough
money for their fares to London, and after a short time there, started a
theatre school in a house on the West side of Clapham Common, paying
the first months rent of £12 from money contributed by the students —
some of them railwaymen from the Nine Elms railway depot. The house
was furnished, after a fashion, by bits and pieces brought by those students
who lived in it. Ewan taught voice and theory, and Joan taught movement,

both of them relying on their instincts, and they themselves learning the whole time. After four months or so, it became clear that they were not going to get to Moscow. The visas had not come through, perhaps as a result of their expulsion from the Party, and even if they had, they had no money to pay for their fares. In 1936, they decided to return to Manchester.

Manifesto of the Theatre of Action

The commercial theatre is limited by its dependence upon a small section of society which neither desires, nor dares to face the urgent and vital problems of today. The theatre, if it is to live, must of necessity reflect the spirit of the age. This spirit is found in the social conflicts which dominate world history today – in the ranks of 3,000,000, unemployed, starving for bread, while wheat is burned for fuel.

The Theatre of Action realises that the very class which plays the chief part in contemporary history – the class upon which the prevention of war and the defeat of reaction solely depends – is debarred from expression in the present day theatre. This theatre will perform, mainly in working-class districts, plays which express the life and struggles of the workers. Politics, in its fullest sense, means the affairs of the people. In this sense, the plays done will be political. The members of the Theatre of Action are actors and actresses, producers, writers, scene-designers and other active supporters of its aims. All interested in its work are invited to become members of the Theatre of Action at a monthly subscription of 6d.

First public performance of items from the repertoire of the Theatre of Action
Round House, Every St, Ancoats

When the Theatre of Action was formed some six months ago, there were tremendous difficulties which had to be overcome, amongst which was the almost insuperable obstacle of creating forms pliable enough to fit any content, which could be cast to any mould.

It soon became obvious that no one specific style of writing or production would solve the problems of the theatre. We propose to show you the varied forms which our productions have taken during this period of growth.

JOHN BULL WANTS YOU
This is an example of tremendous anti-war propaganda. It was customary for these sketches to be performed in the open air, at street corners or at

public meetings, and so a rigid economy was observed with regard to stage design, movement, and even speech.

FREE THÄLMANN by Norman Hall
This is a mass declamation of the type which was so popular with German mass-speaking choirs prior to Hitler's coup. This is a German example of the open platform type of sketch such as *John Bull Wants You.*

THE FIRE SERMON by Sergei Funarov
A young American poet at his best.

A GROUP OF SONGS by Hanns Eisler
Sung by J. H. Miller. Eisler, who is a pupil of Schönberg, and has a considerable reputation on the Continent, has specialised in the writing of musical cartoons. A great number of his songs and choruses have been directly inspired by particular political events, and before the Nazi upheaval in Germany, these were sung at mass demonstrations and other political gatherings.

When Hitler came into power, Eisler was forced to flee the country, and all his published music, in printed form and gramophone records (some of which had a circulation of 40,000), was burnt.

(1) 'Lied der Bergarbeiter'. (2) 'Terner Streiker 40,000 Holzarbeiter'. (3) 'Report on the death of a comrade'.

NEWSBOY
Adapted in montage from the poem by V. J. Jerome, produced by J. H. Miller. One of the most pliable dynamic forms which has yet appeared is the technique utilised in this play. Its essential elements are conflict, mounting, transition and timing. As a form, *Newsboy* is a definite reflection of the quickening process of the clash of modern life. It is pitched at the feverish tempo of industrialisation gone mad. A scene comes and goes with the machine-like rapidity; push a lever, a character springs up like magic; push a button, he disappears, changes to another character. Conflict is the first and primary factor; within a space of sixty seconds four completely separate conflicts take place. The play is built on a series of images placed in juxtaposition to the ideology of the newsboy, and the attempt to draw him to a better level of understanding.

Newsboy
(Extracts)

SCENE I
Amber spot thrown on Newsboy. As the play opens the Newsboy, who represents the establishment bourgeois newspapers, stands in the amber spot

and shouts in staccato symbolic fashion the following words:
News Chronicle Empire (*Repeat.*) *Plans for Royal Jubilee.*
Six Kings at Royal Wedding. Cup Final Latest.

As he talks the spot grows larger till it covers the entire stage. With the growth of the spot comes the growth of the Newsboy, from a symbolic figure of all newsboys, to an individual Newsboy, realistically selling his newspapers. This is the transformation to the second scene.

* * * * *

SCENE 4

...

Enter Third Pedestrian.

UNEMPLOYED MAN (*loud voice angrily*). Hey Mister. How about a tanner for a bite and a bed. This ain't charity. I'm hungry.

PEDESTRIAN. Why don't you go to the Workhouse? What about your Parish Relief?

UNEMPLOYED (*harshly*). I told you I ain't looking for charity.

Pedestrian, frightened, searches through his pockets for small change. He finds a sixpence and with hasty fingers offers it to the man and starts to back away.

PEDESTRIAN. Here ... (*The coin drops*).

UNEMPLOYED (*furious*). Too good to hand it to me are yer?

PEDESTRIAN (*terrified*). ... I – It ... it slipped!

UNEMPLOYED (*growling*). Get out of my sight.

Pedestrian scampers. Unemployed looks after him angrily. Enter Urchin. Urchin rushes for the money. Unemployed kicks him away.

URCHIN. That's mine. I seen it first.

UNEMPLOYED. It's mine! THAT'S MY SIXPENCE!

As he stands there, the money in his hand, a sibilant voice (right) whispers –That's my sixpence – Following this, voice (left) ditto. Then voices everywhere. Voices of the three million unemployed. They come on to the stage, the same people who were in the Labour Exchange scene, with their hands stretched out to the Unemployed Worker, pleading for the sixpence. All the time they keep repeating the phrase – That's my sixpence – so that it sounds like the murmuring of a hungry mob. Above this noise are heard the following lines repeated at intervals of about 45 seconds.
Three million men and women.
As this line is said, the desperation of the mob to get the sixpence rises, and the voices grow with it till by this time they have practically surrounded the Unemployed Worker.

UNEMPLOYED (*raising his fists, crying hysterically*). Tortured in hostels with hymns about saviours!

> *All the other figures follow his hands, building a pyramid of grasping hands as they rise to the top. They do so saying the words:*
> Three million men and women!
> *Then, deathly silence.*

       *   *   *   *   *

SCENE 6

Played in the dark.

WORKER. It's not mine.

PROSECUTER. Be sensible Ali Singh. You know we're going to make you talk.

1ST DETECTIVE. Do you want us to knock it out of you?

2ND DETECTIVE. Come on, own up. Are you looking for a hiding?

PROSECUTOR. Now be sensible Ali. Don't waste my time. Say you fired those shots, and get it over.

WORKER. No.

1ST DETEC. You still say this isn't your revolver?

WORKER. YES.

2ND DETEC. But it was found in your pocket. It must be yours.

WORKER. No! I've never seen it before.

2ND DETEC. Don't tell bloody lies.

WORKER. It's the truth. I swear it isn't mine.

PROSECUTOR. Then how did it come in your pocket?

WORKER. Someone must have put it there.

1ST DETEC. (*angrily*). Stop lying. (*threateningly*). Now you little brown-skinned bastard, is this your revolver?

WORKER. No.

> *A loud crack. A yelp of pain.*

1ST DETEC. Is it your revolver?

WORKER (*sullenly*). No.

> *Another slash. A yelp of pain.*

1ST DETEC. Is it? Refresh your memory.

WORKER. No! No!

> *Two terrified screams. Three loud cracks. Worker cries painfully. Silence.*

PROSECUTOR. Now, Ali Singh, perhaps you will tell us. Is this your revolver?

> *A slight pause.*

WORKER (*almost whispered*). Yes, it's my revolver.

Pause.
In the silence, in the darkness, starting very slowly with pauses in between,
in a stage whisper, the following lines are heard, each word spoken by a
different person.
Tortured ... Framed ... Imprisoned ... Burned ... Lynched ... Murdered
...
These words are repeated three times, growing louder each time until these
words are heard:
Have you heard of Sacco and Vanzetti?
Then the words travel round again until someone takes the line:
Have you heard of Thomas Mooney?
Once round again, then:
Have you heard of tortured Torgler?
And again:
Have you heard of Scottsboro? Scottsboro?
Each time a different voice takes up the line. This continues until the last
time round, then the line is:
Have you heard of Thälmann? Thälmann?
And then the entire group, in mass:
Have you heard?
Lights go up on Scene 7.

*　*　*　*　*

SCENE 7

As the lights come up on the words: Have you heard? *all figures are facing*
the Newsboy, pointing at him. Their hands slowly go down as Newsboy
starts shouting headline:

NEWSBOY. Plans for Royal Jubilee.

He comes off chair, still shouting lines, and asks workers to buy papers. As
he touches each on the shoulder the worker turns round with the 'Daily
Worker' in front until there is a full line of dailies. Newsboy walks to
centre front, as voice talks.

VOICE. Get yourself a trumpet, Sonny, a big red trumpet. Climb to the top of St.
Paul's and blare out the news:
'Time to revolt! Black men, white men, field men, shop men − time to
revolt.'
Get yourself a trumpet, Sonny, a big red trumpet and blare out the news −
ALL. TIME TO REVOLT! TIME TO REVOLT!

Newsboy discards his own placard, takes up trumpet and joins in chorus.

Blackout.

Two

1936–1942
The Formative Years
Manchester: Theatre Union

'That this house will in no circumstances fight for King and Country.' This was the motion passed on 9 February 1933 by the Oxford Union, with 275 votes for and 153 against. It gave a great impetus to the Pacifist Movement in this country, and in the years that followed, up to the outbreak of war in 1939 and even beyond, Pacifism had many followers. The Peace Ballot in 1935 in favour of collective security through the League of Nations and against re-armament secured millions of votes, and even the Tory government, led by Stanley Baldwin, came to power in the same year on the basis of support for that policy. It was against this background that, on their return to Manchester in 1936, Joan and Ewan were asked by the Peace Pledge Union if they would produce an anti-war play *Miracle at Verdun* by Hans Chlumberg.

A very large cast was required, and with the help of the Peace Pledge Union and the Quaker Movement contact was made with amateur groups over a wide area of Lancashire. Students from the University also responded and provided the foreign nationalities that were needed, Nigerian students playing the parts of the Negro delegates. The Friends' Meeting House was put at their disposal for rehearsals, and Joan and Ewan divided the play up between them instead of working on scenes together, as they had done previously. This was only possible now because of the complete rapport that existed between them. Realism was the predominant style of the play, though it did include a scene in which the dead of the First World War rise from their graves and return to their homes. This apart, there was only limited scope for experimental ideas in the production and little opportunity to build on the work done previously in Theatre of Action. Despite that, it was well worth doing. It gave expression to the anti-war feelings of many people of different nationalities, and the opportunity to work together. The play was performed at the Lesser Free Trade Hall in 1936, and was a tremendous success.

There was a wealth of amateur talent in the area at that time, and casting a play to run for a week or so presented no problem. Finding people prepared to give the hundred percent commitment of time and energy needed to continue the work started in Theatre of Action was not so easy. Enough people did emerge from those involved in *Miracle at Verdun* to form a group, which took the name 'Theatre Union', and issued its first manifesto (see page 25). The manifesto issued by Theatre of Action had placed the work of the Group directly in the context of the class struggle. Thus, while still recognising the need to be involved in the social and political struggle, in line with the theatre's long tradition of social awareness, it emphasised the importance of solving the theatre's own particular problems. Theatre Union regarded itself as more than another weapon in the class struggle, it existed in its own right, with its own specific identity.

Artists and craftsmen with particular skills were now being drawn into the Group. They included Barbara Niven, a lecturer at Manchester Art College, Ernie Brooks, artist and illustrator, and Tony Popham and Chris Glover, technicians at Metro Vickers. The painter L. S. Lowry also offered to help. They were all attracted by the concept of a broadly based, left wing theatre, which was not content simply to play to the converted, but to as wide an audience as possible. When civil war broke out in Spain in 1936 it was decided, with this aim in mind, to put on Lope de Vega's early seventeenth century Spanish classic *Fuenteovejuna*, translated as *The Sheepwell*. This story of the uprising of the villagers of Fuenteovejuna against the tyranny of their feudal overlords mirrored in many ways the struggle of the Spanish people against Fascism and the forces of Franco. Apart from being an exciting play to do, it was hoped that this great poetic drama would attract a wider audience and hence more support for the Republican cause and the Spanish Government than any more obvious contemporary propaganda.

The decor group designed and built a set consisting of an abstract backcloth of all the colours associated with Spain, a beautiful large sculpted sheep and a well. Musicians too, were now working with the Group and an innovation was the use of 'live' music. Ewan composed the songs and tunes, but as he couldn't write music or play an instrument, he had to keep them in his head until he was able to convey them to the singers and musicians.

Though I was not yet involved with Theatre Union, it was at this time that I first saw Joan Littlewood. In fact, I heard her before seeing her. A committee meeting of a young Zionist group I was attending was interrupted by terrifying screams from the adjoining hall. Going out onto a balcony, I was completely riveted by a rehearsal that was taking place on the floor of the hall below, and particularly moved by the performance of a young actress. Later I learned that I had been watching a rehearsal of the rape scene from *The Sheepwell* with Joan, then in her early twenties, playing the part of the peasant girl.

Curiously enough, Patience Collier, now an established character actress, had a similar experience:

> Harold Lever told me he would like me to meet a woman of my own age, but of a very different type of character, who was also interested in the theatre. One morning he took me to the Free Trade Hall, up a long winding back staircase, through a small door, and when it was opened, I looked down onto a brilliant light, very very far down. The people looked tiny, and out of the light was coming the most wonderful voice, and it was the voice of Joan Littlewood. She was producing *The Sheepwell* and, after a few minutes, I turned to Harold and said 'Why isn't this woman playing great leading parts in the West End?' and he said 'She doesn't want to, she's not that sort of woman. She's here starting a theatre group called Theatre Union, and I'll introduce you to her some time.' One day he said 'Joan's always in a muddle with organisation, though she's a brilliant director. I think it would be a good idea if you came and met the Group and I'll suggest you become her organising secretary.' So I went to the flat of a painter, her art director, called Barbara Niven, and it was a glorious, muddly evening, certainly, and I was introduced to everyone. They weren't particularly pleased, nor was Joan, but they agreed with Harold because they really did need an organiser.

Harold Lever was, at that time, the Business Manager of Theatre Union. He went into politics, became Financial Secretary to the Treasury under Harold Wilson and, in 1979, became Lord Lever.

The performances of *The Sheepwell* were a great success, playing to packed houses, and were followed by more direct political involvement in the issues of the Spanish Civil War. Sketches and songs were performed at public meetings – sometimes involving comrades who had returned from fighting in the International Brigade – and house to house collections of food for the Spanish people were made.

It was over a year later, in 1938, that I first actually met Joan and Ewan. I was working as a junior clerk in an accountant's office in Altrincham, a few miles outside Manchester. Every lunchtime the Senior Clerk would pop round to the pub next door, leaving me his Manchester Guardian to glance through as I ate my sandwiches. One day I noticed that auditions were being held in a hotel in the city for a production of *The Good Soldier Schweik*. I had dabbled a little in amateur dramatics, so I decided to go along. Though I was only seventeen, Joan offered me the part of An Old Shepherd which, at the time, seemed to me very eccentric casting. I was to learn, over the years, that Joan's apparent eccentricities made very good sense; and I actually found no difficulty in playing the part – or rather overplaying it. Joan later described my character as 'the oldest man that ever lived'. I had no idea, of course, that *Schweik* was to be the beginning of a working relationship with Joan and Ewan that was to last over thirty years.

Patience Collier played the part of the Baroness in this production, and Anne Dyson, who also became an established character actress after the war, joined at that time to play Mrs. Muller, Schweik's landlady:

I had done a bit of repertory acting, you know the sort of things they did in those days – 'Anyone for tennis?' I was asked if I'd play in *Schweik* and I was plunged into something quite different. It was the training I found so useful. It was my introduction to Stanislavski, and it was a revelation and such a change from the mechanical approach to work I had been used to. We took exercises from his book, *An Actor Prepares*, and applied them to the parts we were playing – things like units and objectives, imagination, concentration and so on. There were movement and voice classes and relaxation – everyone knows about that now, but in those days, in the thirties no-one thought about it. I had no political background when I came in, and I wasn't really aware of the importance of the events that were going on around me, the rise of Fascism, the threat of war and so on. In Theatre Union, we began to see these things more clearly. Ewan used to talk a lot about politics, he was very well read, and had this incredible photographic memory. One began to adopt an attitude towards events, and out of the work we were doing, we came to a sort of basic truth. This has stayed with me since those days, and it seems to extend to one's acting work, the truth of what one is trying to do and the ability to discriminate between a good play and a bad play. The one luxury we had in those days was the amount of time we were able to spend on productions, analysing everything in great detail, dissecting right down to the bone and then building up again.

The script used for the production of *Schweik* was a translation of the German adaptation by Erwin Piscator and produced by him in Berlin in 1928. Technically, the production was a big advance on anything done previously; something of an innovation in those days was its use of back projected scenery. A group of technicians from Metro Vickers overcame the problem of how this could be done, when only a short distance was available backstage between the projector and the screen. A more flexible use of light and sound was also made possible by the work this group put in into improving the equipment. The performances in the Lesser Free

Trade Hall in May 1938 were a tremendous success and attracted more offers of help and support.

The amateur theatre was flourishing in the North at this time. Its standard of acting was reasonably high, and casting from its ranks a single play like *Schweik* presented no problem. However, Theatre Union had a long term purpose in view. It aimed to develop a highly trained group of actors and technicians; and the complete commitment of time and energy that this required appealed to comparatively few. The second manifesto (see page 26) was a generalised statement of aims, there was no detailed blueprint of the workings of the Group, and people joined for a variety of reasons. It developed and changed as it went along, benefiting from the growing understanding of its members. Those who survived the first shocks tended to stay a long time. The left-wing politics attracted some, while others like Rosalie Williams simply wanted to work in a theatre which took its job seriously. She stayed and was one of the founder members of Theatre Workshop in 1945:

> I was at university, at the end of my first year; a young, middle-class, liberal-type student, a member of the Stage Society. I went along to Theatre Union, and the impression I got was quite overwhelming. I was interested in movement, having studied dance as a child, and on my first day, Joan introduced me to Laban's theories of movement, something I'd never even heard of. The range and intensity of the training programme that Joan and Ewan had worked out, and the combination of their unique talents seemed quite extraordinary to someone like myself, coming in from an ordinary University training. Each night at seven o'clock we reported to a huge empty room over a furniture store in Deansgate, Manchester, and also on Sunday afternoons and evenings. We started each evening with relaxation exercises, lying on the floor. Then voice production, Stanislavski, ballet, movement and mime. If we managed to finish before it closed, we all trudged to the Squirrel, a very smart restaurant, owned by the father of one of our members. A long table was reserved for us, and we were served with numerous pots of tea in silver teapots, silver jugs of hot water and the best china, for which we paid threepence. I often wondered what the smart diners thought when we trooped in all dusty and dishevelled ... I remember the incredible library of books that Joan and Ewan had – you could study any aspect of theatrical history you wanted to. There were many books on art too – Joan had a great love of painting and it was always a source of inspiration to her. She was always telling us that looking at paintings would give us stimulus and ideas,

and I'm sure they always had a great influence on her work.
International tensions and the threat of war were all around us, and I
am amazed at how politically naive I must have been when I came
into Theatre Union; but Ewan's extraordinary vision and insight
soon encouraged in us a political awareness. This was necessary, but
at no time was artistic excellence and integrity sacrificed to political
expediency. We felt the revolution was going to come, and we had to
prepare for it by building up the finest theatre we could.

... Alongside the practical work, we studied the periods of
popular theatre and their dramaturgy – the Greeks, Molière, the
Elizabethans, the Spanish theatre of Cervantes, trying to find out
what they had in common that had appealed to ordinary people and
which might provide some basis for our own work in the theatre. We
discovered that they all had a progressive approach to topical themes
in their plays, that they attempted to mould common speech into a
lively poetical form and that there is also evidence of a high level of
literary and acting skills. So, from the beginning, we tried to give our
own work some sort of historical perspective, and by also studying
present day theatre in America and the Soviet Union we were able to
learn from what was best in the theatre of our own time. There were
no guidelines to follow and our training was very much an intuitive
process, a period of experimenting and trying out.

Those of us who were lucky enough to have jobs regarded them as a
necessary evil, providing the money for necessities and a bit over to help
out those who were on the dole. Our real work was in the theatre. Joan
and Ewan were able, for a while, to continue their freelance acting and
writing for the B.B.C. We seemed to be able to manage on very little,
perhaps because all our spare time was spent working together. The
flourishing artistic and cultural life of Manchester, plus a vigorous Radical
movement, gave stimulus to the work of the Group. Help was forthcoming
from many quarters, local Jewish businessmen provided materials for
costumes and sets, truck drivers helped out with transport, and the
Manchester press gave serious consideration to productions, even when
the political views expressed ran counter to their own. This affinity with
Manchester and its community expressed itself in the second manifesto,
and it continued after the war when, as Theatre Workshop, the Group
returned again and again to the city.

The next major production, at the beginning of 1939, *The Masters of
Time* by Irvin Kocherga, a Soviet play about the Revolution, was not a
success. It was conventional in style, required naturalistic acting, which the
Group were unused to, and its static quality gave little scope for

imaginative production. This was the period of appeasement of Nazi Germany, the Munich Agreement, and Chamberlain's 'Peace in Our Time'. Political feelings were running high. Public meetings called for a united front with France and the Soviet Union which, it was felt, would halt Nazi aggression, and Theatre Union took part in these meetings with songs and sketches. Despite the sacrifice of Czechoslovakia to Hitler, war broke out in September 1939. In March 1940, in the Round House in Ancoats, Manchester, Theatre Union produced its most ambitious Living Newspaper in the form of a political bombshell called *Last Edition*. It dealt with national and international events from 1934 to 1940 and was based on a research carried out by the whole Company. We were each given a specific subject – say, the Gresford Pit disaster – went off to the Reference Library, and came back with as much information as possible, in the form of facts, not just comment or opinion. Ewan and Joan would decide on the most effective way of presenting each scene, and Ewan would write it:

> We never stopped working on the script. Political situations changed overnight, a juror from the Gresford Trial died and his deathbed statement was incorporated into the show. The staging was a big development on anything we had done before. We'd use the platform available in the hall, plus two other longer platforms that went along the side of the hall so the audience was surrounded on three sides with action; sometimes on all three simultaneously! It was very exciting theatre and lent itself to all sorts of ideas. For instance, we divided the central stage at the back into various levels, each having a different function, one for world events, one for national, one for local. We made use of a lot of the production techniques we had used over the years and we now had a group of people who were used to working together with a common vision of the theatre and a common vision of the world.

In *Last Edition* were amalgamated all the styles that had been used since the days of street theatre (see pages 28–36) – fantasy, satire, agit-prop, music hall, folk song and dance. In content, it covered the plight of the unemployed in the thirties, the Gresford pit disaster and the trial that followed, the Anglo-German naval agreement, the Spanish Civil War, the Finnish-Soviet war, and Munich. The final scene urged the workers not to sacrifice themselves for the capitalist system which in peacetime exploited them; they had nothing to gain by fighting each other, the real enemy was at home. This reflected the view that the only war that could be supported was the class war and that international conflict was against the interests of the working class of all countries who always bore the brunt of the hostilities. This admittedly minority view needs to be set in the context of the refusal of the Western powers to co-operate with the Soviet Union in the pre-war years when the outbreak of hostilities might have been prevented.

Play censorship still existed at this time, and all scripts had to be submitted to the Lord Chamberlain's office for approval. It was all too obvious he would object to most of *Last Edition*, not least to our portrayal of Neville Chamberlain, and many other establishment figures. It was decided to form a club which anyone could join for a nominal sixpence. The response was good, and *Last Edition* played to enthusiastic audiences. Despite the device of club membership, Joan and Ewan were taken to court, where they were bound over for two years, with a surety of twenty pounds each. The real object of the prosecution, which was to have the show taken off, succeeded, but not before it had played to several thousand people in Manchester and some of the small surrounding towns.

To replace our rehearsal room, which had now been taken over by the Civil Defence, we had been offered, by the Vicar, the crypt of All Saints Church. It was gloomy and cold, and honeycombed with old family vaults full of coffins, but it was spacious, free and certainly quiet. We laid down a floor of planking, and commenced rehearsals of an adaptation of Aristophanes' anti-war play, *Lysistrata*. The period of the 'phoney' war, during which time no fighting had taken place on the Western Front, had ended with the beginning of the 'blitz' on London on 7 September 1940. A few months later, just before Christmas, the sirens went and it was Manchester's turn. Some of the Company had sought shelter in the cellar of a warehouse, but this had been hit by a bomb. They had got out unhurt and made their way to the crypt, but the church too was hit, and eventually they were dug out, suffering no more than cuts and bruises. I myself was on Red Cross duty at a hospital in North Manchester where I was working, and there too, the Nurses' Home was destroyed and the patients evacuated to another hospital.

On that terrible night, a world one had assumed would always be there was destroyed. Streets and buildings familiar since childhood were now heaps of rubble. The great warehouses in the centre of the City, stacked with bales of cotton, had become blazing infernos, the fires spreading from one to the other. Everywhere, streams of homeless people, carrying what they had salvaged, some pushing prams, were finding their way to the reception centres; a sight we have now grown all too familiar with. Some of the Company, too, were now homeless, and we had no place in which to work, but we were determined we would keep going as long as possible. We found a large hut, more or less intact, surrounded by devastation, which we were able to share with a reception centre for Jewish refugees. It was less than adequate, but we had to manage as best we could.

We played *Lysistrata* in the Milton Hall in January 1941, and even managed to tour it to Bacup and a few other towns around Manchester. We followed this with *The Flying Doctor*, based on Molière's *Le Médecin malgré lui*, which we were to revive in 1945 as part of Theatre Workshop's first programme.

The last production of Theatre Union was *Classic Soil* (see pages 34–37) which was in two parts. The first, historical, dealt with the ending of handloom weaving in the cottages of Lancashire in the last century, and the forcing of the weavers into factories, then with the consequent revolt against machine work, the Chartist Movement, the Peoples' Convention, and its failure and dissolution. This part was based on 'The Chartists March', a documentary feature that Ewan MacColl had written for the B.B.C. The second part was an attack in poetic terms, on the whole concept of war and the needless and unequal sacrifices it entailed. It did so, not in the specific political context of *Last Edition* but in broader, philosophical terms. It was a plea for sanity in a world that seemed to have gone mad.

By 1942, it was no longer possible to continue as a producing company. Actors who were called up had to be replaced at short notice, often by unsuitable people, war restrictions intensified and petrol rationing and blackouts had made touring of plays impossible. A nucleus of the Group decided to keep in touch with each other in the hope that those who survived the war would be able to work together again some time in the future.

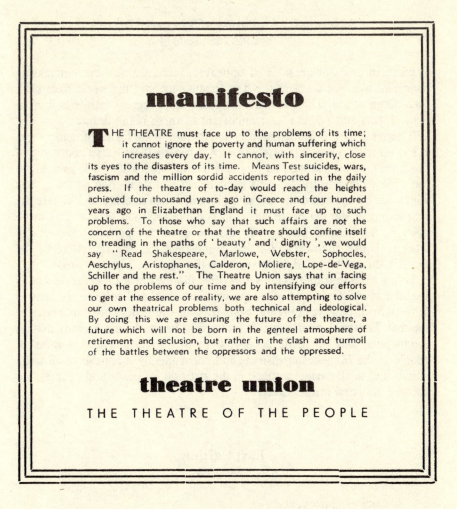

manifesto

THE THEATRE must face up to the problems of its time; it cannot ignore the poverty and human suffering which increases every day. It cannot, with sincerity, close its eyes to the disasters of its time. Means Test suicides, wars, fascism and the million sordid accidents reported in the daily press. If the theatre of to-day would reach the heights achieved four thousand years ago in Greece and four hundred years ago in Elizabethan England it must face up to such problems. To those who say that such affairs are not the concern of the theatre or that the theatre should confine itself to treading in the paths of ' beauty ' and ' dignity ', we would say " Read Shakespeare, Marlowe, Webster, Sophocles, Aeschylus, Aristophanes, Calderon, Moliere, Lope-de-Vega, Schiller and the rest." The Theatre Union says that in facing up to the problems of our time and by intensifying our efforts to get at the essence of reality, we are also attempting to solve our own theatrical problems both technical and ideological. By doing this we are ensuring the future of the theatre, a future which will not be born in the genteel atmosphere of retirement and seclusion, but rather in the clash and turmoil of the battles between the oppressors and the oppressed.

theatre union

THE THEATRE OF THE PEOPLE

I enclose P.O. value .... as I wish to become a member of Theatre Union at 6d. per annum, Unemployed Worker: 3d. per annum, Member of Affiliated Organisation, 3d. per annum (Please state organisation).

NAME, ADDRESS AND DATE:

✱ Please use Block Letters and State whether Mr., Mrs. or Miss.
Further Membership Application forms obtainable from
THE SECRETARY, THEATRE UNION, 111 GROSVENOR ST., M/cr. 1

ELECTRIC [C] PRINTING CO. LTD. [T.U.] MANCHESTER, 8.

Necessity and aims of Theatre Union
(Second Manifesto)

We live in times of great social upheaval; faced with an ever-increasing danger of war and fascism, the democratic people of the world have been forced into action. Their struggle for peace and progress manifests itself in many forms and not the least important of these is the drama.

Theatre Union is Manchester's contribution to the forces of democracy. It has set itself the task of establishing a complete theatre unit consisting of producers, actors, artists, writers and technicians, which will present, to the widest possible public, and particularly to that section of the public which has been starved theatrically, plays of social significance. Where the censorship of the period makes it impossible for such productions to be open to the general public they will be given for private audiences of Theatre Union members. All that is most vital in the repertoire of the world's theatre will find expression on the stage of Theatre Union.

It has been said that every society has the theatre it deserves; if that is so, then Manchester, one of the greatest industrial and commercial centres in the world, deserves only the best. It is for the people of Manchester to see that Theatre Union's goal is attained. Theatre Union intends that its productions will be made accessible to the broadest possible mass of people in the Manchester district, and consequently it appeals to all trade unions and to all parties engaged in the struggle for peace and progress, to become affiliated immediately.

Last Edition
(Extracts)

Munich – Gangsters scene.

ACTOR. Once again we return to the story of Sir Launcelot du Lac and Sir Sigismund the Black Knight of the Twisted Cross. You will remember how, when we last saw them, they had sworn a blood brotherhood. In the following scenes we see the results of this pact. In accordance with our policy of giving you as much variety as possible, what follows is in the style of an American gangster film. Sir Sigismund – or Siggy as he is known in the underworld – is expecting a visit from Sir Launcelot – now known as Lance The Umbrella Man. In the meantime he has summoned a meeting with Muscle In, the Italian killer. This scene is called: 'Who killed Johnny the Czech?'

> *Curtain up.*
> *A desk – up stage, slight right. A chair – left centre. Chair – downstage*

right. Two chairs – up left. SIGGY *seated at desk. He is smoking a cigar and has a hand of cards as if he is playing solo by himself.* MUSCLE IN *enters up right, flashily dressed.*

SIGGY. Hi Muscle!

MUSCLE. Hi Siggy! I gotta your invitation. (*He saunters down right to chair, pauses on seeing the other chairs.*) Say, what's the idea of all the chairs? A party?

SIGGY. Yeah, a party.

MUSCLE. On my way here I sees one of your boys. He says, 'You got a big job on. Plenty good pickings?'

SIGGY. Yeah. Plenty good pickings. (*He pours himself a drink.*) Siddown, Muscle. This is the biggest job since we cracked open the Spanish Bank on 38th Street.

MUSCLE. Yeah?

SIGGY. Yeah! I need your help see?

MUSCLE. Sure sure, Boss. A fifty-fifty deal eh?

SIGGY. What d'ye mean, fifty-fifty? What kinda talk's that? We fixed that you got the pickings from the Spanish job and I take the next. Well, this is it – see?

MUSCLE. O.K. O.K. I getya Boss. I getya. What's the layout?

SIGGY. Listen. There's a store at the corner of 18th Street kept by a guy called Johnny The Czech. You know him?

MUSCLE. Sure. He's gotta plenty big dough. Not so long ago he live in a cheap tenement joint in 14th Street. Now he's on velvet. He gotta plenty cash, plenty boys to take care of him, and plenty good business. Sure sure, I know him.

SIGGY. This guy's poison. He's got to go!

MUSCLE. But Boss, dis guy's plenty tough. Everyone of his boys packs de rod. My boys, dey tell me, every joint on his block packs de machine gun, and we wouldn't stand a chance on dose streets. On no, I tink dis is not such a good idea, yes?

SIGGY. Yeah!

MUSCLE. But listen Siggy. My boys don't feel so good. Look at dat Spanish job. I told de boys it was easy. But it took 'em three years just da same. Don'ta forget Spanish Joe; he was as full of holes as a sieve before he lay down. And I losta plenty of my good boys, and plenty cash. Siggy, you know me. Muscle In is your friend. But no, I can'ta do this.

SIGGY. Ease up, ease up. What do you take me for? A hick from da sticks? What do you tink dis is for, a ball game? (*Pointing to his head.*) Now look. (*He arranges bottles and glasses on desk.*) Dis is Johnny De Czech's joint. And dis is a speakeasy I control – the Viennese Cafe. Now here is the territory of Lance The Umbrella Man, and just across de street is Eddy, his echo. Now

Johnny The Czech thinks dese two guys is his buddies see? Well are they?

MUSCLE. Boss dose guys is nobody's buddies.

SIGGY. Dat's just what I think. Now listen, who is it that nobody loves? Huh?

MUSCLE. I don't tink dat nobody loves me Boss.

SIGGY. Don't be so dumb. De guy nobody loves is Joe De Red, see?

MUSCLE. Sure sure, dat guy gives me a pain.

SIGGY. Yeah. But he gives Lance and Eddy a worse pain. Dose two guys is scared stiff of him, dey'll play ball with any guy who's willing to take a packet at him.

MUSCLE. I getta you Boss, I getta you. You means you's de guy?

SIGGY. No, I mean I want dose guys to tink I'm going to take a packet at him. And in exchange dey double-cross Johnny De Czech. And then — well, I double cross them. A double-double cross, get me?

MUSCLE (*laughing*). Gee, Siggy, dat's wonderful. You tell 'em you fight Joe De Red, if dey take a run-out powder on Johnny De Czech, and den you take a run-out powder on them. You know what I tink Boss? I tink dat's beautiful. I tink you're a genius.

SIGGY. Sure we get de Indian sign on 'em.

Knock on the door. SIGGY *and* MUSCLE IN *dive for their guns.*

Come in!

Enter LANCE *and* EDDY. *Greetings are exchanged. Everyone is seated.*

Well boys, you know what my terms are. Johnny The Czech's joint in return for a battle with Joe The Red. O.K.?

LANCE. Well, I don't know. Eddy here ain't so sure. I ain't so sure we can trust you Sig.

SIGGY. I'm trusting you, ain't I?

LANCE (*reaching for his gun*). What d'ye mean?

SIGGY. Siddown Punk. Right now my boys are breaking in on Johnny's territory. All you gotta do is to send one of your boys over to Johnny's place and tell him to quit or else! Tell him you say so.

EDDY. I think that Monsieur Siggy does not realise that this job is so — difficult. Do not forget Johnny The Czech is under the impression that I am his friend, and the double-cross is not so good for one's reputation.

SIGGY. Aw, can that bull. Stop talking like a sky-pilot. Let's have the answer, yes or no.

EDDY. But, Monsieur, you forget Joe The Red. He also is Johnny's friend.

SIGGY. Yeah. Dat's where you come in. You gotta make Johnny break with the Red.

EDDY. But how?

SIGGY. You know how. Just give him some of that high falutin talk. Put it over big. Tell him Joe's bad for his health. And if dat don't work, threaten him.

Tell him he'll be taken for a ride, see?

EDDY *shrugs.*

LANCE. What about Joe. When do you start operations on him?

SIGGY. As soon as I've cleaned out Johnny.

LANCE. Can we count on that?

SIGGY. Yes. I give you my word.

MUSCLE. Sure, and I give you my word too. My boys' shirts may be dirty, but dey sure do hate that Red guy.

SIGGY. Is it a deal then?

LANCE and EDDY. It's a deal.

EDDY. And now that that is settled, I think perhaps we had better get back.

SIGGY. Wait a minute. The job ain't finished yet. I gotta make sure youse guys don't double-cross me, and I gotta way of making sure. (*He walks to the door and shouts.*) O.K., bring him in boys.

> Two henchmen bring in JOHNNY THE CZECH. *They shove him across the room.*

LANCE and EDDY. Johnny The Czech!

SIGGY. Yea. Johnny The Czech. We're gonna bump him off, the four of us.

JOHNNY. Listen Eddy, and you too Lance. You're ma buddies. Dis guy's nuts. You can't let him croak me like dat.

LANCE. No? You were tied up with Joe The Red weren't you?

JOHNNY. Yeah. But I was tied up with you too. Look, I ain't done a thing. I kept out of your territory didn't I? I kept to myself. All I did was run my own joint and try to keep de peace wid you boys.

SIGGY. Aw, can de sob stuff. You gotta go Johnny.

LANCE. Sure. And after you Red Joe.

EDDY. I'm afraid so, Johnny. It is destiny.

MUSCLE. Sure, dat's a very good word.

JOHNNY. O.K., O.K. But don't forget you birds, dat Siggy'll double-cross you. He'll two-time ya. Den you'll be on de spot.

SIGGY. Shut up! O.K. boys, give him de woiks.

> *They have drawn their guns.*

LANCE. Hold on youse guys.

> *He puts his umbrella up to cover the four guns. Shot.* JOHNNY *falls. Closes umbrella.* LANCE *takes a rubber ball out of his pocket.*

O.K. He's all washed up. And now let's play ball.

> *He throws the ball to* EDDY, *who throws it to* MUSCLE, *who is just about to throw it to* SIGGY *when* SIGGY *refuses.*

SIGGY. What's de prize?

LANCE. Joe The Red's territory.

SIGGY. No, I don't play.

LANCE (*to* EDDY). Did ya hear what I did? He won't play ball. (*To* SIGGY). You dirty little double-crossing rat. What about you Muscle?

MUSCLE. If he don't play, I don't play.

LANCE. O.K. This is war, war to the knife. This is war.

> *They all take up their pistols and fire.*
> blackout.
> curtain.

* * * * *

NEWSBOY. Disarmament conference decision. Anglo-German naval agreement reached.

> WORKER *approaches him from centre platform.* 2nd WORKER *comes from auditorium. They each buy a paper.*

JOE. Funny kind of a disarmament conference.

ARTHUR. Bloody funny. Ever since the last war Germany's been asking for equality. While it was a democracy nobody listened but as soon as Hitler comes they get a fleet.

JOE (*reading*). Lord Lothian says 'A stable Germany will ensure peace. Hitler has done much to bring order to Germany ...'

ARTHUR. That's another way of saying he smashed the trade unions.

JOE. And now Britain's going to help him to build a new German fleet.

ARTHUR. Yes, with our money. Listen to this: 'The Bank of England has granted a £750,000 credit to Germany in order to facilitate the mobilisation of German commercial credits.' That money comes from our pockets, every single penny of it.

JOE. Well, they can't squeeze me any more. If there's another rise in the cost of living I'll be paying the boss a wage to let me work for him.

ARTHUR. They'll squeeze and squeeze until they've milked you dry and then they'll take the skin off your back to make purses with. Hitler's paved the way for this grand ceremony, that's why they're so friendly with him.

JOE. And why call the ceremony 'disarmament'?

ARTHUR. For the same reason that they call hunger 'malnutrition' or a blackleg a 'loyal employee'. Because they want to give dung a fancy name and make it smell like a wallflower. Have you read what Sir Thomas Inskip said in an article to the Press yesterday?

JOE. No ...

ARTHUR. He said: 'In actual fact there is no great difference between the totalitarian and the democratic systems of government.'

JOE. He's talking through his hat. Why, you can't open your mouth in Germany without having the secret police on your track. Just read this, for instance.

ARTHUR. 'It is announced from Hamburg that John Schier and Rudolph Schwartz, the well-known German Communists, have been executed for high treason.' Now just take that news item. You be Johnny Schier and I'll be a Gestapo official. (*Turning to* NEWSBOY.) You be an S.S. man.

NEWSBOY. How can I be a fascist without a uniform?

ARTHUR. Don't worry about that. Fascism doesn't always wear a black shirt.

JOE. Well, what do we do now?

ARTHUR. You walk ahead of me three paces. I have a black automatic pistol in my pocket and it's evil-looking muzzle is trained on the small of your back, so that if I move the trigger just slightly the bullets will smash right into your spine in the way they did when Maria Engelman, a Hamburg woman worker, tried to escape from the camp at Oranienburg.

NEWSBOY. What do I do?

ARTHUR. You watch him carefully, ready to shoot at the slightest gesture from me, because you have been taught that Reds are animals. The Marxists stabbed Germany in the back. They burnt the Reichstag. Plotted to sell Germany to the Jews and the Bolsheviks. Marxism is a disease, a livid sore in the heart of Germany. Adolf Hitler has saved us from this pestilence.

NEWSBOY (*ecstatically*). Heil Hitler!

> *They have walked slowly centre stage and stand centre. There is a chair on it.* ARTHUR *turns suddenly menacing to* JOE.

ARTHUR. Sit down.

> JOE *sits.*

JOE. Where am I now?

ARTHUR. You are in the guest chamber of the Moabit prison, Berlin. Many of your friends have been visitors here. Some are guests here now.

JOE. Thälmann, for instance?

ARTHUR. Yes Thälmann. You were in touch with the illegal Communist centre in Hamburg. You had contact with the factory groups. You were in daily contact with Rudolph Schwartz. You needn't answer, we know all this. What we should like to know is who else was with you? Who were the others?

> JOE *sits silent.* ARTHUR *looks at* NEWSBOY *who advances on* JOE.

ARTHUR. Who were the others? You have a bad memory Mr. Schier. Perhaps our friend here can help it to function. We have a way with bad memories. (*He makes a gesture towards* NEWSBOY.) Who were the delegates chosen by the factory groups who were members of the Centre? (NEWSBOY *accompanies questions with short blows to* JOE's *head*.) You Red bastard.

You'll be glad to talk before I've finished with you. (*Strikes prisoner.*) Who were the others?

> *Pause.*
> *He hurls the chair away with his foot.* JOE *crawls to the wall.* ARTHUR *draws gun.*

I'll give you sixty seconds to open your mouth. Who was in the Centre? Speak, who was in the Centre? Half a minute left. Who was in the Centre? Better talk now. You can't fool me with your silence. I've seen too many rats not to know how to deal with vermin. Who was in the Centre? Who were the others? Your sixty seconds are up. Who was in the Centre?
Shoots the prisoner.
Blackout.

NARRATOR. Schier and Schwartz, the Communist leaders who, for years, have been engaged in stirring up class hatred in the Fatherland, were today shot while attempting to escape from the Prison Camp at Dachau.

> *Lights go up.* NEWSBOY *is on centre dais.* JOE *and* ARTHUR *are reading papers.*

ARTHUR. Now another news item.

*   *   *   *   *

NARRATOR. Honour for ever to the International Brigade
They are a song in the blood of all true men.
The men of each nation showed qualities of their own.
The Swiss formidable – their dour obstinacy
And their concentrated, fretful impatience when hot attacking;
The Poles – kind-hearted, romantic, dashing, and absolutely fearless;
The English treat the war as a kind of job that has to be done;
And they do it well – (the pacifists from the English universities
Making excellent machine gunners). The Bulgarians
Have a preference for the hand-grenade. They resemble
The Spanish 'Dynamiters' who storm machine-gun positions
With hand-made grenades. The French have the greatest number
Of deserters, because it is easier for them
Than for the others both to come and go.
The French who remain are men of prodigious valour
And impetuosity. The Americans are an elite
By reason of their sober courage
And their keen intelligence.
The Germans are the best that Germany can give,
(And that is saying much) – many of them
Hardened by persecution and with much to avenge.

Mr. Chamberlain was not moved — M. Daladier was unaffected.

The lights go up on platform, centre. WORKER *stands near left prosc. arch. Centre stage: a table around which sit half a dozen men wearing character masks, playing dice. At each throw they all bend forward and gasp contentedly. An obvious* REPORTER *enters down left carrying a notebook etc., pauses undecided, turns to* WORKER.

REPORTER (*tentatively*). Excuse me, who are these people?

WORKER. They're English gentlemen. The first is Captain Cassallet and the one next to him is Sir Arnold Wilson, and the next Lord Redesdale. The one in the centre is Sir Henry Page-Croft, the next Sir Nairn Stewart-Sanderson, and the end one Mr. Lennox-Boyd. What do you want to know?

REPORTER. Excuse me Sir — Captain Cassallet, I presume. I represent the Press, Suppress, Oppress and Depress. My paper would like your views on the Spanish Civil War.

CAPT. CASSALLET. Franco is the leader of our cause.

REPORTER. And your views, Sir Arnold Wilson?

SIR ARNOLD. I hope to God Franco wins.

REPORTER. And you Lord Redesdale?

LORD REDESDALE. General Franco is holding a crusade for all that we in England hold dear.

The REPORTER *hesitates.*

REPORTER. Excuse me Sir. Isn't Miss Unity Mitford your daughter?

LORD REDESDALE. I believe so.

The six men raise their hands in salute.

REPORTER. Sir Henry Page-Croft?

SIR HENRY P. I recognise General Franco to be a gallant Christian gentleman.

REPORTER. Sir Nairn Stewart-Sanderson?

SIR NAIRN S-S. I want Spain under Franco.

REPORTER. Mr. Lennox-Boyd.

MR. LENNOX-B. I cannot understand the argument that it is in our interest to stop Franco winning.

REPORTER. Thank you Gentlemen.

Throughout the foregoing passage, at each mention of Franco the six men stop the game for a second, raise their hands in the Fascist salute, and immediately go back to the Game. REPORTER *hesitates. Crosses to* WORKER.

REPORTER. Excuse me, but what are they doing?

WORKER. They're gambling away the lives of the Spanish people.

REPORTER (*going*). Well well, I thought they only did that with the English workers!

Blackout.

Classic Soil
(Extracts)

Part One
  Opening scene.

ACTOR. The play has started. The lights are focused on the central figure of the first scene.

A spot picks out an OLD WEAVER.

He is your father. He came before you. He fought for you against the darkness.

OLD WEAVER. We speak out of our graves marked with unscribed stones. The dust is in our dead mouths. We have lain quiet for a hundred years. It is too long. We who died in cellars speak to you who live in cellars.* We have a request to make, it is this. Remember our dreams. Do not let your children die – don't let them die.

ACTOR. They came before us. A hundred and fifty years ago they were born. And they lived in a small stone cottage which stood on the downslopes of the hills in Lancashire or Derbyshire or Yorkshire. In winter the wind blew cold from Pendle Hill across the valley below, and in summer it had the smell of heather in it. It may not have been Pendle Hill. It may have been Wadgate Edge or Saddleworth Moor or Pikanase, but the view was more or less the same.

YOUNG WOMAN. Work, work, work. Oh God, the noise of the hand-loom is driving me mad. It's making an old woman out of me. It's killing us Luke, I can't stand it. Will there ever be time when we can sit back and rest for half an hour, or when the dry wood-clacking of the loom won't fill the house?

MAN. We canna stop work or we'll get behind. We mun keep at it lass, or go under.

ACTOR. They were hand-loom weavers and worked in their own cottages. Every two or three days, one of them would go down to the village with the finished work and collect a few pence that kept a whole family going from one day to the next. Then more work would be given out and the routine of endless

---

* A reference to the air-raid shelters in Part Two.

labour would start again. But the machine came, and everything changed.

[*The essence of the production was flexibility – characters could change in front of your eyes. For instance:*]

ALL. We said we'd rather starve than work in't factory.

An actor springs round and becomes 'Overlooker'.

ACTOR. You'll starve then. The factory can hold out longer than you can. I'll give you three weeks to come crawling to me and in three weeks you'll be too late.

[*It moves from direct talking to the audience to a realistic intimate scene between characters. For instance:*]

ACTOR. The factories won. The hand-loom grew rusty in the cottage and the town grew up in the valley. Here in Manchester the population grew and grew. Progress was on the march and four fifths of the population lived in cellars.

WILL. Liz, how are you feeling lass? Are you alright? It's so dark in here I can hardly see you. Fancy having a child here. It's no fit place for any human creature.

[*This scene between husband and wife ends in her death and developes into:*]

OLDER WOMAN. You canna bring her back wi' grief.

WILL. I'll have to watch childer grow like her ... see 'em grow sick and old and the machines destroying 'em.

MAN. Aye, the machines are destroying all of us.

ALL. Aye. Smash the machines!

They all turn.
Blackout.

ALL. They've set fire to Arkwright's – they're smashing the machines.
They've marched to Kay's Mill and smashed t'looms.
They're throwing warps into t'canal.
They're smashing t'machines.

From the back.

They're bringing soldiers in.

Mass movement.

NARRATOR. Richard Lund of Haslingdon – shot through the stomach.
James Rothwell of Haslingdon – shot through the breast.
James Lund of Newchurch – shot in body and head.

Mary Simpson of Clough End – shot through left thigh and bled to death.

Movement back.

VOICE. Mills attacked at Accrington, Hough Hey, Blackburn, Darwen, Manchester. Windows and machinery smashed.

ALL. Down wit' machines.

Blackout.

Part Two
A scene of poetic prose between the young lovers. He has received his calling up papers. The time is the early days of the war.

CHRIS. Instead of sunlight, everlasting darkness.
Winter instead of summer.
They've plunged the earth into eternal night and turned our towns to jungles.
They have conspired with darkness and produced a blight upon mens' souls as blow flies to on apples.
All that is decent, generous in man has been forsworn by governments of tigers.
Progress, discovery and invention have gone awry.
Love is malformed, kindness turned bitter, hope an abortion, charity a bleeding afterbirth.
They've plunged the whole world into night's damnation and fed men's minds into a maelstrom.
Men are turned ants and labour at the instruments of their own death.
Gross toads have become kings and ministers of justice.
Apes are turned prophets and mouthers of sweet words.
Swine are become leaders of men.
There never was such darkness as is now.

JULIE. It can't go on for ever. There must be an end sometime.

An air-raid siren sounds.

CHRIS. Nature devised the lion's roar and the wolf's howl
And the cackle of the jackass but it needed man to conceive
Such an abominable noise as that.

Bomb explosion distant, then near.

JULIE. This is our last night together.

CHRIS. Not our last, dear heart. Perhaps we'll find a way into the light.

A warden hurries past. Then a woman.

CHRIS. We'd better go.
JULIE. Where to?
CHRIS. Where they have gone. Into the earth, the shelter or perhaps the grave.

They kiss. A loud explosion near.

CHRIS. Our love has made the tigers mad.

They run out.
Blackout.

THEATRE UNION
Presents

LAST EDITION
A LIVING NEWSPAPER
DEALING WITH EVENTS FROM 1934-1940
Edited by Theatre Union

AT THE ROUND HOUSE
EVERY ST., ANCOATS
on MARCH 14th, 15th & 28th, 29th at 7-30 p.m.
MARCH 16th & 30th at 2-30 p.m.

ADMISSION BY MEMBERSHIP CARD ONLY
Collective Membership fee of 2/6 per annum
for Trade Union Branches, Co-op. Guilds, Etc.

I enclose P.O. value............, as I wish to become a member of the Theatre Union at 6d. per annum (Unemployed Workers 3d. per annum).

Name

Address

Will you send ...... Membership Application forms for my friends.
The Secretary, Theatre Union, 111 Grosvenor St., M/cr. 1

THE BLACKFRIARS PRESS (T.U.), CLEGG'S COURT, CHAPEL STREET, SALFORD.

Three

1945–1946
Learning the Hard Way
Kendal – Theatre Workshop's first year on the road

Though it was no longer possible, in wartime conditions, to continue producing plays, we felt it was essential to try and develop our theoretical work and to study in depth the great theatres of the past, to find out what were the characteristics they had in common. With this in mind, we decided that each one of us should study a different period of history and exchange the results of our research, trying to maintain contact with each other wherever the war might send us. Many exciting discoveries were made in this way, for instance, that the character of Falstaff recurs throughout dramatic history from the pre-Roman Atellan farces, through the mumming plays, in Plautus as 'Miles Gloriosus' and in *The Three Estates* as the Braggart Captain; this led to the tracing of the antecedents of basic characters in the Classical theatre. So we were able to develop a greater understanding of popular theatre and the vigour of its language. The war inevitably took its toll; Graham Banks, who had acquired a profound knowledge of Greek theatre, was killed in a bombing raid over Hamburg and was sadly missed. He had joined us straight from Grammar School, a shy gentle lad, who, quite suddenly and unexpectedly, developed into a fine actor with his performance in *Master of Time*. Another great loss was Bill Sharples, a gifted sculptor and scenic designer, who was blown up in an oil tanker.

During the early part of 1945 it became clear that the war in Europe was at last nearing its end. The Germans had thrown everything into their offensive in the Ardennes in December 1944, and this had been defeated. The Russians had taken Warsaw and Budapest, and by the end of February the Allies had cleared the entire Rhineland. At home, the blackout was relaxed in September 1944, the Home Guard had been stood down in December, and in March 1945 air-raid fire watching duties had been abandoned.

Though I had had contact with Joan, Ewan and others when on leave and through correspondence, I was never quite convinced that we'd work together again, and was reconciled to the idea of a prosaic, if somewhat more secure life in hospital administration. However, for better or worse, this was not to be. When I was still in the army in Belgium a letter arrived from Joan urging that we start a full-time company as soon as possible. This was March. A month or so later I was in Manchester in my demob suit. How I achieved civilian status in so short a time is another story. The nucleus of the Group was now very few indeed. Some had decided, when it came to the crunch, against an unknown and uncertain future with Theatre Workshop, and others went into the established theatre. Bunny Bowen was still in the army and was to join us later. So Joan Littlewood, Ewan MacColl, Rosalie Williams, Gerry Raffles and myself met to plan for the future, in a small top flat in Lower Mosley Street, so near to Central Station that trains appeared to be rumbling through the adjoining room, making normal converstaion sometimes very difficult. Gerry had joined the Group in 1940 after seeing a performance of *Last Edition* and was to play a significant part in its work right up to his sudden death in 1975.

A few weeks later David Scase joined the company. He had met Joan during the war at the B.B.C. where he was working as a sound technician, after being invalided out of the Merchant Navy. He was to become a key member of the Group both on the technical side and as an actor. His lack of training could only be regarded as an asset as conventional training was geared to the needs of the theatre of the time and had little relevance to our work. The small experimental theatres were amateur and the emergence of Fringe theatre lay years ahead. Though there were productions of the classics, J. B. Priestley and even the occasional Sean O'Casey, the majority of plays being produced at this time were purely escapist, written for the entertainment of the upper and middle classes who formed the major part of the theatre-going public. Plays like *Kiss and Tell* by Hugh Herbert, Noël Coward's *Sigh No More* and *Under the Counter* by Arthur Macrae were typical of the West End successes in the immediate post-war period.

There were also the repertory theatres who, with a few notable exceptions followed the safe policy of playing the previous year's West End successes and the hardy annuals like *Ma's Bit o' Brass*. What was needed in the new company we were now forming was an understanding of what we were setting out to do, imagination, a capacity for hard work and no pre-conceived ideas of acting. Today regulated entry into the profession and the existence of the Equity shop would make it very difficult to take actors 'off the streets' as it were, and, with the new methods of training, probably unnecessary anyway. As a co-operative company, with no management other than ourselves, there was no Equity contract that could be applied, and the Union turned a blind eye taking the view that if we were crazy enough to work all the hours of the night and day for two pounds a week, that was our business – provided we were all suffering equally.

Auditions were held, and they weren't easy for anybody. We sat through several aspiring Hamlets and Lady Macbeths with perhaps a bit of Noël Coward for light relief. With the set pieces out of the way Joan could start the real audition. She asked for some form of improvisation. After recovering from the initial shock of being asked to do something 'off the cuff', the applicant's imaginative power – or the lack of it – began to emerge. Then followed the informal but all important 'chat' which gave some indication of whether he or she could work with us or indeed, if by this time, they still wanted to!

James Gilhouley, Nicholas Whitfield, Arnold Locke and Phyl Gladwyn were invited to join us, and Pearl Turner, an attractive blonde with a beautiful singing voice who had appeared in one of Joan's radio programmes, during the war completed the first Company. Our initial capital of about £400 came from the pooling of our savings, demobilisation money, and compensation Gerry had received for an accident while working in the mines. This would enable us to cover expenses during the rehearsal period and pay ourselves between two and three pounds a week, which was sufficient, in those days, to pay for digs, the occasional drink and even cigarettes, though, for a time, smokers received a small extra payment. As soon as we started playing, the box-office receipts would take care of things – or so we thought. We had yet to learn it wasn't quite as simple as that. We still had some curtains and odd props from before the war, and Emmanuel Raffles – Gerry's father – generously gave us enough to buy lighting equipment and other necessities; the first of many occasions on which he was to help us.

On 8 May 1945 – VE day – we joined the jubilant crowds in Piccadilly, Manchester, celebrating the Victory in Europe. I remember Gerry Raffles carrying me around on his shoulders, and as we sang and cheered we felt we were celebrating, not only victory, but our own joy at being alive and together again. These were wonderful, euphoric days. It all seemed quite simple. Fascism was dead. The Soviet Union was our friend, in peace as she had been in war, and together we would forge a just and happy future for all mankind. Our own contribution would be to build a theatre worthy of that future, and this, with all the confidence in the world, we were setting out to do.

A building in which to rehearse and play had been offered to us by John Trevelyan, Director of Education for Westmorland and a friend of Joan's. It was in Kendal and had been requisitioned during the war, but when the time came it was still not available. Nevertheless, we decided Kendal would be a quiet, pleasant place in which to experience our birth pangs. So we rented the large top floor of the Conservative Party headquarters, and during June we moved there from Manchester.

We worked long, hard hours, but we were doing what we wanted to do and life was good. For around twenty-five shillings a week we had comfortable digs and full board. There was no time or money for luxurious living but enough for the odd visit to the pub, and after three and a half years in the Army, what more could one ask for than an evening stroll by the beautiful River Kent, an exploration of Kendal's old yards and alleys or a Sunday hike in the Lake District?

The Labour Party had turned down Churchill's offer to continue the wartime coalition government, and a general election was held on 5 July 1945. The results were not declared until 25 July to allow time for ballot papers from service units overseas to be sent in. It was a Labour landslide and the Conservatives worst defeat since 1906 – 393 seats for Labour, 213 for the Conservatives, 12 for the Liberals and 22 Independents, which included two Communists. On 26 July, as successive Labour victories followed those declared during the night, our top floor echoed to cheers and jubilation, while down below in the Conservative H.Q. all was silence and gloom. However, they were not denied their moment of triumph. As the Westmorland result came through on the radio, with the election of Lieutenant Colonel Vane, Conservative, a small dignified procession, led by Miss Hilary Ovary, agent, carrying a Union Jack, made its way up the stairs, through our rehearsal room, and up a ladder onto the roof, where the flag was duly unfurled! It was a theatrical gesture we all appreciated, and, in our hour of victory, we could afford to be magnanimous. The swing to the left, which was echoed all over Europe, had been influenced, to some extent, by the enormous part played by the Soviet Union in the defeat of Nazism, and an emotional response to the sacrifices of the Soviet people. Basically, it was a reaction against the Old Order, and an expression of an overwhelming desire for change. What better time to build a Popular Theatre than in this time of post-war optimism? We gave no thought to the difficulties that might lie ahead, and our manifesto reflected our confidence:

Manifesto

The great theatres of all times have been popular theatres which reflected the dreams and struggles of the people. The theatre of Aeschylus and Sophocles, of Shakespeare and Ben Jonson, of the Commedia dell' Arte and Molière derived their inspiration, their language, their art from the people.

We want a theatre with a living language, a theatre which is not afraid of the sound of its own voice and which will comment as fearlessly on Society as did Ben Jonson and Aristophanes.

Theatre Workshop is an organisation of artists, technicians and actors who are experimenting in stage-craft. Its purpose is to create a flexible theatre-art, as swift moving and plastic as the cinema, by applying the recent technical advances in light and sound, and introducing music and the 'dance theatre' style of production.

Ambitious perhaps, even pretentious, but in our very first production we came near to achieving it. This was *Johnny Noble* by Ewan MacColl; a ballad opera which used traditional tunes and poetry as linking narration and drew on research done by Joan in Hull during the war. It brought together and developed many of our pre-war ideas on the orchestration of light, sound, voice and movement, and it merits discussion in some detail. It told the story of the love of a young merchant seaman, Johnny Noble, played by David Scase, for his girl Mary, played by Rosalie Williams, against the background of 1930's unemployment, the Spanish Civil War and the war years. All transitions in time and space were made by sound, light and sung narrative, as illustrated in the opening sequence:

The curtain opens on a completely dark stage draped in black curtains. On either side of the stage stand two NARRATORS. *A man and a woman dressed in black oilskins. They are pinpointed by two spotlights. Very simply the man begins to sing.*

1ST NARRATOR (*singing*). Here is a stage.
2ND NARRATOR (*speaking*). A platform twenty-five feet by fifteen feet. (*Or whatever were the dimensions of that particular stage.*)
1ST NARRATOR (*singing*). A microcosm of the world.
2ND NARRATOR (*speaking*). Here the sun is an amber flood and the moon a thousand watt spot.
1ST NARRATOR (*singing*). Here shall be space
Here we shall act time.
2ND NARRATOR (*speaking*). From nothing everything will come.
1ST NARRATOR (*singing*). On this dead stage we'll make Society appear.

    An acting area flood fades up discovering three YOUTHS *playing 'pitch and toss' up stage centre.*

The world is here.
2ND NARRATOR (*speaking*). Our world.

    Up boogie-woogie music. A WOMAN *enters, dances across stage and off. Fade out music.*

1ST NARRATOR (*singing*). A little gesture from an actor's hand creates a rolling landscape:
1ST NARRATOR (*speaking*). Or a desert.
2ND NARRATOR (*singing*). A word from us and cities will arise.
The night be broken by screaming factories.

> *Up burst of machinery. A red spot is faded up discovering a half-naked figure of a* MAN. *He mimes raking out a furnace in time to machinery. The light and machine noise fade out together. The* MAN *goes off.*

1ST NARRATOR (*speaking*). Yes, we speak of days that linger in the memory like a bad taste in the mouth. Come back with us a dozen years or so, back to the early thirties, to the derelict towns and the idle hands, the rusting lathes and the silent turbines.

> *An* UNEMPLOYED MAN *enters. Stands left centre, yawning.*

Here is the man of those years, a man without hope, without work, a man burdened with time.
UNEMPLOYED MAN. Time to sign on.

> *He exits. A* CHILD *enters, a small lonely figure in a pool of white light. She begins a queer, abstracted, hopping dance.*

2ND NARRATOR (*speaking*). Here a child grows up in a desolate land.
1ST NARRATOR (*singing*). Here is a street in any seaport town.

> *Two distant blasts of a ship's siren.*

It could be anywhere.
Where a man's work is the sea.

> *The pitch and toss players begin to intone their calls.*

1ST YOUTH. Heads.
2ND YOUTH. Tails.
1ST YOUTH. It's mine.
2ND YOUTH. What is it?
1ST YOUTH. Heads.
2ND YOUTH. Tails it is.
1ST YOUTH. My shout.
2ND YOUTH. Shout!
1ST YOUTH. Tails.
2ND YOUTH. It's mine!

> *Fade and hold behind following sequence . . .*

The 'Pitch and Toss' sequence and others, were produced with stylised, semi-dance movement; and it was interesting that these transitions into song, mime and dance were readily accepted by the audience as quite normal and indigenous to the play. They didn't analyse it or identify it as a 'style', they simply enjoyed it, though they must have been quite unused to this form of theatre. What we were presenting, though revolutionary in this country, was a development of ideas in staging that had prevailed on the Continent, particularly in Russia and Germany, since the turn of the century.

The evocative use of light and sound is illustrated in the station platform scene that followed Chamberlain's declaration of war:

Up level drone of planes behind the foregoing sequence. Cut in on last word with music, hold at peak and cross-fade with heavy ticking of clock. Hold behind following.

MICROPHONE VOICE. Passengers for Preston, Lancaster, Carlisle and Glasgow will leave on number three platform at 5.43.
ANOTHER VOICE. Not much time left.

Two groups of figures, each composed of a man and a woman, are discovered embracing in two yellow pools of light.

1ST WOMAN. Don't forget your sandwiches, Jim. I've put them at the top of your case. And let me know your address as soon as you get there. I'll send you a parcel. Must keep talking, Jim we must keep talking. It's queer the minutes are bleeding away and all I can talk about are the things furthest from my mind. Do look after yourself Jim, and don't forget to send anything you want washed. Four more minutes and it'll be the end. Oh God!

Towards conclusion of this, fade up clock backed by voice.

ANOTHER VOICE (*whispering*). Hurry etc.
MICROPHONE VOICE. The train for Crewe, Hereford, Birmingham, Pontypool and Bristol will leave number eleven platform at 5.58.
MARY. Go on talking, Johnny, please go on talking. If we stop talking we'll start thinking. Take care of yourself Johnny, and please write as often as you can. Oh so much to be said and no words to say it with. If you need anything just write and I'll send it to you. Only a few minutes left and then ... Perhaps it won't be for long. I'll be waiting for you. Oh, if only the clocks would stop for ever.

Ticking of clock at peak. Sudden high pitched blast of train whistle.

MICROPHONE VOICE. Johnny ... Noble ... Able Seaman!

JOHNNY *looks round.*

JOHNNY. It's time, Mary.

MICROPHONE VOICE. James ... Munroe ... Bricklayer!

1ST MAN. It's time lass.

MICROPHONE VOICE. Young men, it's time to say Goodbye.

> *The couples embrace. The men go off. The two women, lonely figures in the pools of yellow light, stand without moving. There is a sudden loud blast of escaping steam, and the women begin waving handkerchiefs. The train gets underway, and as the light fades there are two short, melancholy blasts of the engine's whistle as it passes into a long tunnel.*

MICROPHONE VOICE. If only one could choose one's moments of eternity. But inexorable Time divides and sub-divides again, until nothing is left of a moment but an acrid memory.

> *Complete blackout.*

We knew that many of our audience had themselves been in a similar situation only a few years before, and by deliberately not using settings to define the location of the station, we left their imaginations free to evoke their own place and memories.

David Scase, who had been a merchant seaman during the war until he was wounded, describes how Joan was able to synchronise movement, sound and light:

> She would pick out the one sound that somehow epitomised that moment, and with her direction and the right sound, she could create the most extraordinary effects. I can remember something she did which was absolutely brilliant. I was sitting on the deck and another man was standing. I was taking the pitch and toss of the boat, the forward and aft movement, whereas the man who was standing was taking the roll of the boat, starboard to port. So in fact, we were side by side, moving in slightly different directions. On the side of the stage, to emphasise that, she had the green and port light going up and down with the ship moving at sea. This was all there was on the stage, two actors, two lights and the sound of the engine going 'debum ... debum ... debum ...' People have told me they were literally feeling seasick at the end of the scene. Now this was genius.

David also gave an example of how Joan was able to make use of an actor's background and draw on his experiences:

> Five men and a gun, fighting off an attack on their convoy. Joan asked me to show what each member of the gun crew did. By repeating the movements over and over again, the orders and the

shouts, Joan actually created a ballet, a dance sequence out of it; but by incorporating realistic sound, bombers coming in, guns and shots, the scene had all the drama of a gun crew fighting off an aeroplane.

Johnny Noble ran for an hour, so to make up a double bill, we re-rehearsed *The Flying Doctor*, which had been in our repertoire before the war. It was based on Molière's structure plus notes made by Domenico Biancoletti, an actor in the Commedia dell' Arte. I was Sganarelle, the valet, and aside from the sheer pleasure of playing the part (which I continued to play on and off for nearly twenty years), there were 'perks' in those earlier performances in the shape of raw eggs! Posing as a doctor, I had to extract a 'palmed' egg from the housekeeper's mouth, a part played by Joan. I then had to break it into a glass and swallow it down. Though eggs were still rationed to one or two a week per person, Joan insisted the scene should not be cut. Sometimes a friendly corner shop would supply the nightly egg in the cause of Art. Failing that, my fellow actors had to hand over their ration, and a roster ensured equality of sacrifice. So each performance I had the luxury of an uncooked egg sliding down my throat, preceded, in the first scene, by a luscious peach. The odd bad egg served to offset the envy of my less fortunate colleagues!

Bill Davidson, who was to join the Company later, as an actor, was spending his summer holidays with us, and he was roped in to build the *Flying Doctor* set. It needed to be light and portable, but also strong enough to carry the weight of the actors, and as Bill was a trained engineer, we reckoned he would know how to do this. Joan wanted a round platform, twelve feet in diameter, supporting a wall, a door, and a window, and it was to be revolved by two actors, in full view of the audience. Bill brilliantly constructed it on aeroplane principles, using a system of tensioned wires. The platform was in two halves, and the flats, canvassed and painted on both sides, slotted into metal pockets. It was made in the carpentry workshop at the local boys' school, and a nearby timber yard helped us out with wood, which was still in short supply.

Bill had no training or experience in the technical problems of theatre, but he did have understanding and sympathy for our work and found no difficulty in adapting his skills towards solving the practical problems. We were to find, time and again, that a lack of technical training in theatre was no disadvantage and, indeed, often resulted in a more imaginative approach.

Though it was four years since any of us had worked together it took surprisingly little time to get back to our rhythm of work; and those new to the Group were able to benefit from the experience of the old hands. We worked long, hard hours rehearsing as well as training in voice, movement and relaxation. We felt it was as necessary for actors to continue training as it was for musicians, dancers and singers, particularly as movement and dance were to be so much a part of our productions.

It wasn't all sweetness and light, and there were the inevitable clashes of personality and emotional upheavals within the Group. Personal relationships would break up to form new ones with the resulting jealousies and antagonism. Differences of background affected attitudes to problems, the clash between the genuine working class and the middle class aspiring to be working class. Some were more politically committed than others. It all had to be accommodated to a situation where we were living on top of each other most of the time, but usually our overriding sense of purpose managed to prevail. We were grateful for the opportunity to work in peace, and we were full of ideas. We believed the people were waiting with open arms to receive our sort of theatre. All we had to do was to book halls, put up our posters and, provided we were good enough, the rest would take care of itself. We were to learn the hard way that the ingrained habit of not going to see plays wasn't going to be changed overnight, by us or by anyone else.

Our experience of theatrical administration was minimal and there was no-one we could turn to for advice on the organisation of tours. The few small Arts Council tours had their own minority following and were lucky enough to have their subsidy anyway. I was made business manager as I had worked in an accountant's office and could add up. Broad lines of policy were decided upon at Company meetings, and I had to write the letters, book the halls, get posters printed and do general secretarial work as well as paying the wages. In the time left over I rehearsed and played leading parts. There was a great deal to do and everyone mucked in, making costumes, props, typing: some of us even developed specialist skills, becoming experts on weapons, jewellery and so on.

Joan always had great difficulty facing up to the unpleasantness of telling an actor or actress that they had to go. Over the years, her solutions to this problem were many and varied, but perhaps the most bizarre, probably because she was new to it, occurred not long after we had moved to Kendal. She was worried that an older member of the Group would not be able to stand up to the strenuous work and the rigours of touring. Rather than tell him this, she devised an elaborate plan that consisted of calling a Company meeting for the purpose of telling the Group that we were going to have to disband. Everyone except the actor in question had already been told that it was all a device in a good cause, and that they were to go back to their digs and hide, returning the following day for rehearsal. Fortunately we were spared this elaborate charade, which almost certainly would not have worked, as the actor in question found out, understood the situation perfectly and left on the best of terms.

We opened on 13 August 1945 in the Girls' High School, Kendal, with our double bill *Johnny Noble* and *The Flying Doctor* ... 1/6d unreserved, 2/6d and 3/6d reserved. We were well received, and thus encouraged we set off on our first tour. The itinerary of this tour (see page 201), which took us to the end of the year, reveals how much we had to learn. We were an unknown company, playing unknown plays, hoping to attract audiences for a week in Grange-over-Sands, Workington and Penrith. In the middle of a tour of the Lake District, we had the expense of travelling down to Wigan and then back again, and a return three-day visit to Grange in the middle of November. Even at the bare minimum wage of three pounds, sometimes less, we lost money. Ewan recalls:

> We booked any place we could afford – often where there were few people who had ever been to the theatre – perhaps a village hall where you would literally have to construct the stage. We'd go to a town like Blackburn: there was still fuel rationing, there'd be more people on the stage than there were in the audience, and those few had brought hot water bottles! We were standing there in a scene from *Johnny Noble* in our bare feet, trying to suggest we were sweating in the hot sun of the Mediterranean.

Sometimes we travelled with our gear in a hired lorry, or on longer journeys, by train, the gear travelling free in a goods wagon, but having to be loaded and unloaded from a lorry at each end of the journey. We were carrying a lot of stuff; the set, lighting equipment, curtains, costumes, props, curtain rails, battens, sound equipment and speakers and sundry skips and crates, plus a large switchboard and dimmers on wheels – designed by our electrician and requiring four strong men to lift. All this had to be loaded, unloaded, rigged and de-rigged. Sometimes it had to be carried up and down several flights of stairs! But for the time being, at least, it did not happen every night – the one-night stands lay ahead in the early fifties.

Each hall was different, and we soon became adept at coping with the varying sizes of the stage and facilities; but our hearts would sink when, on the odd occasion, we would be faced with an immaculate, highly polished, bare wooden platform and the inevitable anxious caretaker. He would hover over us with growing resentment as we piled up our mountain of equipment on his spotless floor, and when we finally heaved our switchboard onto his stage, his resentment became burning hatred. He naturally would forbid us to put in screws and nails, but to his disgust we would manage to complete the rig all the same. We all had our own jobs – rigging curtains, ironing costumes and so on. John Blanshard became our expert in the skilled job of putting up curtains and making sure they hung correctly without the pins showing.

We returned to Kendal in October to rehearse *Don Perlimplin* by Federico García Lorca, who was killed by the Fascists in Granada during the Spanish Civil War. We were fortunate in having with us during rehearsals Dr. Luis Meana, then Professor of Spanish at Manchester University, a friend of Lorca's and a member of his travelling theatre in Spain before the civil war. Joan was always faithful to Lorca's text and his sources of inspiration, church ritual, perhaps, or a historical painting; and she maintained during rehearsals – 'I know this is how Lorca would have produced it.' After a run-through, Luis Meana commented: 'It's marvellous, Lorca would have loved it, but it's completely different from his production!'

The Love of Don Perlimplin for Belisa in his Garden, to give the full title, was a beautiful, poetic, evocative play about the love of an old man for a young woman. We played it within a semi-circle of green velvet 'pillars' which changed in texture and shape with the changes in lighting. Quite different from our first two productions, both in its atmosphere, and use of language, it was an important extension of our work.

Don Perlimplin opened with *Johnny Noble* at the end of October in St. George's Hall, Kendal, and at once became a *cause célèbre*, dividing the theatre-goers of the town. Some were so disgusted they crossed the street to avoid me – I was playing Don Perlimplin. Others came up to congratulate me. Today, even Mary Whitehouse would let it go without comment, but I suppose it's not surprising that in that time and place some people were disturbed by an old man's obsession for a woman young enough to be his daughter and by lines like 'between my thighs the sun swims like a fish', sung by a beautiful Swedish actress Kristin Lind.

Despite a warning from the Allies that the weight of attack on their country would be increased, the Japanese had given no indication that they were prepared to surrender, and on 6 August 1945 an atom bomb was dropped on Hiroshima. It killed seventy thousand people, more than all those killed in the air raids on Britain, and was followed by a bomb on Nagasaki, which killed forty thousand. On 14 August the Japanese surrendered. Suddenly with the advent of nuclear weapons war had acquired a new and horrible dimension. Bill Davidson, who was now an actor in the Group, put forward the view that we could not simply ignore its implications:

At the time of the dropping of the bomb, the Americans had published the Smythe report, which covered in detail the work of the Manhattan Project that had produced the bomb. Obviously some things were kept secret, but an extraordinary amount was released, and it seemed to me a play could be based on it, which would explain how the bomb worked and which would also have a social message.

Ewan agreed, but couldn't quite see how to express it in theatrical terms. I was only an engineer, but our electrician, Alf Smith, had a degree in physics, and he was able to explain the actual fission process. The idea then evolved of incorporating an atomic ballet, the neutrons and protons dancing, and splitting with a character called Alfie Particle – the Alpha Particle.

Ewan's enthusiasm for the idea was tempered by his lack of scientific knowledge:

We considered ourselves a theatre with a powerful social dynamic, and this was really our meat, but very few of the Company could understand what was being discussed in the scientific papers. Bill and Alf said they would give me a crash course in Atomic Physics. My knowledge of science came from the odd lesson we got at Grecian Street School in Salford, which I left when I was fourteen, and the odd bit of litmus paper that changed colour: that was my concept of science. I still remember the first book they gave me, called *Crucible*. It was fascinating; written for ignorant laymen like myself, it gave the basis of a philosophy behind scientific discovery. In the end, I decided, you just couldn't write a script about the Atom Bomb. You needed to explain the whole history of Atomic Energy. So I did this; in many scenes, in a whole series of different styles. Energy as a gang boss in a Hollywood gangster movie, Max Planck and Niels Bohr explaining the quantum theory as a couple of knockabout comics with phony German accents. Einstein as a comic figure.

My abiding memory of *Uranium 235* is of the costume changes. There were fifteen scenes and fifty seven characters, played by a company of twelve. I played eight parts, and quick changing, always in the wings, became an art in itself. Everyone found a space to pile up their clothes in precise order of use. Wing space was usually very limited and speed was of the essence, and as entrances were made to music cues, they had to be on time. George Cooper reminded me of one of the very rare occasions when things went wrong. It was during a tour of Sweden, and in this case, lack of space wasn't to blame:

Johnny Armstrong had carefully laid his trousers for the scientists scene on top of a grand piano in the wings. We dashed off to make our change and Johnny finds a large Swedish stagehand asleep on his trousers. He couldn't make the change, so when the scene started, there we were, all doing this rhythmical movement, five of us in trousers and white coats – and Johnny in his white coat and bare legs! The Swedes must have thought it deeply symbolic of something.

Touring in 1946 was much more extensive (see page 201) and included our debut in London at the Park Theatre, Hanwell, and the Assembly Hall, St. Pancras. Some of these bookings were disastrous! Windermere brought in sixteen pounds. At a performance in Workington, there were fewer people in the hall than on the stage, and the week there brought us twenty pounds. We were stranded in Bury, having taken eleven pounds in three days, and were rescued by the goodwill of Gerry's father, who paid for a heavy lorry to take us back to Kendal. During the week in Stockton I had to leave Ewan sitting on our cases in the hotel while I went to find money to pay the bill. At these moments of crisis – and they were to crop up quite frequently in the years to come – there were no wages at all. I paid out as mealtimes came round, 2/6d for lunch, I recall, and we relied on the Saturday night takings to pay for the digs. If there was money to spare, it was allowed for non-essential items such as soap and toothpaste; unless there was some that could be shared. The struggle to survive forced us into minor acts of dishonesty, like the occasion when Rosalie Williams and myself discovered a large restaurant in Leeds on two levels. On the upper level we could have a three course meal and get the bill. On the lower level we could have a cup of tea and get a second bill, paying the second one only on our way out. On another occasion, I took an over-generous tip of 2/– from under a saucer and replaced it with 6d., justifying my action on the grounds of greater need. Technically I had stolen the 1/6d, but as it was the difference between having a meal and going hungry, I prefer to view it as sharing a perk between the waitress and myself.

There were good times too. Our share of the takings for a week at the Dewsbury Empire was one hundred and twenty pounds – pretty low by commercial standards, but for us, something of a triumph. Sometimes we were able to save money on digs by accepting hospitality from well-wishers. But there was a price to pay. After rigging and performance, sometimes followed by notes from Joan, our hosts not unnaturally expected interesting chats after supper, often into the small hours. However, there were clear signs that our work was becoming known and appreciated – performances were sometimes sponsored by local Arts Groups, who guaranteed a fee, and then worked hard to make sure that people came and that the guarantee was covered. Glasgow Unity Theatre invited us to their Queen's Theatre for a week, and the W.E.A. Theatre Group sponsored a special performance of *Uranium 235* at the St. Pancras Assembly Hall, enabling us to play to a much larger audience than we could possibly organise with our resources.

Individuals too, like David Mitchell, at that time a Unitarian Socialist in Glasgow, were coming forward to help us. He was greatly impressed with *Uranium 235* and invited Michael Thompson (then our business

Manager) and myself to visit him in his digs. We had sherry, talked about our work, and left with a small brown leather attaché case containing a new pair of handmade boots, a Penguin copy of Graham Greens's *Brighton Rock* and one hundred pounds in crisp one pound notes – a lot of money in those days, particularly to us. Our next port of call was to the Business Manager of Glasgow Unity to collect our share of the week's takings. It hadn't been a good week, and Leon Shuster, Unity's Manager, was worried that our share wouldn't cover our wages, as we obviously lived from week to week. So he thought that perhaps we ought to have a bit more. We agreed with him fervently, and I clearly remember pressing my feet firmly against the sides of the case, fearful it should somehow fly open and reveal our new-found wealth. It had been a red-letter day, and Mike and I felt justified in celebrating with lunch at Pettigrew and Stevens – a large department store – spending, if I recall correctly, all of five shillings each on a three course meal.

We also held a number of week-end schools and a summer school during this period, led by Joan and Ewan, and they were always well attended. Apart from supplementing our income, they were extremely useful as an extended audition for anyone wishing to join the Company. A week-end of classes, discussions and social get-together was an ideal way of finding out all you needed to know about anyone.

The dramatic impact of *Uranium 235* was acknowledged, but was it scientifically accurate? Any doubts we may have had were dispelled when we played to a group of scientists who had worked on an atomic energy project in Britain during the war. They were very excited by it and could fault it in no way. In fact, a professor of physics speculated as to how he could use it as a teaching aid for his students. Even more gratifying was the enthusiasm of the audience at Butlin's Holiday Camp in Filey, where we played five performances in May 1946. Ian McKay wrote in the News Chronicle:

> Of all the bizarre and unexpected things you come across in this amazing phantasmagoria of a place there is nothing so surprising as the brilliant band of young strolling players who have been packing the giant camp theatre this week.

The response of the working-class holiday audience was less restrained than the scientists, as might be expected: every scene, including the Atom Ballet was applauded, sometimes cheered, as though it was indeed a Variety show. *Uranium* was not an easy show – it was telling an involved story through many different theatrical styles – but the audience were thoroughly absorbed. So much so that when the time came for me to 'interrupt' from the auditorium as part of the action, I was man-handled by a large, outraged lady, and told to 'get out if you don't want to listen'.

Joan Littlewood rehearsing *Volpone*, Stratford, 1955.

...tion group

production	**Joan Littlewood**
stage direction	**Ewan MacColl**
dance training	**Rosalie Williams**
sound	**David Scase**
decor	**Gerald Wilkinson**
costume	**Ruth Brandes**
secretarial	**Howard Goorney**

Ewan MacColl (2) in 1946; Joan with the first Theatre Workshop company (3) in Kendal, 1945; and the stable block of Ormesby Hall (4), the Company's rehearsal room in 1945. Background: two pages from Theatre Workshop's first brochure.

t h e

theatre wo

artists, writers

Kendal, We

terrupte

during the last

artistic beliefs.   Their obje

creative art and the lives of the ord

★   They believe that the return of the young

Britain to their homes will bring about a great change

values, the young men and women who have f   for

civilisation will want a richer,   d

their childre

r k s h o p

5

6

Foreign Tours. 5: Kristin Lind and coach driver, Germany, 1947. 6: Leaving Hitler's bunker, Berlin, 1947. 7: In Olomouc, Czechoslovakia, 1948. 8: Dinner in Sweden, 1948. 9: Shirley Dynevor, John Blanshard and Maxwell Shaw (l. to r.), Paris, 1955.

7

8

9

The warm response of the Butlin holidaymakers to *Uranium 235* was a confirmation of what we had always believed – that there was no necessity to play down or compromise when faced with a working-class audience. Our performances at Filey came to be regarded as something of a milestone, and we felt we had come quite a long way in a short time towards creating a popular theatre.

Four

1946–1948
The First Real Crisis
Ormesby Hall – Isle of Man – Isle of Wight – London

In the summer of 1946, after we had been touring for a year, we had an unexpected piece of good fortune. We were offered the use of the east wing of Ormesby Hall by Lieutenant Colonel and Mrs. Pennyman, after they had seen our performance of *Don Perlimplin* in the St. John's Hall, Middlesbrough. Purchased by James Pennyman in 1600, it was extensively rebuilt in the mid-eighteenth century, though the east wing still dated back to the earlier period.

It was situated a few miles out of Middlesbrough in pleasant parkland, and provided us with living accommodation, workshops and a large rehearsal room over the stables. It was obviously cheaper to live communally, we paid ourselves £1 a week for pocket money and personal needs, and there was enough space to enable those who could take just so much of living together to get away on their own when they felt they had had enough. There was a large refectory and kitchen, and above this, round three sides of a cobbled courtyard, were the bedrooms: basically furnished, but enough for our needs. We even had an office, a secretary and a phone number, which made the life of our business manager, Mike Thompson, a lot easier. Ruth Pennyman recalled our stay at Ormesby:

We had an old quadrangle, roughly furnished, which had been used by various groups connected with the Arts. Theatre Workshop brought with them much excitement and interest, many problems, and always drama, on and off the stage. By good luck the old wing survived them and was not brought down as a result of the experiments with the ageing electric wiring, and many splendid plans and productions were hatched there. One recollection will always remain with me, of Ewan MacColl pacing up and down the Georgian kitchen singing, or should we say chanting, 'The Bonny Earl of Moray'. One realised at once (with Joan it took months to discover) that Ewan was a liar, but in a delightfully Celtic and frivolous manner, also that he became easily and frequently amorous. This caused a certain amount of embarrassment. At the week-end schools, organised in collaboration with the local authorities, girls would emerge from his bedroom looking flushed, excited, and in some disarray. A purely fictional member of the Group was 'The Admiral'. He existed three-dimensionally as a sort of Guy Fawkes, and he wore an ancient naval uniform discovered amongst my theatrical clothing. He led a legendary life created for him by the fertile imagination of Theatre Workshop.

'The Admiral' was only one of several fantasy characters that shared our lives at Ormesby, most of them the creation of Joan and Ewan. Some of them were never actually seen, but were constantly referred to and discussed. There were dummy figures like 'Birdie' who was to be found swinging from a meat hook in the kitchen; and 'The Twins' who were always asleep together in bed. They were constantly being separated, but, somehow, they always seemed to finish up together. These three wore beautiful bird masks made by Ruth Brandes, our costume designer at this time, for a projected production of *The Birds* by Aristophanes that did not materialise. A short term visitor was a lion that Gerry had sent from Chipperfield's Circus. He was locked in a garage for three days, until Colonel Pennyman insisted he was sent back. The detail that went into the creation of this particular fantasy, plus Gerry's known fondness for strange acquisitions, made even this highly unlikely visitor almost plausible.

'The Admiral' was the most believable of them all, and he became so much a part of our lives that many of the Company were never quite sure whether he actually existed or not. The climax was his departure from Ormesby which was as carefully stage-managed as anything that went into a production. He was struck down by illness and had to retire to bed. A friend of Jean Newlove's, unknown to the rest of the Company, was persuaded to act the part of a nurse, and she was kitted out in full uniform. The admiral sat up in bed, supported by pillows, clad in his uniform – which he insisted on wearing, and looking, from a distance, remarkably real. The illusion was made even more convincing by Ewan, who lay under the bed for a while, coughing, breathing, and making all the other appropriate noises one might expect to hear. Jean organised the passage of trays and bed-pan so that they went through when all the Company were around to see them and everyone was asked to keep as quiet as possible, creating an atmosphere of concern for the well-being of our friend. One evening, when fit enough to travel, he was taken out on a stretcher to a waiting ambulance, and driven all the way to the St. Neot's naval home in Scotland. Colonel Pennyman, who entered into the spirit of all these charades, had provided the ambulance in his capacity as president of the local St. John's Ambulance Brigade. We were, of course, sorry to see the admiral go, but he continued to keep in touch with us. Letters arrived on headed 'St. Neot's Home' notepaper giving us his news. The notepaper was printed for us by William MacClellan, a Glasgow printer and a director of Pioneer Theatres, the limited company created to 'present' Theatre Workshop.

Ormesby Hall was a wonderfully relaxed setting in which the imagination could run riot. The cobbled courtyard, the outbuildings and the extensive grounds, provided an ideal location for the shooting of 'Westerns'. Baddies were pursued along low rooftops, hurling themselves off onto waiting horses. Chases, gun battles and hand-to-hand fights took place in the moonlight, Ewan shouted directions, and the cameras whirred!

We lived simply, there was no money to do otherwise; but the luxury we really enjoyed was the sheer space. Even indoors, the refectory was big enough for those who couldn't bear conversation at breakfast to get away on their own. Bill Davidson was in charge of catering:

> Wartime rationing was still in force, and I had to collect all the ration books and organise the cooking of two meals a day for twenty or so. There was a daily roster for spud bashing and so on, and, as far as I remember, we lived mainly on sausages and mash. We enlivened the time between rehearsals and classes with playing games; Ewan and I were very good at the Marx brothers. I can well remember John Bury, now head of design at the National Theatre, arriving as a young lieutenant in the royal navy, in uniform, complete with beard. I can see him in my mind's eye, flat cap and all, he didn't actually salute, but he was every inch a model officer. He wanted to be an actor, and he played quite a few parts, but he wasn't very good and eventually got more interested in design. On another occasion I remember Billie Whitelaw arriving with her mother. She had been to a weekend school. She was only fourteen or fifteen and Joan gave her an audition. She was really electrifying, it was a fantastic performance for a young girl. It had a kind of magnetism and everyone was very impressed, but her mother didn't approve of us and wouldn't let her join.

A few hours after his arrival, John Bury was lying on the floor of the rehearsal room, in his uniform, doing relaxation exercises. We already had two or three 'Johns' in the Company, so having found out his nickname at school was 'Camel', this was quickly adopted and he was rarely referred to by any other name.

As Bill Davidson recalled, meals were fairly basic, except on one memorable occasion when lunch was prepared by Ernst Ulman, an

Austrian actor in the Company. With great pride, he placed in front of us small portions of an Austrian delicacy. We took this to be an hors d'oevre and looked forward to his main course. There wasn't any; that was the meal. Not only were we still hungry, but Ernst had managed to spend several days' food money on this carefully prepared treat.

It seemed almost appropriate that in a world where fantasy and reality lived side by side and sometimes overlapped, there should emerge an extraordinary story of mental breakdown. Benedict Ellis, who had joined the Company only a few months previously, was rehearsing in *Operation Olive Branch*, Ewan MacColl's adaptation of *Lysistrata*, which was to open in January 1947 in St. John's Hall, Middlesbrough. Ben had been blown up on D. Day, was invalided out of the army, and as a result was, as he himself put it, 'living on a knife edge':

> I recall a lot of happenings which I didn't fully understand and wasn't let into. My morale was getting lower and lower by this time. In the large hall at Ormesby, somebody said something very ordinary, and this has always been my experience of mental breakdowns, like 'why are you taking so long to screw up that plug?,' and I suddenly felt the need for air. I went out and walked about for a couple of hours, trying to get myself together. I came back, went to bed, I can't exactly remember what I did, but I know I slashed my wrists, and I remember tearing up my notebooks and breaking my bust of Beethoven. I have a vague recollection of being held down and a doctor being called, and I finished up in St. Luke's Mental Asylum. A male nurse said 'Put him on those scales' and 'Have you got the certificate?' I was sufficiently sane to know that if they had the certificate, that was it. I was given an injection, and when I woke up next day in bed, a nurse said 'we're going to keep you here.'

Fortunately for Ben, and all of us, the young doctor in charge of the case had different ideas. He realised that if Ben was not allowed to play his part in *Operation Olive Branch*, he would probably be in an asylum for the rest of his life. Ben was escorted to the theatre each night in a taxi. As he was not allowed to look in a mirror because he would try to break it, Gerry had to make him up in a separate room. No-one is ever likely to forget the tension on the stage for the first night in Middlesbrough. Ben, playing a slave soldier, was digging the wooden dagger he carried into his wrists to keep himself under control; and when, during the action of the play, he had to hurl this dagger at Gerry, we knew that it was being thrown with real force.

All this served to heighten the tension in the scenes, which was all to the good, and though the audience must have been aware of the atmosphere without knowing the real reason, they could only ascribe it to our acting abilities. All was revealed to those who happened to read the *Reynolds News* the next Sunday, which carried a detailed account of Ben's breakdown, and of the performance, by Tom Driberg M.P. The shows continued for a week and the treatment worked. By the time the company went to Germany at the end of January, Ben was cured. The tour, which is described in the Chapter on 'Foreign Tours,' lasted until the end of March.

We spent the months of April and May rehearsing and training, and in June commenced our Summer Tour at the Esplanade Pavilion in Felixstowe, during which time a series of very successful week-end schools were held at Ormesby, run by Joan, Ewan and Jean Newlove, who had joined the Company as a Laban trained movement teacher. For Jeanne Goddard, who had joined us at Ormesby to be in charge of costumes, it was her first introduction to touring with the company:

I remember being so happy with this life, and I was working on making some costumes for *Lysistrata* when John Blanshard came in and told me we were all going to have a pound each that week, and I didn't want to take mine. This sounds a bit idealistic and sentimental, which it was, as it shows how happy and fulfilled I was. I felt it was such a privilege to be allowed to work in such an atmosphere, as long as I was fed and housed, I didn't need to be paid!

During the mealtimes we queued up with our plates at the hatch, and nearly every day there would be one or two 'strangers' – tramps, I suppose, who joined the queue. Nothing was ever said to them, Joan handed them a plate, and they had the same as us, and then shuffled off!

In Felixstowe we played to poor houses and had so little money that we all went to a little old lady who ran a café at the front. In the morning, she'd give us a plate of broken biscuits and a glass of milk for threepence; and in the evening, after the show, we'd go to the fish and chip shop for sixpennyworth of chips – and that was our diet for the week! Nobody complained as everybody was treated alike, including Joan and Ewan. I remember going out of the Stage Door behind John Bury, and being very amused to notice that his espadrilles, which looked all right when seen from above or from the side, were a sham. From behind, I realised, both rope soles were completely worn through, and he was really walking on his bare feet! None of this poverty worried me a bit, though it would have worried my parents if they had known, as I was only eighteen and living life to the full! It's no wonder we didn't make any money on the tours; they were the craziest tours one could think of. After a week in Felixstowe we went for a week to the Isle of Wight, to Ryde, and then back to the mainland and up to Liverpool to cross over to the Isle of Man for two weeks, one in Castletown and one in Douglas.

In 1951 we were to return to one night stands and booking our own halls, but for the time being we were playing in theatres, and these could only be booked through agents. As might be expected, they didn't regard our shows as popular attractions and we had no star names to offer, so we were never offered seaside theatres at the height of the season. Playing off season affected our takings at the box-office, but at least it helped Kristin Lind find digs for us in the Isle of Man:

Joan and Ewan had heard of an interesting rich woman, a Miss C., who owned a big hotel somewhere. Why not take a chance there! 'I have a feeling you'll do it,' said Ewan. So off I went. I had lots of time to think as I was walking along the green lanes. How many times had we not hunted for digs! In all the smokey towns of Lancashire, Liverpool, Glasgow ... One knew where to look. In the workers' narrow streets, with their long rows of equal houses, and the same friendliness. You knocked at the door: 'Have you a room to let for the week?' – 'Are you theatricals? What are you putting on? Never heard of it ... I haven't time for such luxury. And my old man likes football. How many are you? ... we can take two of you. The children can move into our room and there you have a nice big double bed. But won't you have a cup of tea deary? You look frozen ...' And one didn't mind a bit having to walk half a day, or drink a dozen cups of tea. I'll always remember their generosity. Those were the audience we wanted and those were the people Ewan wrote for and for whom Joan expected us to give our best. It was not hard to be a 'digs-finder'.

But this time it was different. This 'Miss C.' would surely only cater for rich tourists. On the main road a car stopped and I got a lift. The driver told me that the 'Chateau' of Miss C. was quite near, just outside Castletown. I could phone her. I found a booth. A very dark voice answered. I had rehearsed my speech, but before I had finished the voice said; 'Where are you dear? I'll come and fetch you immediately. Stay where you are.' Soon a car arrived, driven by a blonde middle-aged woman. We drove through a park and up to a large country mansion. It was almost dusk. We entered a hall with subdued lighting, soft carpets. Behind a bar stood a man, quite small and stout. He had dark, very fascinating eyes and thick brown hair. 'Welcome. Have a drink.' I felt very uncomfortable. This film-like setting was a world I was not familiar with. But one has to play many parts. I thought I recognised the voice but could not remember from where. His very kind and sad eyes watched me. 'Your name is Kristin, you said. Mine is ...' – and she mentioned a woman's name and came out from behind the bar. Now I understood: 'he' was Miss C.! She was very small but enormously fat. With short arms and legs. And then that beautiful face and expressive eyes! I hoped she did not notice my confusion. She must have been used to being stared at. I felt a great pity for her. 'Won't you have something to eat?' I started to talk about our theatre. Hoping to create a theatre for the people and not only for the well-to-do and 'cultured.' Not a very smart thing to say in these surroundings. I explained our very difficult financial position and that it would mean a lot to us if we could find somewhere to stay without paying too much. 'I'm glad you came. Let's drink and enjoy the evening. You are really lucky, Kristin, this is off season. Already next week we are booked out. But I want no service problems. You have to clean your own rooms and make your own beds ...' 'Of course! Of course!' It was done! But how should I get back. She must have guessed my thoughts: 'This evening you stay here with us, and in the morning we'll drive you back. Get a good bath and a good night's sleep.' And off she went, kissing me gently on both cheeks.

When we got there she ordered us to our different rooms. We all showed great respect for her wishes. We rehearsed all day. Had quite a good audience in spite of the off season. When we got back in the evenings she greeted us with all kinds of surprises in the way of food. As the days went on we all grew very fond of her, and she grew fond of us, although she ordered the boys about like a military sergeant. We all felt sorry for her. So lonely in the midst of her big mansion, friends and lovers. Always on guard. And her fascinating eyes searching for love and understanding. Perhaps we did understand her. The last evening when she had seen our performance, she prepared the big 'surprise'. In an enormous Grecian urn she poured bottles upon bottles of wine, and filled the tables with delicious dishes. We sang all our songs. She listened, her eyes filled with that same sadness. We were many, we 'belonged': she was alone. When we left next day in our lorry she looked at us as if she really was going to miss us. 'Bugger off all of you. Glad to get rid of you crazy lot!' It was difficult to keep your eyes dry. Her girlfriend, though, looked rather relieved!

This strange, generous woman remained long in our memories; always in red or blue corduroy trousers, which seemed to emphasise her stoutness, a cigarette in one hand, a gin and tonic, which she referred to as a 'snifter', in the other, and never seeming to eat or sleep. She would waken us in the morning with shouts and curses up the stairs. It would have been simple for her to have offered hospitality only to Kristin, who no doubt attracted her, but she chose to take the entire Company under her roof. Our work, and perhaps our way of living seemed to evoke sympathy and help from many different types of people, and it is doubtful if the Company would have survived so long as it did without it.

In August and September 1947, the Company played a successful first season at the Manchester Library Theatre, then known as the Intimate Theatre, with *Operation Olive Branch*, *Johnny Noble* and *The Flying Doctor*, and in October we went to London for a season at the Rudolf Steiner Hall just north of Baker St.

Looking back on this period, and in the light of experience, it becomes clear that our plans were unrealistic, and that we had, to some extent, lost our sense of direction. An unknown Company, playing unknown plays, we had booked a hall used only occasionally for theatrical performances, hoping to attract audiences for three weeks. To make matters worse, we had very little to spend on publicity. We were learning that, though our audiences enjoyed our shows and, hopefully, spread the word, this in itself was not enough to ensure good houses. In fact, audiences were sometimes so poor at the Rudolf Steiner, that we had to cancel the show. Even in those days, digs in London were expensive, and our £3/10/- a week didn't go very far. One good thing that emerged from this rather low period was the opportunity it gave us to work on voice production with Nelson Illingworth. We spent many tiring but useful hours working on exercises and on specific voice problems arising out of the current play we were performing. (See also Chapter Eleven.)

When we finished at the Rudolf Steiner, at the end of October, all the Company had in prospect was a week in December at the Dolphin Theatre in Brighton, the less successful of the two commercial theatres in that town. For over a month, therefore, there would be no income at all. It was decided we might do better in Brighton with a more conventional style of play than *Operation Olive Branch*. It was perhaps foolhardy to set about rehearsing a new play, finding costumes and building a set for one week's booking. No doubt we hoped it might attract further bookings or bring in enough money to make it all worth while. That we based our possible future on this sort of conjecture is an indication of the extent to which we were now completely at the mercy of events. It was decided to put on *Professor Mamlock* by Friedrich Wolf, a leading figure in the German theatre at that time, who had seen and admired our work. The play was set in Berlin in 1933, at the time of the Nazis' rise to power, and dealt with

the humiliation and suicide of Mamlock, a German-Jewish surgeon.
Perhaps not the wisest choice at a time when most people were trying to
forget the horrors of Nazism.

A sympathiser offered us a basement in South Kensington for
rehearsals, and we went through a difficult period of re-writing, re-casting
and set problems. We were not at our happiest when coping with this sort
of play. Edmund Bennett remembers our arrival at the Dolphin Theatre
with our gear, the first commerical theatre we had played:

> We had been used to moving everything ourselves, and when we
> arrived at the theatre a crew of stage hands was waiting. Gerry went
> up to them and said 'Hello, I'm Gerry.' They couldn't have cared
> less who he was, all they wanted to do was get the stuff in. There we
> were, the actors, standing around wondering what to do, and the
> stage hands looking at us, wondering what sort of idiots we were!
> They were there to do all the work and we were wanting to do it!

Our attempt to woo the public with realistic drama was a failure; at the
end of the week in Brighton we owed £950. We returned to London with
no plans for the future but with the intention of keeping together as long as
possible. Some of the Company had homes in London and others found
hospitality with them or with friends. We read plays and did training
classes in the Old Vic rehearsal rooms, which had been made available to
us. On 24 December we joined in the Old Vic Christmas dinner, and
Gerry produced six bottles of wine. On 26 December we made our way to
Nelson Illingworth's bungalow on the banks of the Thames at Staines, for
intensive voice classes. It was decided that Manchester would be a more
propitious place in which to try and establish a base than Ormesby,
pleasant and useful though it had been, and Joan and Gerry went there to
see what they could find. On 5 January 1948 a meeting of the Group
decided that there was no alternative but to disband the Company for the
time being. We went our separate ways and it was ten weeks before we all
met together again in Manchester.

THEATRE WORKSHOP

RNATIONAL
OURING CO.

Rhymney Church Hall.
South Wales Tour.

HGreene 1951

Harry H. Greene '51.

Feb 1951   177A, OXFORD RD, MANCHESTER.

Sweden
1957
H.H.Greene.

'ORNASHALS' THE
LUXURIOUS HOME
OF DOCTOR MARTHA
PSON HENNING, AT
HALSINGBORG, WHERE
GEORGE COOPER &
I STAYED

'DIGS'
Early morning call
on tour, in South Wales, 1952 H.H.Greene.

Five

1948–1950
Going Commercial

The return to Manchester – Alice in Wonderland on tour

Joan and Gerry went back to Manchester at the beginning of 1948 determined to get the Company together again as soon as possible, and in a few weeks Gerry had managed to clear the outstanding debts. The source of this windfall and others that were to come our way from time to time was not revealed, and it is idle to speculate. It was sufficient that they enabled us to keep going, and for that we were grateful. In March, Gerry came very near to securing a lease on the David Lewis Theatre in Liverpool, as a base for the Company, but there was a last minute hitch. We had a second season lined up in July at the Library Theatre in Manchester. Ewan was at work on a new play, *The Other Animals*, to open there, and Joan decided the Company could not remain apart for any length of time. She felt that, if necessary, the Company should try and get temporary jobs in Manchester and work together as 'amateurs' in the evenings – there was, after all, many a precedent for artists having to earn their living doing other things. In March, a large house suitable for the Company to live in was found in Wilmslow Road, and from another mysterious source or perhaps the same one, there was enough money to pay six months' rent in advance.

Joan expressed her feelings at this time in a letter to one of the Company:

> What we are living and going through hell for is a great theatre and such things were never born easily. Compromise is no way out – we must do great plays even though people would say it is impossible to exist in this society without compromise. At the moment they appear to be right but we shall come together again and the Company will be stronger than ever. It is always like that.

It was at these periods when there was no income and no wages that the struggle intensified and we became more and more unscrupulous. Private savings of new members of the Company, if not carefully guarded, would be ferreted out and prised away, or a sizeable sum could become an indefinite loan. Even small amounts were coveted. Julia Jones somehow managed to hold on to her £3 in the Post Office, but Edmund Bennett with a larger sum in Post War Credits found himself paying for part of the *Professor Mamlock* set and the wages of some of the Company. His contract read: 'The Company will endeavour to pay you a living wage' which turned out to be £61 for seven months' work in 1948 and £95 for six months' work in 1949. In his diary for 27 January 1949, his shopping list read:

Loaf   4¹/₂d
Grapenuts   10d
Sausages   1/3
Fish   6d
Tomatoes   1/3
Coffee   8¹/₂d
Toothpaste   1/1
Apples   10d

In decimal coinage, a total of 34p which indicates how it was possible to survive on the low level of wages. There was still some food rationing, which helped to keep the prices down.

The house in Manchester became affectionately known as the Parrot House after the wallpaper design in one of the rooms, and the Company gradually began to take up residence, bringing their sheets and cooking pots. Camel planted peas and beans in the garden. We survived in various ways, some managed to draw the dole, others found jobs. Edmond Bennett was, for a short period, a copy boy at the *Daily Express*, John Blanshard, a skilled toolmaker, worked in an engineering factory. Camel somehow managed to qualify as an analytical chemist working in Green's Food Factory and brought back various food dyes to brighten up the menu, on one occasion turning the rhubarb a very unnatural red.

However, it soon became clear that *The Other Animals* needed more than part-time rehearsal. It was the most difficult play we had tackled so far, both in its structure and in its use of poetic speech and choreographed movement. Enough money was found for communal feeding, and a rehearsal room which we didn't have to pay for, so we were now able to resume full-time theatre work.

Many hard and useful movement classes were held in the Art of Movement Studios in Oxford Road – the Laban Studios, run by Lisa Ullman and Sylvia Bodmer, some of the classes being taken by Rudolf Laban himself.

About this time, in the spring of 1948, the possibility arose that we might take over the Library Theatre as a permanent company, and voices were raised on our behalf. The *Daily Herald* said: 'Theatre Workshop hopes to take over the Library Theatre and start a "This is the North" renaissance', and in the *Evening Chronicle*, Fred Isaacs, a supporter of the idea, quoted Wilfred Pickles: 'Joan is the one person who would give the Manchester public something different'.

Perhaps the powers that be were afraid it might be too different, for nothing materialised, and a year later, when Charles Nowell, Chief Librarian and licensee of the theatre, proposed to the Libraries Committee that a series of companies should be approached, rather than a resident one, Theatre Workshop was not even on the list! It eventually did go to a resident company run by Peter Cotes, who was rightly regarded as more respectable and more predictable than Theatre Workshop.

However, spring 1948 also brought manna from heaven in the shape of a Flying Fortress of the U.S. Special Air Service. It was carrying equipment used in the entertainment of troops on the Continent, and it crashed on Bleaklow Hill in Derbyshire, scattering stage lighting equipment including some large spotlights, all over the moors. Camel led the Company on a hike of several miles from the nearest road to the scene of the crash, and we each shouldered a piece of equipment, and staggered back to load it into a van. We cleaned it up and made good use of it for several years.

We had, of course, very little money to spend on the materials needed for the costumes and setting for *The Other Animals* and had to rely on local good will, which was never lacking. We were also fortunate in having in Kristin Lind, a young woman of unusual persuasiveness. Using her charm and Swedish accent, which nearly always proved irresistible, she arrived back from one expedition in a large car with several rolls of very expensive material for costumes. Lack of money was no deterrent if Kristin had a journey to make, and many a railway ticket collector fell victim to her 'helpless foreigner' act. Even air travel came within her scope. After our tour of Germany in 1947, Kristin had the idea of a tour of Sweden, and she went there from Hamburg to put out feelers. She had no money for her fare back to England, and we had none to send her, so she managed to get herself adopted as a football team mascot, and travelled back with a charter flight of footballers returning home. As payment for the trip she had to attend a few football matches.

Tom Driberg M.P. was a close friend of the Company's, and brought Aneurin Bevan, at that time Minister of Health, to the opening night of *The Other Animals* on 5 July 1948 at the Library Theatre. Seen through the mind of a political prisoner in solitary confinement, the play showed his conflicts with society through memories and creatures projected onto the stage by his imagination. It was a complex philosophical play which

explored the problems of absolute truth and conscience and was by no
means a play which was easy to understand. Ewan's reply to those who
complained on that score was that symphonies were listened to more than
once, and that anyone who found it interesting but difficult could always
see it again. The Manchester press reacted favourably, and it was
encouraging to see how they now accepted us as a Group with an aesthetic
and an identity, rather than as an ad hoc company putting on plays. The
Manchester Guardian said it 'should be seen, not only because they give a
new idea of the theatre's potentialities, but because they are unique in this
country. The acting is always good. Joan Littlewood's production has an
air of conviction rare in the experimental theatre.'

Kristin now prepared to return to Sweden to organise a tour to follow
directly on from a last-minute tour of Czechoslovakia, arranged through
the good offices of Tom Driberg. (These are discussed in detail in a later
chapter.) We were due to leave England on 7 September for a period of
eight to ten weeks. We had to vacate the Parrot House, so it was necessary
to find somewhere to store all the equipment we had accumulated and
which we were not taking with us. Someone hit on the bright idea of Mrs.
O'Leary, a wonderful working-class woman, who had helped us in all
sorts of ways, from mending costumes to speaking up for us at public
meetings. She had made a particularly forthright speech at a meeting called
to support our taking over a building in St. John's Square as a theatre,
though this, sadly, came to nought. Kristin asked her if we might 'store a
few things in her house' and what followed was calculated to stretch even
Mrs. O'Leary's friendship to its limits. We arrived at her small two-up
two-down in Moss Side, with a large, fully loaded van, and proceeded to
cram her upstairs front room with large crates, sets, lighting equipment
and other paraphernalia, until it spilled out onto the landing. It was
nothing short of a miracle, and a tribute to the long-dead builders that the
floor didn't collapse under the weight. Accustomed as she was to our
vagaries, even Mrs. O'Leary was taken aback by the extent of the
invasion.

We arrived home at the end of 1948 after our triumphal tour of
Czechoslovakia and Sweden, but still lacking any official support or
recognition in Britain. The Arts Council had been formed in 1946, and in
1948 local authorities were empowered to support cultural activity
through the rates, but it was to be some time before we received any help
from either of these sources. Theatre was just beginning to be recognised
as an integral part of the life of the country, and repertory theatres were
re-opening after the closures during the War, but it was not until 1958
that the first new, professional theatre since 1938 was built – the Belgrade,
in Coventry.

Gerry found us another large house, this time in Bury Old Road in North Manchester, complete with stables into which – to Mrs. O'Leary's relief – we moved our gear. It was rented from a Dr. Schlosberg, so it immediately became known as 'The Schloss'. Individuals reacted differently to communal living. The more sociable shared the kitchen for cooking; the others, like myself, prepared a series of monotonous meals on a small electric ring in their own rooms, lived in a continuous smell of cooking, and constituted a 'living unit' of one. Edmond Bennett, who shared a living unit with Julia Jones and Dennis Ford, recalled:

> There were rows as to who should have the top of the milk. Our unit shopped at the Co-op and collected the 'divi' and on the day the Directors of Pioneer Theatres Ltd. came for a meeting, we had to spend our divi money on providing tea for them. I remember Peter Varley getting into trouble for secret eating – taking food out of the larder.

These 'Directors' acted in a purely advisory capacity. At this time they were James Ford, a schoolmaster from Wallasey; Hugh MacDiarmid, the Scots poet; William MacLellan, Scots Publisher; and Frederick Piffard, theatrical manager. Hugh MacDiarmid had known of our work before the war and the others became interested after seeing our shows. We rented a room in a Polish club, not far from The Schloss, where we did movement and voice training, Stanislavski exercises and rehearsed a version of *Twelfth Night* for schools. I was given the job of organising bookings within an area of about thirty miles. At £15 to £20 a time we had to work hard to keep going, but bookings were not too hard to obtain, and we managed to pay our way. There were no Theatre-in-Education companies at this time and few opportunities for children to see plays in their own schools, so we were made very welcome. An additional perk was a school dinner provided at low cost and often comparing favourably with our own efforts at cooking.

In July we returned to the Library Theatre with a new play of Ewan's, *Rogues' Gallery*, a contemporary satirical comedy. The press were somewhat disappointed by our handling of it. The *Manchester Guardian* said:

> *Rogues' Gallery* is not Theatre Workshop's line of country ... naturalistic acting is required. We missed the music, movement and cinematic construction.

They were now looking to us for a unique style of production.

We followed this with *The Flying Doctor*, Chekhov's *The Proposal* and *Don Perlimplin*, a programme we called 'Summer Fare', and we decided to take these to the Edinburgh Festival, joining what was then a very small 'fringe'. We booked the Epworth Hall, owned by the Church of Scotland, so it was not surprising that the local vicar, on seeing a rehearsal of *Don Perlimplin* decided it wasn't quite suitable for that building. We turned Kristin onto him, who in tones of outraged innocence, convinced him she wouldn't appear in any play that had any suggestion of immorality. Again the spell worked and we were allowed to stay. Our programme was something of a sensation. We were described by the *Edinburgh Evening News* as 'the highlight of the Festival', and even the vicar must have been appeased when the highly respectable *Scotsman* described *Perlimplin* as 'the work of a sensitive poet'. The *Yorkshire Post* went even further: 'I do not think that any straight production, while keeping within the bounds of propriety, could have achieved the gripping, exotic and perfectly characteristic atmosphere, worked up by Joan Littlewood.' We were not quite sure what that meant, but it saved us from any further arguments with the Church Authorities.

We played *The Other Animals* for the last week of the Festival to an enthusiastic audience and press, and returned to the Library Theatre to play *The Gentle People* by Irwin Shaw. An impressionistic play invoking the atmosphere of the Brooklyn waterfront, it had been written for the Group Theatre in America. According to the press, we seemed to have solved the problems in acting style that had bedevilled *Rogues' Gallery*. The *Daily Telegraph*: 'It calls for a technique over which Theatre Workshop shows a considerable mastery'.

We rehearsed our second Shakespeare, *As You Like It*, and played it in the schools till the end of November, followed by *The Gentle People* in Kidderminster.

In December, rehearsals started on an adaptation by Joan of *Alice in Wonderland* and *Through the Looking Glass*, taking the best bits of each. We billed it as 'A sheer delight for young and old.' It was certainly, for us, an elaborate production. Two dancers were brought from Sweden to dance in a Chess Ballet on a giant chess board. Music was specially composed by Jack Evans. Costumes were many and elaborate, and the sets were ambitious. Many hours were spent creating shapes out of thick wire – giant flowers, rocks, a mushroom and so on, which were then sprayed with a new material, one of the first of John Bury's many discoveries, a form of spun latex used for making spiders' webs in film studios. It was strong and practical when it hardened and looked most effective, painted and lit. The show had all the ingredients of a success, and it probably would have been had it been played in the right places. The tour was booked through an agent who we imagined knew what he was doing. It is painfully clear, in retrospect, that the last place to play *Alice in Wonderland* at Christmas, opening on Boxing Day, was to an audience of Yorkshire miners and their families, packing the Theatre Royal Barnsley; but this is what we did, and it was an experience none of us is likely to forget. A note in Edmond Bennett's diary reads:

We hear that Barnsley has the toughest audience in the country. Apparently Wilfred Pickles got the bird, and the Young Vic was a flop until they mustered the schools. Musically, Barnsley must be unique. The trumpeter is always sharp and the clarinet always flat.

From time immemorial the seasonal fare in that theatre had been pantomime, usually third rate, sometimes downright tatty, but always with the recognisable ingredients; the Dame, the Principal Boy, the blue jokes and the chorus girls. Habits of a lifetime are not be changed overnight, and faced with a weird assortment of strange creatures including a gryphon, a caterpillar on a mushroom, Tweedledum and Tweedledee and a Mad Hatter holding a tea party, our audience were far from amused. You could say they even felt cheated.

It was my misfortune to be playing the Ugly Duchess. Dressed beautifully, with a large farthingale and an enormous decorated wig, I could easily have been mistaken for the Dame. Unfortunately I was. Hopes rose in the audience that the fun was at last about to start and cheers greeted my entrance. My heart sank – I knew what I had to offer, and as I started to sing 'Speak roughly to your little boy' rocking the baby violently and with never a joke in sight, the audience realised they were on to a loser and had no hesitation in showing their disappointment.

When we took the curtain call, which was a pretty hasty affair, pennies and halfpennies landed on the stage. It took me some little time to realise where they were coming from – I thought they may have been dropped by someone on stage. I was unaware, in my innocence, that this was an old established method of expressing disapproval. When booing broke out, the truth dawned, and I lost my temper and booed back. As we were due to play three performances a day for six days and there were many more of them than us, I soon gave up doing that, and we all accepted defeat as gracefully as we could.

John Blanshard was the worst to suffer. Dressed as a gryphon and standing on a rock, he had the unenviable task of trying to persuade an incredulous audience to join in the chorus of 'Beautiful soup so rich and green!' Needless to say, he failed completely and consistently, until about halfway through the week, when he just lost his voice. It didn't make all that much difference as far as the audience was concerned, but it was very upsetting for John. The doctor could find no physical cause; there was nothing wrong with his vocal chords. The reason for the disappearance of his voice was entirely psychological. Under the circumstances it was perfectly understandable.

Some of us had to get through the three shows without even the comforting thought of some kindly mother figure of a theatrical landlady and cosy digs to retreat to. All I had been able to find was a bed in a lorry drivers' dormitory. After the first night, a married couple in the Company were kept waiting in the hall of their digs for five minutes, and then hustled into a room with a single bed that was still warm when they got into it and with the clothes of the previous occupant still lying about the room.

Saturday night was New Year's Eve and twelve o'clock struck as we finished loading our gear into the railway truck in the deserted goods yard. We passed round a bottle of wine and sang Auld Lang Syne with great fervour, celebrating the coming in of the New Year and our departure from Barnsley. It had been an exhausting, nerve-racking week but at last it was over.

It wasn't that we had a bad show on our hands, quite the contrary. Nor did everyone dislike the show. We had had letters of appreciation, and a local vicar tried to organise parties of children to come and see it. We just had to face the fact that the bizarre creatures of Lewis Carroll's imagination, and his strange sense of humour, just did not have universal appeal. How the management of the theatre were persuaded to take the show in preference to the traditional panto for Christmas week will remain a mystery. It was an experiment they were not likely to repeat. Nevertheless, we made money that week which was something of a compensation. A family visit to the theatre at Christmas, regardless of what was on offer, was a tradition. So houses were good.

On Sunday, New Year's Day, we travelled to our next booking, Llandudno in North Wales, and suddenly our lives were transformed. We were met by members of the local Drama Group, who swept us off to a slap-up tea, and when we had eaten our fill of the sandwiches and gooey cakes, we were taken into their homes and mothered. We found hospitality, help and an appreciative audience. It did not escape us that it was all rather cosy and middle class, but we were ready to be grateful for anything that would restore our morale. We decided to accept with good grace the creature comforts that were being offered to us, and moralise about it afterwards. After all, four weeks of the tour still lay ahead, and it didn't look all that welcoming. It was a happy coincidence that Lewis Carroll was something of a local hero in Llandudno; it is said that he wrote part of *Alice* there and a statue of the White Rabbit stands on the promenade in commemoration. It was rather like coming home!

We made the most of our week there and headed for our next booking in the East End of London, the Theatre Royal and Palace of Varieties, as it was known then, in Angel Lane, Stratford-atte-Bow. So, for better or worse, this tour introduced us to the theatre that, three years later, was to become our home. It was run down, but despite that, it had all the evocative atmosphere of the genuine Victorian Theatre. Our work was now beginning to be known, and we attracted a number of people from other parts of London, though *Alice* proved no great attraction to the locals: a foretaste of what was to come. Then followed Hastings and Weymouth, not ideal places to play in the depths of winter. Weymouth, particularly, seemed almost deserted, and the hall in the Alexandra Gardens was situated on the Promenade, on the edge of the sea. The wind howled around us, rattling the doors and windows, the waves lashed at the foundations, and we had the feeling at times of actually being out at sea. The landladies had fled to warmer climes, there were no visitors, and we were left more or less on our own to get on with it.

The last week of the tour was at the Theatre Royal, Leigh, in Lancashire – a sad, broken down, neglected theatre. Though the Mayor and local dignitaries attended our first night and every effort was made to welcome us, all I really remember about the week was an incredibly filthy dressing room, with orange peel and used contraceptives littering the floor.

Perhaps the one who suffered most consistently on the tour was our composer and Musical Director, Jack Evans. It was sheer agony watching his attempts to coax a tune he could recognise from the three or four inadequate musicians that usually composed the pit orchestra. Even if some of them did have the skill it simply wasn't the sort of music they were used to, and they were reluctant to make the extra effort required. Certainly Jack, sensitive and gentle as he was, was the last person able to persuade them. The dancers too, had a nasty time, adapting quickly to whatever sounds might come up from the pit, which were rarely the same two nights running. It would be an exaggeration to say it drove Jack to drink, but who could blame him if he sought refuge in alcohol when things got quite impossible.

George Cooper had joined us just before *Alice in Wonderland*, and he summed up his introduction to the Company:

> Barnsley was the only place I've heard beer bottles rolling down the aisles during a performance. It was my baptism of fire. I was playing the Executioner, Tweedle Dee and the front legs of the White Knight's horse. David Scase, a well-built chap, was playing the White Knight, so I'd quite a bit of a weight to carry. When the tour finished, I just collapsed physically, I got tonsilitis and was in a real state.

The tour, despite Barnsley, had been pretty disastrous financially but we managed a return visit to Hastings with *The Gentle People* by Irwin Shaw, and a Jewish charity show on a Sunday evening at the Adelphi in the Strand consisting of our 'Summer Fare' triple bill, *The Flying Doctor*, *The Proposal* and *Don Perlimplin*. We played the same programme at the

Alexandra, Stoke Newington and the King's, Hammersmith, both theatres no longer in existence, and after another charity show at the Adelphi of *The Gentle People*, we were once again completely broke. In March the Company disbanded for the time being, and we went our separate ways.

FOLLOWING THEIR SOUTH WALES TOUR OF "URANIUM 235"

Theatre Workshop

presents

LANDSCAPE *with* CHIMNEYS

By EWAN MacCOLL

Produced by JOAN LITTLEWOOD

"Landscape With Chimneys" is the story of a street and the people who live in it. There is nothing extraordinary about this street; its prototype could be found in Glasgow, Manchester, Cardiff . . . . anywhere in fact.

—And the people who live in it? Ordinary people; hard-working, patient, persevering; the men and women who's lives pass unrecorded . . . dockers, housewives, engineers, factory hands.

And yet, this compact community of ordinary people is rich in the raw material out of which drama is made. For the street is a world in miniature and by recording a year of its life, its tragedy, its hopes, its humour, its flashes of gaiety, Theatre Workshop offers you a play full of truth and simple humanity.

. . . . IT CAN BE SEEN . . .

Jan. 8—CWMAMAN	Jan. 15—PENTRE	Jan. 22—RHIGOS
Jan. 9—ABERDARE	Jan. 16—RHYMNEY	Jan. 23—COLBREN
Jan. 10—BEDLINOG	Jan. 17—CWM PARC	Jan. 24—RESOLVEN
Jan. 11—TREHERBERT	Jan. 18—PONT Y CYMMER	Jan. 25—GORSEINON
Jan. 12—WATTSTOWN	Jan. 19—BRYN CETHIN	Jan. 26—CWMAVON
Jan. 13—CYMMER PORTH		Jan. 27—YSTRADGYNLAIS

Six

1950–1952
Theatre to the People
South Wales and the North East – one-night stands

In the autumn of 1950 the company re-assembled in Manchester to re-rehearse *Uranium 235* in preparation for a tour of the Rhymney Valley due to start at the end of November 1950. We were about to embark on a two year period of one-night stands. A new or even a reasonable second-hand lorry could have saved us many hours of discomfort and recurring breakdowns; but we had no money and had to manage as best we could.

On New Year's Eve 1950, in quite heavy snow, the lorry broke down just outside Shrewsbury. Some stayed in the lorry with the gear and brought in the new year with a bottle of rum. They were the fortunate ones. Four of us who had gone to find a hotel in Shrewsbury ended up singing 'Auld Lang Syne' with a group of prison warders who had been brought in to guard a condemned man in Shrewsbury jail. A more depressing start to a new year would be difficult to imagine. We hitched to South Wales the next day, and the lorry arrived just in time for the first booking a few days later.

John and Margaret Bury, who had the thankless task of organising these tours, often managed to find hospitality for us; and in some places, well-wishers, sometimes local Union officials, would organise the selling of tickets for us. A guarantee of twenty pounds for a show would usually result in enough tickets being sold to cover that amount, and we would then have a reasonable audience. When we had to do all the work ourselves, it usually proved an insuperable task. Putting up posters and persuading a local shopkeeper to act as ticket agent for us just wasn't enough. There was no habit of play-going, and interest had to be stimulated in some way. When we tried selling tickets door to door, the man of the house would often be ready to buy tickets for his wife and daughter, but wasn't prepared to forgo his evening at the Club in order to see a play. Apart from some of the bigger places we played, the professional and middle classes were few and far between, and we relied on the support of the mining community. We wanted working class support, so in one village we distributed leaflets at canteens and pits, offering a free ticket to anyone who produced one of these leaflets. Far from being crowded out by this method, we had a very small audience indeed. Those who came were usually glad they had done so. But we soon became aware, more so than on the previous tours, that we were trying to do even more than change the habit of a lifetime, for theatre had played no real part in the lives of these communities for *generations*.

Our financial situation was usually bad, and on one occasion, Barbara Young, our youngest and prettiest member, was given the task of appealing to the audience for money for the Company after a show. One member of the audience was so moved by the performance, or perhaps Barbara's appeal, that with tears in his eyes, he donated fifty pounds! We were willing to try anything. I recall escorting Barbara to a factory canteen, noisy with talk and clatter, and the complete silence that fell as it was announced 'Now we have this young lady who's going to sing you a few songs.' I don't recall that this particular attempt to woo an audience met with any more success than the leafleting, processions or other stunts. In the final analysis, it came down to organisation of ticket selling over a period of time. Word of mouth had no value as we only played for one night in each place, though we played two or three times over a period, and the build-up in audience varied from place to place. We usually managed for necessities, and there wasn't any real need for anything else – except on one occasion when there wasn't enough to pay the digs. A sister of one of the company, after receiving a desperate telegram, was fortunately able to rescue us from a very nasty situation.

Sometimes we would stay in one village for a few days and travel each morning to others in the vicinity. The work was demanding; unloading, rigging, de-rigging and loading every night, often getting back to our base in the early hours of the morning. We learned to adapt to small and ill-equipped stages. In a show like *Uranium* involving six or seven quick changes for each member of the company, the efficiency of the show depended on complete co-operation and making the best use of the wing space available. In one hall, the dressing room was under the stage, and the only way onto the stage was up a ladder too narrow for two people to pass each other. We had to work out who had right of way at any particular time during the show.

We relied on an elaborate lighting rig, and sometimes had difficulty obtaining the amount of current we needed. John Bury, on one occasion, had to connect up to the tramways system outside the hall. Things could go wrong in all sorts of ways. George Cooper:

At Colbren, the electricity supply for the hall came from the local colliery, and it was direct current. Our sound equipment wouldn't work on DC and I was sent to Swansea to get a transformer. I was the last person they should have sent and I got the wrong thing, so that evening we used a hand operated gramophone for sound, and the lights on the dimmers were flashing and sparking with the DC current like Blackpool illuminations.

On the South Wales tour we recruited Harry Greene, whose talent for scrounging things we couldn't afford to buy and for making sets and props for next to nothing was to stand us in good stead on many occasions. After seeing a show at Rhymney and chatting to Joan and Ewan, he gave in his notice as an Arts and Crafts teacher at fifteen pounds a week (a decent salary in those days) and, a few weeks later, joined the company:

I got to Manchester, and as I walked down the long, dreary road from the station, I thought 'What have I come to? There must be a theatre somewhere or a big house.' 177a, Oxford Road I was looking for. It was off the main road, over a second-hand car salesroom, dusty, dirty, blokes hanging round the corner. I stepped back and looked up – a dismal three-storey building. Could this be the right place? I knocked at the door and as it opened, laughter, music, the smell of cooking. Oh this is fine – up the steps into the passageway – on the right was the kitchen and a booming voice said 'Come on, here he is, he's come. Come on in and eat.' Gerry Raffles. There was John Bury, bearded; Maggie, Joan other people milling around, and the smell of the cooking was very inviting. Then the joke started that a mouse had been put into this large pressure cooker to give the food flavour! It put me off because I believed it. Why should I not believe it? I didn't eat. I went to bed hungry. I was shown to the top of this building. Half the room was given over to camp beds lining the one wall, and the other half to curtains hanging up, and in between the curtains, stacks and stacks of things, crates, skips, lighting in another sectioned-off part. Someone said 'That's your bed.' I thought 'Oh no, what the hell have I come to?' Bare floor, no curtains at the windows. I'd never been farther than Barry Island in South Wales. I think I'd been once out of Wales. George Cooper was sleeping in the next bed. There was laughter, there was gaiety, there was a great sort of feeling which I was to learn was part of Theatre Workshop. There was bonhomie, a family feeling, and they made you feel good. Anyway I ate two bars of chocolate I'd bought at the station in bed that night underneath the army blankets, for my supper – and I must admit, I felt down! Any way next morning, light coming in through these big tall windows, into the room, peoples' movement, the smell of coffee downstairs, the clink of cups and so on, and work started straight away! Joan came in and said 'Right, get something on' and then we had some exercises of some sort. I thought 'what the hell is going on'. I couldn't believe it. This was a Sunday! 'There must be a rest day' I thought. Not on your life, we worked harder that day than I'd ever worked before. They were preparing to do a schools tour for the coming week, and I remember loading and unloading, rigging and de-rigging, fixing lights and being the general dogsbody. Suddenly, from the first day, one was swept up in it. Joan had, still has, this quality of taking people under her wing, almost like a mother hen, and filling them with her enthusiasm. The first week I was there on trial, and I didn't expect any wage. I thought the three pounds I received was a bit of generosity on their part − to buy a bottle of wine or something. I didn't know the financial state of the company − that they were literally struggling. But it didn't seem to matter, it really didn't.

By cutting out some of the less interesting characters, and doubling and trebling the rest, Joan had devised a lively and entertaining version of *A Midsummer Night's Dream* for our schools tour. As well as providing us with a guaranteed audience and income − and cheap school meals − it was good to play to a demanding audience. Children are quick to let you know if they've lost interest or don't believe in what's going on. I had to change from Oberon to Quince and vice versa behind a cut out tree on the set. When it worked it was magic and the children loved it; when they spotted what was going on, they lost no time in letting us know.

Our tour of Norway and Sweden in February and March with *Uranium 235* is described in the chapter on Foreign Tours. On our return and after a short break, we prepared for a tour of the North East with *Uranium 235* and *Landscape with Chimneys*. The lorry that had been left on a croft while we were abroad had been completely vandalised by the local kids and had to be replaced. George Cooper recalled:

Because I'd been connected with the building trade, I was put in charge of putting the top of an old furniture van, bought for three pounds, onto a 1938 Post Office lorry that Gerry had bought for about thirty. I somehow managed it and we set off with the fifteen or so members of the Company travelling in the back. I remember sitting in the front with Gerry driving and watching the iron supports swaying with the load of the lights, the curtains, costumes and everything else, and praying the top didn't drop off on the way.

It was painted up by Harry Greene and George Cooper and emblazoned with the words 'Theatre Workshop – International Theatre Company' and a list of the places we'd played here and abroad.

After an enthusiastic reception in Scandinavia by critics and audience, the packed houses and the luxury living, coming back to the hard slog of one-night stands was something of a shock. We had chosen to do it and, in the final analysis, we thought it was worth while, but it was an uphill task. It would have been nice not to have had to stint and scrape all the time, to have been able to afford adequate transport and above all, not to have had to wage a constant battle against what seemed an inbuilt indifference to theatre. Those who did come shared the enthusiasm of our foreign audiences but the interest in our work was certainly less widespread.

On returning to Manchester, we played *Uranium 235* at the Library Theatre, and in August 1951 ran two summer schools at Appleby in Westmorland and Newbattle Abbey College near Edinburgh. These provided a welcome break, and an opportunity for training and relaxation in congenial surroundings. Students came from all over the country and abroad, we had informal discussions and pleasant chat, and Ewan talked about his new play *The Travellers* analysing its structure and the relationship of the characters to each other. We did Laban movement on the lawn with Jean Newlove and voice production with Joan and Ewan, and one of the students, Frank Elliot, joined the Company. The first week of the Edinburgh Festival we were at Newbattle, and we played *Uranium 235* at the Oddfellows Hall. We received enthusiastic praise from the press and the B.B.C. Arts Review, and we played to capacity. The *Daily Herald* described the show as 'The only striking feature at the Festival' and the *Scotsman* wrote: 'This is not an ordinary production or ordinary acting ... gives critics the feeling that in comparison with this, most acting is uninspired.'

An attempt was made to create a form of Alternative Festival aimed at attracting support from the Labour Party and other left-wing groups. Organised largely by Norman and Janie Buchan it included Theatre Workshop, Glasgow Unity Theatre, clowns, folk singers and a group of Scots poets led by Hugh MacDiarmid. Any suggestion of commitment was suspect in those days and apart from *Uranium 235* and Unity's *Time of Strife*, it was largely ignored by the media, and the People's Festival lasted for only two years.

We followed with a short tour of Scotland and a return to South Wales for a six week tour, playing *Johnny Noble* and *The Flying Doctor* followed by two plays new to the repertoire; *Hymn to the Rising Sun* by Paul Green and *The Long Shift* by Joan Littlewood and Gerry Raffles, a study of a group of colliers in a Lancashire pit and a fall at the pit face. On our return to Manchester we prepared for a longer tour of Scotland. Gerry was

ill and unable to go, which left us without a driver. Nothing daunted and
with only three days to go before we set out, he took Harry Greene (who
had previously only driven a motor-bike and tractor) around the side
streets on a crash course of driving lessons, and somehow arranged a
driving test for the Friday. A lady examiner arrived in her car, set off in
the lorry with Harry, twisting, backing and turning down the side roads.
He passed the test, and the next day we set off. How it was all done so
quickly remains one of the many mysteries that surrounded Gerry's
dealings with authority. We just accepted and didn't ask questions.

It was now late November. Snow and ice covered most of the roads in
Scotland, and incidents with the lorry were many and varied, but mostly of
a minor nature. A narrow escape from what could have been a real disaster
is described by Harry Greene:

We'd unloaded at the Hall and we were told we could get fish and
chips in Bathgate, on the main Glasgow to Edinburgh road. We
found ourselves driving alongside the main railway line which ran on
the left of the road with big heavy wrought iron railings – six foot
high, with a forty or so foot drop below. Gerry had told me to get the
pull and push rod attended to but he didn't say it was urgent and I
hadn't had an opportunity. It controlled the steering and our lives
depended on the damn thing. We were driving along this very busy
road at forty or fifty, Frank Elliot was sitting beside me, lots of
singing going on in the back. The steering wheel suddenly spun in
my hand for some reason. I didn't panic. I turned to Frank and said
'Do you want this?' and I just spun it! I tried to brake gently with
the clutch and the lorry veered slightly to the left. I thought what I
had to do was jam on, gauging how fast we were travelling, how
much it would veer, hoping we wouldn't tumble over the great
void, down there onto the line, thinking of the fourteen people in the
back of the truck. Within about forty feet we crashed onto the
railings. The front wheels were spinning in the air over this bloody
drop. We were balanced on a knife edge. I rushed round to the
back. Faces began to appear over the edge of the tailboard, everyone
having crawled from the front of the lorry – it was empty of props, of
course, at the time. You had a cracked finger and cuts and bruises on
your face. If we'd had all our stuff on the back, six or seven tons of
it, and those railings had not been quite so strong, we would have
been right over the edge. Do you remember Frank Elliot suddenly
leaning on the railings and screaming 'There's the train we would
have been under' as an express thundered by a minute and a half
later.

The lorry was towed away and repaired, only to be condemned a few weeks later in Aberdeen High Street after it had shed various parts and a police woman had kicked the mudguard which had promptly fallen off. We were told we could use it to get us back to Manchester, but, as Avis Bunnage recalls, it didn't quite make it:

We had just got to Shap Fell when a lorry driver behind us kept flashing his lights. We were all sitting in the back with the props, and waved cheerfully at him. He finally got through that something was wrong, but it took ages before Harry, in the cabin, heard us shouting. Finally, he stopped, and we found the wheel was coming off. The girls had to sit on the side to balance the lorry and the boys walked by the side watching the wheel till we got the nearest town. It couldn't be repaired that night so some of us started to hitch to Manchester. We got a lift in a lorry, two boys, freezing cold in the back, and two girls in the cabin with the driver. When we got to Salford I only had a halfpenny and a farthing in my purse and someone gave me a shilling for the bus fare.

The lorry, of course, played a large part in our lives during these touring days; our lack of money to buy a reliable one and the resulting breakdowns put an additional strain on the Company. We spent many hours in the space that was left after the gear had been loaded, it became like a second home. We made the best of it, but Harry Greene was one of those who actually enjoyed it:

The amusing incidents that one could recall day after day – George picking up a walking stick, using it as a microphone to improvise, putting a hat on telling a funny story. Ewan, with his right hand cupped round his ear, head tilted, singing folk songs. The journeys were the highlights for me, it was marvellous.

Ewan's subsequent success as a folk singer must surely owe something to these sessions but not all his captive audience shared Harry's enthusiasm. Harry Corbett's recollection of these journeys is somewhat different:

Squashed in amongst the scenery, Joan was striking matches, giving notes at twelve-thirty in the bloody morning. This was a regular occurrence. You felt as if you were in a dressing room. The standard answer was 'Yes, Joan, definitely' – that was it. I don't think it registered because she never paused. Her notes were copious, but good and to the point.

Harry had joined the Company at the beginning of 1952 in time for our return visit to the North East.

I wasn't thrilled by the idea of a tour in January and February. I started listening to the tales, like a recruit joining the army. What happened and what didn't happen in the past. 'We get 2/6d a day for meals!' All the horror stories: 'We get hospitality, we knock at doors and say will you take in some actors.' I had sprained my foot dancing about, there were those cracks in the floor. I thought 'this a perfect excuse to get out, I can't be doing with this at all. It's madness, the whole thing. What are we in for?' I didn't really know. Anyway I went off with them. We played this mining play *The Long Shift*. John Bury had painted the set with real coal dust and it kept coming off. We had genuine miners' shorts, donated by miners, and we played it and Gogol's *The Overcoat* round the mining villages, on trestle tables usually, the audience helping us to shift the tables. They were helpful and generous. I remember when a chap died in the pit and they closed it and cancelled the show, they gave us our twenty-five pounds, which was as well, as we desperately needed it for petrol.

In March 1952 we gave two performances of *Uranium 235* in St. Andrews Halls, Glasgow. Over the years we had attracted a great deal of support in Scotland, and a 'Friends of Theatre Workshop' committee had been set up to help us and to sponsor these performances. Morris Linden, Chairman of the Committee, wrote in the programme:

> The state of British Theatre is unquestionably very low ... This impoverishment of the spirit is perhaps best shown in our Edinburgh Festival ... It was in this atmosphere of frustration that members of this committee first encountered Theatre Workshop at the Edinburgh Festival three years ago. It was an exciting experience. By comparison, the offerings of some of the other famous companies seem to be stiff-jointed and inarticulate. It was with a jolt that we realised how much one's standards had been reduced by the general lack of vitality in present-day British theatre. But in Theatre Workshop we found a group of dedicated players, led by a producer of genius. Here was something fresh, delightful and stimulating.

We were to return to Scotland again for the Festival, but in the meantime we went back to Manchester where Michael Redgrave and Sam Wanamaker saw us re-rehearsing *Uranium 235*. On the strength of what they saw, they presented us, in May 1952, at the Embassy Theatre in London, for a short season. In the publicity leaflet, Michael Redgrave wrote:

> Several weeks ago I saw the Theatre Workshop actors rehearsing in a

cold, bare basement in Manchester. There were no lights, no costumes, none of the trappings of a complete performance. But those of us who saw that rehearsal were spellbound, and are still under that spell.

Others had attempted to compound drama and ballet, verse and mime, burlesque, revue, satire and song, but this seems to me to achieve a synthesis, and one that is moving and exciting.

The organisers and actors of the Theatre Workshop are not offering some high flown idea which has been cooked up overnight. They attempt to rediscover what is the essence of drama and theatre, and have rigorously trained themselves for over seven years, to express it.

In any case, the result is unique in this country, and I think without parallel elsewhere. There is no knowing what they may not achieve in the years to come.

Let us support them now.

Oscar Lewenstein, who was managing the Embassy Theatre at that time, became a friend of Joan's and Gerry's and was to be of great help to the Company for several years to come. The show was highly praised, as always, by the critics; *The Times* describing us as 'A model of what a theatre group should be.' We then played for two weeks at the Dolphin Theatre in Brighton, and a short season at the Comedy Theatre – our first visit to the West End.

Despite the critical acclaim and the recognition of our work abroad, we were not yet in a position to break down the bastions of the West End. We didn't fit in to the accepted pattern. The Company and Joan were not yet sufficiently well known to replace star names. *Uranium 235*, as far as the West End was concerned, was 'avant-garde' theatre, and, as such, suspect and to be avoided. So by the summer of 1952 we were as hard up as ever. We gladly accepted an invitation from Tom Driberg to pitch our tents in the gardens of his home in Bradwell-Juxta-Mare in Essex, and rehearse *The Travellers* for the forthcoming Edinburgh Festival in a barn. Frank Elliot would go off at four in the morning to shoot rabbits and John Blanshard would cook them over an open fire for breakfast. How we raised the money for food and the fares to Edinburgh is told by Harry Corbett. He had come up earlier than the rest of us, had been found farm work by the local Labour Exchange and was, by now, conversant with the local farmers' requirements:

I started contracting fields from farmers, and I took everybody down and we did stooking for hours – getting a lot of corn together and putting it in stooks. I had plenty of cheap labour! I had vicious

stand-up arguments with Joan: 'You can't have him for rehearsal, I
need him for stooking.' The new society of share and share alike
disappeared in an orgy of private enterprise, after all it was money we
needed to get us from Bradwell to Edinburgh.

Some of this money went to individuals, most of it to the Company and
after a lot of stooking and other back-breaking tasks, we raised enough for
petrol and other necessaries. What we didn't have was money to spend on
the elaborate set needed for *The Travellers*. How this came to be built for
less than five pounds is such a remarkable achievement it deserves
recounting in some detail.

Harry Greene, with Karl Woods as his assistant, was sent up to
Glasgow with a hammer, a bag of nails and four pounds, to build the set
and have it installed in the Oddfellows Hall, Edinburgh, ready for the
arrival of the Company. Harry takes up the story:

We stayed at Norman Buchan's house. I slept on the settee and Karl
slept on cushions on the floor. They were marvellous to us, Norman
and his wife Janie, they introduced us to people, got us to places. I
knew the size of the set Joan wanted. It was to be a simulated train
with a first class compartment, a third class compartment and a
guard's van and platform. It was to extend between the audience,
from the stage end, right down to the entrance to the hall.

There had been an item in the local paper about Harry and Karl's task,
and help was soon forthcoming. They were introduced to Barney Levin,
who offered them the use of his machines, timber for the basic structure
and space in his factory in which to work.

We scrounged ironwork from a dump and Karl and I humped it to
the factory and we had it cut on a metal saw to size, and got it welded
for the third class carriages. We got some timber for slats for the
seats and screwed it all together. We pre-fabricated a lot of it. What
was missing was the cloth for the first class seating. I was introduced,
by David Murray, to Morris's, a big furniture manufacturers. Went
to see the boss. He wanted a drawing for a Press advert for the local
paper, and I did one for him. I said 'I'll do a black and white of this,
you donate the cloth.' I gave him the measurements of the set, he
made a calculation – and next morning, the cloth was delivered. Not
only that, he sent us one of his upholsterers, who upholstered the
whole of the seating for the first class compartment. We then had to
get it from Glasgow to Edinburgh, and one of the firm's lorries was.
loaded one night. The three of us went up to Edinburgh, unloaded
it that night, set it up, worked through the night again, cups of tea
and benzedrine. We then went to bed. Oscar Tapper had come up to

Johnny Noble, 1945: (10) hauling in the nets.
The Flying Doctor, 1946: (11) (l. to r.) Isla Cameron, Rosalie Williams, Howard Goorney.
Don Perlimplin, 1949: (12) Joan Littlewood (2nd left).
The Proposal, 1949: (13) Howard Goorney, Rosalie Williams.

10

12

13

14: *Operation Olive Branch*, 1947. 15: *The Other Animals*, 1948.

15

16: *Uranium 235*, 1951.

7

The Alchemist, 1953: (17) (l. to r.) Howard Goorney, Harry Corbett, George Cooper.

A Christmas Carol, 1953: (18) Yootha Joyce with Howard Goorney as the young Scrooge; (19) Howard Goorney (left) as the old Scrooge with Murray Melvin (centre) and Stella Riley.

18

20

An Enemy of the People, 1954:
(20).
Red Roses for Me, 1954: (21)
Gerard Dynevor and Company.
The Good Soldier Schweik, 1955:
(22) (l. to r.) Gerard Dynevor,
Maxwell Shaw, Howard Goor-
ney.

21

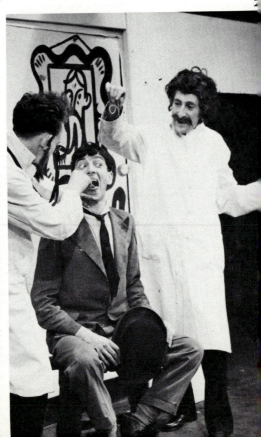

help and he found us some digs. We slept from early morning to lunchtime. As we got back to the Hall, the Company were just going in through the door. That afternoon they were rehearsing on the set!

It was beautifully made and a joy to work on, a tribute to sheer determination, hard work and a very special talent for transmitting enthusiasm to others. It also reflected the enormous amount of good-will on the part of all those who had helped Harry and Karl in so many different ways. It had cost less than five pounds; 3/9d for screws, 4/- for washers, bolts and nuts, 6/4d for paint. The largest item was 30/- for six hours of welding done through the night.

The setting contributed a great deal to the success of *The Travellers* at the Festival. Downstairs, the audience faced in to the train on either side, and upstairs, a horseshoe shaped tier of seats looked down. Using sound, light and the movements of the actors, we created the impression of a moving train, and the audience had the feeling of being involved as passengers on the journey, rather than as passive spectators. The train was crossing Europe to an unknown destination and the passengers were of different European nationalities. The journey symbolised the nations heading towards war and the differing reactions to this situation. Ewan described it as a political thriller. There was nothing to spend on props and costumes. These had to be improvised, and those who could provided their own. Harry Corbett needed a suit and, fortunately, actually possessed one — a relic from his more affluent repertory days. George Cooper was able to come up with a railwayman's long dark raincoat, inherited from his father, a beret and a pair of army boots.

Despite the lack of resources, the show looked good and received generally very favourable notices. There was the exception. The Spectator commented:

A melancholy evening is to be spent at the Oddfellows Hall where Ewan MacColl and and his fellow-travellers' sermon is ingeniously produced by Joan Littlewood. Theatre Workshop is a very model of devotion and zeal. A good Company and a good Director devoted to the presentation of propaganda thinly disguised as experimental drama.

About this time, there had been a growing feeling amongst some members of the Company, of a need for stabilisation, for a building of our own where we could play and rehearse. The house in Oxford Road Manchester was adequate for rehearsals, even provided living accommodation on a primitive level, but there was no possibility of its being used as a theatre. In any case, the lease ran out at this time and we could not afford the amount asked for its renewal. The Company moved to

Glasgow after the Festival in a determined effort to find a suitable building there. It seemed logical to try and settle in the city where we had received so much interest and encouragement. The Company lived in a house in Belmont Street belonging to an eccentric millionaire. Everyone received a pound a week, which was handed back to pay for food, and those who could drew dole or Public Assistance. Some actually saved out of their dole. Others, like Harry Greene and George Cooper, lived it up and made a weekly trip to the local Chinese restaurant for a meal and a bottle of Sauternes. Harry Corbett recalls Belmont Street:

> We were all duty cooks for a week. I'll never forget George Cooper's first meal. It was water and three dumplings. It was unbelievable and at the end of the week he had about ten pounds left out of twelve and we chased him up the road pretending to kill him! Then Gerry got a wine importer's licence and we all sat around drinking, it was 3d a glass, you kept putting your hand up and a mark went into his little book but as we never got any money out of him anyway and some of us hadn't got any, we wondered how we were going to get round to paying this off. The place was littered artistically with all kinds of empty wine bottles, chianti bottles hung from the ceiling, and we were having one of our big, end of the week type meals when a load of 'Friends of Theatre Workshop' came to see the starving actors, and there we were half drunk, raucously shouting out those terrible songs which were always traditionally sung on these occasions – revolutionary German songs of the 1920's.

A schools tour of *Henry IV* was organised to keep the Company working and earning while the search for a theatre building went on. A cinema, then a church came up as possibilities, but the amount of money needed just couldn't be raised. There was a real desire that we should settle in Scotland, but finding the money for a suitable building proved to be beyond the resources of private individuals, and there was no public money available to us at this time, or indeed, for a long time to come. Support for the Arts was in its early days, and the Arts Council was in no position to assist us. Even when they were, they didn't, but that is another story.

At the end of 1952 when our future was in the melting pot, Gerry announced that the Theatre Royal, Stratford, in London E.15 was available to us.

All black drapes, isolate acting
Accident area   areas with
                     lighting

"THE
LONG
SHIFT"
by
Gerry
Raffles.

Black Drapes

Manager's Office

Coal
face

From rear of
theatre actors
enter to
crawl to
coal face

Prelim. sketch of acting
areas based on Joan's
production ideas for
Gerry's "The Long Shift" 1952

The 'fall' is the most
difficult effect! Piles of
stones & talc on the
collapsible platform is
awesome enough for
Joan!

b -------- Pull →

← Hinged

Donated miner's hats & lamps by
friendly South Wales ex-miners
at Bargoed and Rhymney.

Scaffolding poles easy to erect each afternoon, but
heavy to carry to the lorry each night!

authentic
props; these
have actually
been used by
the miners
underground!

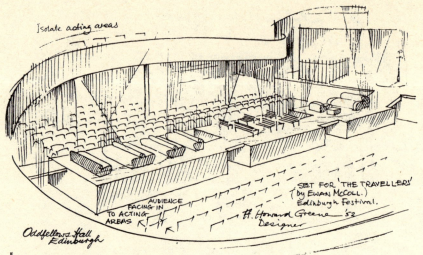

Isolate acting areas

SET FOR 'THE TRAVELLERS'
(by EWAN McCOLL.)
Edinburgh Festival.

AUDIENCE
FACING IN
TO ACTING
AREAS

H. Howard Greene '52
Designer

Oddfellows Hall
Edinburgh

" THE PLATFORM IS WITHOUT FEATURE OR IDENTITY
AN ISLAND OF CEMENT AND SHADOWS; BARREN OF SHELTER,
A WALK THAT TERMINATES AT NOWHERE
AND YOU, THE TRAVELLERS, DO YOU KNOW WHERE YOU ARE GOING?
WILL YOU RECOGNISE YOUR DESTINATION? "

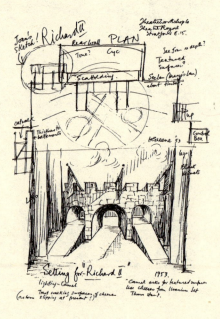

Joan's Sketch! Richard II

Rearwall PLAN

Tone? Cyc

Scaffolding.

Theatre Workshop &
Theatre Royal
Stratford E.15.

See Joan re depth?
Textured
surfaces?
Stela (Mary's Law)
about timber

catwalk

Thickness of battlements

HGreene '53

Setting for "Richard II"   1953.
lighting - Camel
(actors working surfaces of cheese
slipping at present!)   'Camel asks for textured surface
like cheese from Uranium Set
Throw stent.

Seven

1953–1958
The Struggle to Survive
The move to Theatre Royal, Stratford East

A company meeting in Glasgow in November 1952 took what was to prove the most momentous decision in the history of Theatre Workshop: to take over the lease of the Theatre Royal, Stratford, London E.15. A majority felt that we had endured the strain of touring for long enough, and that we should opt for a situation which might offer some sort of recognition for our kind of theatre, and the hope of a measure of financial and artistic stability. John Bury puts this point of view:

We couldn't go on waiting any longer. We had to get into a theatre through our own efforts, through our own cash-raising, and – through our own organisation – build it up. Stratford, at least, gave us the opportunity to do this. Being in London, it gave us a much bigger theatre public to draw on than, say, Glasgow or Manchester. Even if we only got a tiny percentage, we got enough to keep us going. Of course, it could have been the Angel, Islington, or somewhere like that, but it had to be somewhere cheap – it couldn't have been Kensington or Hampstead – it had to be an unpopular area. I don't think it was a question of conscious choice – it was the only thing to do at the moment. We often found ourselves in that sort of situation. Having to take a certain course of action because there was no real choice. For example, we would go back to Manchester when we had no money left because it was the only town where most of us had places to stay. We went to Glasgow because we had friends there. There were certain courses of action one felt were more defeatist than others, or more possible, but there was no yardstick to measure our progress against, we just had to keep going.

Some of the Company were attracted to Stratford, not simply because it was cheaper than, say, Hampstead, but because it was in the East End of London and therefore provided the possibility of building up a working-class audience rather than attracting existing theatre-goers. If it was not taking theatre to the people, as we had tried to do in the past, we might, instead, become part of a working-class community. Ewan saw the dangers of a move to any part of London that was within reach of the critics:

> There was a feeling that it was time we settled down in a place where we could get the attention of the national theatre critics. I felt from the beginning that this was a mistake, and a number of other people did too. We felt that to suddenly change our policy in mid-stream was to abandon all the experiences and all the gains of those six years' hard work. Before this, the level of discussion had been 'What are we doing wrong when we take a play about mining to the Welsh coal villages and the miners don't care?' This is a perfectly valid question, and by answering it we could formulate a way of dealing with the situation. But the new questions were going to be, 'How are we going to get Harold Hobson? What is he going to think of us?' I don't think anybody at that particular time realised what was involved in trying to make the critics happy.

Certainly, not even Ewan could have fully foreseen the far-reaching effects that critical acclaim was to have on the Company at Stratford.

David Scase and Rosalie Williams, founder members of the Company in 1945, had already left. Kristin Lind had returned home to Sweden, and now Ewan MacColl, who had worked with Joan in the theatre since the thirties, felt he could not go along with the move:

> Some of us believed that this was just going to become another West End type theatre providing its audience with culture. A situation had arisen in the Company by this time where the management could more or less impose a policy, because they were holding the purse strings ... a feeling of them and us was developing which was disastrous. There was also a lack of political training inside the group – a tendency, once we were functioning, to believe that politics would take care of itself. I was only asking that we should at least know what was happening politically in the world around us, not just take refuge in broad generalisations about struggle, about peace and so on ...

The extent to which policy was being imposed by Gerry Raffles as General Manager is dealt with later in this chapter. Gerry would have argued at the time that if he was holding the purse strings and trying to find something to put in it, it was because no one else was prepared to do so and that his aim was to create conditions under which some sort of work by Joan could continue. That was always his main consideration.

As has already been made clear, Ewan's contribution to the Company as a writer and in his formulation of artistic policy was considerable. The late Jack Pulman, who worked as an actor in Theatre Workshop for a short period, later becoming a television playwright, felt very strongly about the value of Ewan's work.

I think the only style that was ever unique about Theatre Workshop was given to it by Ewan's writing. Ewan is right. Joan should have stayed out of the West End if she had really wanted to create a theatre of dance, music and light and all the other things she talked about. The moment Theatre Workshop came to Stratford, it became virtually a try-out theatre for the West End. It wasn't the kind of theatre that Ewan had helped to found. Had it survived within his notion of it then I think twenty years later we may have had a theatre that really was quite unique.

It is possible to agree with Jack Pulman's analysis to the extent that plays like *Uranium 235* and *Johnny Noble*, written by Ewan, directed by Joan with a trained company, were the nearest we ever got to the sort of theatre we set out to create, but there's no need to discount completely, as he does, the rest of the work. To have created Ewan's sort of theatre at Stratford, assuming the will to have been there, would have required a continuing and realistic level of subsidy. In its absence, the sheer struggle to survive took over.

In 1880 work began on transforming a wheelwright's shop in Angel Lane, Stratford E.15, into a theatre, and in 1884, after £3,000 had been spent, the Theatre Royal opened with *Richelieu*, starring Charles Dillon. In 1886, it was sold to Albert O'Leary Fredericks who set about extending the depth of the stage from eighteen feet to thirty-eight feet, making it one of the deepest stages in London, and it remained in the Fredericks family till 1932. It was intended as a theatre for the local market traders, railwaymen and dockers and has had a very chequered career. In 1902 it was damaged by fire, was closed in 1933 and re-opened in 1936 by John Williams, with a stock company. He lost all his capital, and after the war David Horne took it over for a season of revivals. It was closed in 1950, to be re-opened again in 1952, now known as the Theatre Royal and Palace Of Varieties. The production that preceded the arrival of Theatre Workshop was a striptease revue *Jane of the Daily Mirror*. It was by this time suffering from years of neglect, and the auditorium and stage were badly in need of redecoration and repair.

Gerry Raffles and Harry Greene formed the advance party. They left Glasgow at four in the morning and drove to London in an old shooting

brake, stopped to pick up the key of the theatre, and made their way out to
Stratford. Harry Greene recalled their arrival:

It was dark when we arrived. The theatre was situated in a back
street amongst back-to-back terraced houses, a street market
smelling, after the day's trading, of over-ripe discarded fruit, rotting
vegetables and paraffin lamps. May's cafe was recommended for a
snack. Our first meeting with Bert and his ham sandwiches and large
mugs of steaming tea. The theatre inside was damp-smelling and
dismal, the drains were foul, there was the staleness of old clothes,
old make-up and lack of ventilation. Plans went ahead so quickly
there wasn't time to stop and think. I was ordering posters, booking
advertising space, designing front-of-house publicity posters and
pictures, organising local labour to clean up the dressing-rooms
ready for the arrival of the Company. Gerry dealt with
administration, newspapers, box-office, catering, local authorities, all
essential to the setting up of a repertory theatre. For that was what we
were to become.

In January 1953, the Company made their way down from Glasgow.
George Cooper describes his arrival and settling in:

The rich ones came down by train, I hitched with my rucksack on
my back. I remember walking into this rather broken-down theatre.
We just couldn't afford digs, so we had to sleep in the dressing
rooms, which is against the rules. After a few weeks we discovered
that the lady in the box-office had been 'dusting the till' − I think
that is the euphemism. Gerry sacked her, whereupon she went to the
local council offices and said there was a bunch of gypsies sleeping in
the theatre, so the local sanitary inspector arrived. Gerry had to take
him round the dressing rooms and show him the beds, which he said
were just day beds for the actors to relax on before the show. The
really vital bits like gas rings and other illegal devices were hidden in
dark corners. So we got away with that. I had quite a nice time in my
little dressing room. I devised all sorts of gastronomic marvels, like
apple omelettes for breakfast.

Harry Corbett too has vivid memories:

I remember every bit. Taking your turn to go down into the cellars
and get that terrible anthracite boiler going. You never had enough
coal and you could only burn it when the audience came in. Sleeping
in the dressing rooms. We had this password 'Will Walter Plinge
come down for rehearsal please' whenever the fireman came in to
inspect. You rushed into whichever room you were nearest to and

tidied things away. My bed used to go up against the wall, like in a Marx Brothers' film, the ropes fastening it went round coat hooks and underneath a notice said 'Props. Do not touch'. We had a deal that the non-smokers could have the chocolates that were left in boxes in the auditorium. I had the stalls for cigarettes. George Luscombe had the circle. Joby Blanchard had the gallery for chocolates – poor sod, they ate more chocolates down below. The hard centres with teeth marks in, Carol, the box-office girl, had. We drew very little money but you could buy off-cut ends of bacon for sixpence a plate in Angel Lane. We couldn't have survived without Angel Lane and its cheap food.

The street traders and shopkeepers of Angel Lane indeed took us to their hearts, which made our lives a lot easier than they might have been, particularly Bert and May at the Cafe L'Ange, where extra large helpings and credit were always available. Though we were around for a long time, I don't think the locals ever quite accepted us as part of the community. We were regarded rather as entertaining eccentrics who didn't seem to mind working long hours and always being hard up. There were times when we couldn't even afford the modest prices of the Cafe L'Ange, and food was cooked in large quantities, for the entire Company, by Isobel, John Blanshard's wife, on an old cooker in the corner of a tiny room off the gallery.

Our survival depended on our willingness to accept conditions which, had we been working for an employer, would never have been tolerated. Harry Greene recalled:

> Working eighteen hours a day and almost twenty-four on a week-end changeover, we managed to paint the theatre, repair seating and damaged carpets, design and print our own posters in the damp, dismally lit basement under the stage. Bill-sticking in the middle of the night on the tube became a necessity. George Cooper's early morning exercise sessions on the flat roof were one of the diversions, as well as rare visits to a good foreign restaurant in the dock area with Joan and Gerry.

Two years were to elapse before the various leases and sub-leases ran out and Gerry obtained money to buy the building. In the meantime there was no money for re-decorating, or even essential repairs, and our efforts to build up an audience certainly weren't helped by the lack of comfort. The central heating system was antiquated and erratic, and regulars soon learned to dress warmly; some even brought blankets. There were usually too few of them to provide warmth for each other. The big draughty stage and the high grid created arctic conditions on the stage itself, and the wings

and backstage were littered with containers to catch the drips from the
leaking roof, high in the flies. Anyway we slapped whitewash on the
dressing room walls, cleaned and scrubbed, and looked forward to the day
when there would be money to spend on restoration. Peggy Soundy was
the founder of the Supporters Club, and a pillar of strength in those early
days:

> The place was in a terrible mess, and it was obvious it was going to
> fold up. When I heard the Workshop was coming in I was delighted.
> I was sitting in the almost empty circle, watching Ewan's *Paradise
> Street* soon after your arrival and got quite carried away. You could
> forget the theatre was cold and not too clean, that the seats weren't
> comfy and there were only twenty people in the audience. I felt I'd
> got to do something to help keep this going. I did a lot of cleaning,
> and gradually we began to collect people. In 1954, on the first
> anniversary, we had a party and started the club, charging five
> shillings a year. At its height we had two thousand members. I
> remember Gerry telling me the Company were totally broke and we
> had to raise some money. We organised a party charging three
> shillings and sixpence a time. There was no Sunday licence for a bar,
> so we had a Speakeasy in George Cooper's dressing room. Anyone
> who wanted a drink was directed up there. It was all highly secretive,
> but we made money – hundreds of people came, many of them
> locals.

Though Ewan's active participation in the Company's work now
virtually ceased, with the help of the Supporters' Club, he organised
'Ballad and Blues' concerts on Sunday evenings. He invited many well-
known folk singers and musicians to take part and they always attracted
good houses. There were also club performances of the plays, followed by
a discussion between members of the Company and the audience, on the
production and our methods of working generally. We made many friends
in this way, and their help was invaluable during these early difficult years.
But it soon became clear that some form of public subsidy was needed. It
was Abe Woolff, a member of West Ham Council, who set the ball rolling:

> I quickly realised that all this talent and effort would be wasted if
> something wasn't done fairly quickly. To watch the cast working
> their hearts out to an audience consisting of, sometimes, less than a
> dozen, was heartbreaking. My first step was to arrange a meeting
> between Joan, Gerry, myself, and leaders of West Ham Council.
> After a couple of meetings, West Ham agreed to help the theatre
> with a small, but reasonable, sum of money. From there I got my
> colleagues on the Council to sponsor an approach to the Councils in

the catchment area. i.e. Hackney, Stepney, Bethnal Green, Leyton, Ilford, Barking etc. A meeting was held with representatives of all these Councils. It was unanimously agreed that the theatre was something needed in the area, and should be helped. It was also agreed to set up a permanent liaison body, to meet every three months to report progress, and I was appointed its first chairman. Each authority contributed a small nominal amount, to show goodwill, and we approached the L.C.C. for help. Later the Arts Council was contacted.

This, of course, all took time, and it was not until 1957 that Local Authority support got underway (see appendix). In the meantime I had to make an appeal for money from the stage after each show with the cast lined up behind me shuffling their feet and cringing with embarrassment. There was a white box in the foyer to receive donations.

We soon realised that, in the initial period, the support didn't warrant running a play for longer than two weeks, and that we were no longer in a position to play only in black drapes. This led to developing a new style of scenic work, as John Bury describes:

We were soon to be doing Chekhov, Ibsen and O'Casey, and, of course, these plays don't work in black drapes. They have to have an ambience, one has to sit down, they need a table, a door, a wall. How *much* of this you need is open to debate. We didn't say it all had to be there in the tradition of the full box set of that era. We were taking the elements we needed out of naturalism, out of realism, to create our own form of settings.

For a short while, young, progressive designers were brought in, who were keen to work with Joan. However, they were unfamiliar with the staging techniques and lighting methods we'd built up over the years, and the way in which settings developed out of rehearsals, from the ideas of director and actors. They would arrive with a model of what they regarded as a finished set. They didn't realise that Joan accepted it simply as a basis, that it would be subject to changes as rehearsals progressed, and that they were expected to construct the sets themselves, with help from the Company, and more often than not, scrounge the materials to do so. So we dispensed with designers, and for quite a long time, the settings were designed by Joan and constructed by the Company under the supervision of John Bury. A situation would be improvised, a door would be needed here, a window there, and gradually, out of stock materials, a set would be put together. Sometimes, we didn't have the right materials. To make the huge ramps for *Edward II* we hired scaffold planking, scrounged off-cuts of hardboard from a local factory to cover the cracks, got out the old canvas rolls, and created, for about twenty-five pounds, a set which, even in those days, would have cost five hundred. We didn't have to pay for labour, of course, all of us working through the night on Saturday changeovers. It was agreed that six hours sleep was sufficient for anyone, so we were released six hours before our call the next day, and John Bury laced our coffee with benzedrine to make sure we kept going. On these occasions, Sunday was a working day. We were breaking all the known Union rules but we had no alternative. We were working for our own theatre and chose to do it. If we hadn't, we would quite simply have had to pack up.

Since joining the Company, John Bury had developed a great expertise in stage lighting, and he realised that the techniques he had developed required their own form of setting:

> The setting had to be a sounding board, as it were, to the light. You couldn't do the sort of lighting we wanted to do inside a box set, so our early settings became an extension of our lighting technique. You needed clear angles, you needed textured rather than painted surfaces.

Textured surfaces, scaffolding and planking, though effective, made for heavy sets. The flats for *Red Roses for Me*, for example, were covered in concrete and then had stones thrown all over them. The cursing and swearing as we moved them during the intervals must have been heard by the audience.

The wardrobe was a ramshackle room high in the roof of the theatre, with a door leading out onto the flies from where we could look down onto the stage. Here Josephine Wilkinson and Shirley Jones toiled, improvising and putting together costumes and with only a few pounds to spend on each show. The budget was gradually increased, but even *Arden of Faversham* and *Volpone*, the shows that swept the Paris Festival in 1954, were both costumed for £10. Josephine Wilkinson:

> Everything was done to economise. Sometimes we tried to eke out our money by sorting out some rags and taking them along to the rag and scrap bloke who had a yard just along the road. Our regular places for cheap materials were the surplus and ex-service stores in East India Dock Road and the Mile End Road. We'd go around the second-hand clothes shops, there was a particularly nasty dirty one opposite the theatre. When things got a bit more prosperous we would go up to Soho to Berwick Market to Gaber and Nicholls and we would wander round Les's stall and pick up cheap off-cuts. When we persuaded Gerry that there was no alternative to hiring we

would go to the Old Vic costume place, just off Drury Lane, presided over by Mr. Arnos.

At first there was only the old treddle machine which I believe was 'lifted' from the house in Glasgow. A faithful friend in spite of its age and worn out parts. Shirley brought her own machine when she came, then Gerry acquired an industrial machine from his father. It had to be bolted to the table, it shook the floor and made a frightful noise, so it couldn't be used during shows. It was a great boon, it could manage thick material and even leather.

We had plenty of voluntary helpers. A steady stream of friends, wives and girl friends who helped sewing on buttons and unpicking things. I don't know how we'd have managed if materials hadn't kept turning up. Gerry produced a bale of khaki wool shirting, Shirley's father provided some sheepskins for a lion costume and a local firm came up with a mass of reject stuff called 'Stayform'.

Shirley Jones added her recollections of those difficult days:

We always had to abandon our first ideas because of lack of money. Mostly we spent our time rehashing old clothes, always with an eye to the shows ahead. We had to be careful not to take too much liberty with a garment in case we shortened its life. We had favourite costumes which lent themselves to an incredible number of shows, and there were some we hated and longed to destroy, but dared not. Some were sacred and apparently indestructible like the 'Sganarelle' costume from *The Flying Doctor* which was used in almost every period play for years! We had a small and precious collection of boots and shoes which had to adapt to all periods. Size was the problem, those of the Company with very large feet had to finish up with 'doctored' wellies.

Tights were difficult to make, and expensive knitwear was the only material available at that time for making them. Fortunately we were given some material and a girl joined the Company who knew how to make them. So Jose and I turned out tights like maniacs and dyed them in the top bar!

Schweik was the show that gave us the most work. We had eighty costumes, all in black and white, to make in two weeks. Jose and I were up several nights on that. Finally I bought black tape and glued and stuck on all the details instead of trying to sew them on. We had a few awful wigs that we tried to manage with, but on the odd occasion when we just had to hire, there was always an awful row about the cost.

When an actor had to look smart to go up to Town, we lent him our 'best clothes.' We had one or two good shirts and suits in a second-hand hoard which fitted some of the Company, and they could be made to look quite respectable. We always tried to supply actors with a mock-up of a costume for rehearsals, particularly for period plays. We could then cope with snags as they arose, things that fell off, costumes that had to fit over or under without showing, pockets to be hidden, how to make it easier for an actor to move, and so on.

The result was that the actor felt that what he was wearing belonged to him and was not simply something a designer had thought up after reading the script.

During the early years, management had been a company task, performed by the person best able to do it at that particular time. Tours had been organised by John and Margaret Bury, and I had managed the Company in the Kendal days, and on the earlier visits to the Edinburgh Fringe and some of the schools tours. When we had run out of money, we went our separate ways, coming together again when more money had been raised, usually by Gerry. He was now full time manager of Theatre Workshop Ltd. and two years later in 1955, he obtained money to buy the theatre when the various leases ran out. He now had the task of keeping a roof over our head. The overheads went on week after week even when the theatre was dark. Electricity and gas, which could be cut off for non-payment, somehow always got their money, but stamps for insurance cards could be put off, and when the day of reckoning came, the money to buy them was never there. On one unfortunate occasion, all the cards, fully stamped of course, somehow got incinerated in the boiler. John Bury, who was Gerry's close friend, understood, perhaps better than anyone, apart from Joan herself, the problems he had to face:

> Gerry's contribution was absolutely enormous. He had the worst job of the lot of us. You see, Joan was having a ball. She had her own theatre troupe, she had her own theatre. She was in a position to do a lot of what she wanted to do. The only thing that hampered us all was lack of money. She didn't lack talent in her actors. She didn't lack the scripts or scenic devices. She had an enormous amount of help, but she didn't have enough money. This was Gerry's terribly difficult job, because most people who arrange the finances of organisations have a very strict control. They say 'This is how much is going to be spent' or 'This is what we are going to do' but Joan, myself and the Company never accepted this from Gerry. We did what had to be done and Gerry had to go out and find the money. He had to make the books balance at the end of the week, and of course, they never did. He had to scrounge a lot of money. One knows that

his family helped us a lot, and for that we are always enormously grateful. When driven to his wits' end he used to actually have to get into conflict with Joan about sizes of cast, how long we could play and so on, and this was very upsetting. There was Gerry in the 'top office' and we expected to get, not a salary, but our pittance at the end of the week, because we are talking about just enough money to keep going, and often there wasn't enough for that. I don't think anyone in the Company would have swapped Gerry's job, nobody else could have done it.

One of Gerry's less demanding managerial tasks was dividing the free Abdullah cigarettes amongst the smokers. They worked out at seven and a half each and Gerry would cut the halves with a razor blade. The credit 'Cigarettes by Abdullah' dutifully appeared in all the programmes, including *Richard II*. To counteract the cigarettes and the somewhat monotonous diet, I doled out vitamin pills and cod liver oil supplied by a local G.P. Dr. Elliot of Ilford, a keen supporter of the Company, who generously took upon himself the task of keeping an eye on our physical wellbeing. I had to enter the doses in a little book he gave me with a column for noting minor ailments.

We continued to function as a co-operative in the sense that we all received the same money. We didn't have Equity contracts because, strictly speaking, we didn't have a management and couldn't afford the Equity minimum anyway. In theory, all members of the Company continued to have a right to participate in policy-making, but after our arrival in Stratford, Company meetings became more and more a formality, and only decisions on minor issues could be influenced. Gerry's phrase 'If you've got a dog, why do the barking yourself' rather summed up the situation. He would sit calmly smoking his pipe, listening to the argument and discussion, knowing that, in the final analysis, Joan, John Bury and himself would make the decisions. In that particular situation, perhaps it was the only way we could function efficiently. What is arguable, and it was certainly argued by Ewan, was whether it was the right sort of situation for our sort of company to be in. However, most of the Company were happy enough to get on with their acting. Harry Corbett put it this way:

We never really argued about the policy in Company meetings, looking back, because everything that was presented to us was wilder than our wildest dreams. I mean, who's going to argue with *Volpone* or *Richard II*? Or *Arden of Faversham* and *The Dutch Courtesan*? Or *Hobson's Choice* and *Schweik*? Who's going to argue?

Certainly we were all pleased that we now had the opportunity and the facilities to put on a wider range of plays. It was the end, also, of the uncomfortable journeys in the back of the lorry, the nightly rigging and de-rigging, the irregular meals and the ever changing 'digs'. Sleeping in the dressing rooms of the Theatre Royal was no luxury but it offered privacy and the comforting thought that when exhaustion took over, a bed in familiar surroundings was near at hand. We had no longer to face the booking of halls, publicity and all the other problems connected with one-night stand touring. It didn't take long to discover, though, that we had exchanged one set of problems for another and that life, while different, was not all that much easier. There was no ready-made audience, so we now faced the task of trying to build one up and that meant mounting a new production at least every two weeks. It involved rehearsing and playing all day and changing over the set every other weekend. We were now a repertory company, but we weren't putting on the usual run of repertory plays. We no longer had the length of rehearsal period needed for the sort of play we were doing, so rep experience was an advantage. Avis Bunnage:

> There weren't many girls in the company and they were inexperienced, so, having had so many years in repertory, I got all the best parts. I was playing dumb blondes and all sorts of parts I would never normally play.

Most of the Company now lived in the theatre, and apart from popping down to the Cafe L'Ange in Angel Lane for a midday meal, when they could afford it, they rarely had any occasion to leave it. After overheads had been paid, we relied on what was left from the Box Office for our basic needs, and it was just as well there was no opportunity to spend money. The amount available varied from week to week, and on one occasion when there was nothing at all, the entire Company had to be helped out by the local Social Security office. It wasn't easy explaining to the bewildered clerk that we couldn't sign on for dole because we weren't actually available for work and that it really was possible to work 12 hours a day, every day, and still have no money at the end of the week. During the first year or so, wages averaged around £2 a week; in 1955 around £4. It soon became evident that more time for rehearsals was essential, and after a year we changed over to three weekly repertory. In the first two years we put on thirty-six plays (see Appendix) all either classics or plays written or adapted especially for the Company. This concentrated period of training, rehearsing and playing enormously strengthened the Company and made 1954/55 and 1956 the vintage years at Stratford. The technical staff too, though working on small budgets, benefited from the adequate space and workshops now available, and they were able to build more complicated sets and experiment with new techniques in design and construction.

24

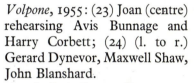

Volpone, 1955: (23) Joan (centre) rehearsing Avis Bunnage and Harry Corbett; (24) (l. to r.) Gerard Dynevor, Maxwell Shaw, John Blanshard.

An Italian Straw Hat, 1955: (25) (l. to r.) Shirley Dynevor, Peter Bridgemont, Robert Gillespie, Maxwell Shaw; (26) Veronica Wells, Maxwell Shaw.

26

25

Richard II, 1955: (27) Harry Corbett as Richard.
Arden of Faversham, 1955: (28) (l. to r.) Barry Clayton, Howard Goorney, Peter Bridgemont, Maxwell Shaw; (29) Gerard Dynevor, Barbara Brown.

30

31

The Quare Fellow, 1956: (30) Glynn Edwards, Gerard Dynevor and Company.
Macbeth, 1959: (31) opening scene.
Fings Ain't Wot They Used T'Be, 1959: (32) Miriam Karlin, Glynn Edwards.

32

33

33–35: Movement classes conducted by Jean Newlove (bottom left, 34), 1959.

34

George Cooper recalls our opening production:

> Previous to our arrival the theatre had dropped down to a sleazy
> fourth rate variety set-up, with drag shows and God knows what,
> and when the local people saw the show billed as *Twelfth Night* I
> think they thought it was a bedroom farce or something. I was
> playing Malvolio with this enormous hat on, and as soon as I got on
> the stage there were cries of 'Big head, big head'. They threw toffees
> on the stage, they threw pennies, they really had a ball.

The extent to which Theatre Workshop succeeded in building up a
local audience was always a matter for conjecture, but it was certainly
never sufficient to keep the theatre going without support from other parts
of London. As costs increased and no subsidy was forthcoming, even that
wasn't enough and we had to look for transfers to the West End. Harry
Corbett had no illusions about the audience:

> We never appealed to the working class. All I could ever see were
> beards and duffle coats every time I peered into the audience. It was
> the day of the angry young whatever. No way was there a local
> following, only in the sense of a few eccentrics – Johnny Speight was
> one – and they were leaving their working-class environment. Never
> a solid working-class audience in any way.

The argument gets bogged down in definitions of 'working-class' and
'local'. The Supporters Club, founded by Peggy Soundy, had a
membership at one time of two thousand. They cast their net wide and no
doubt many of them couldn't be described as working-class; but if we
accept 'local' as being a radius covered by five miles, then we can
undoubtedly claim a following in that area. In addition, the Club was a
great morale booster to the Company, stimulating active interest in our
work and providing us with some good friends.

There was the inevitable disagreement about the right sort of play.
George Harvey Webb thought the emphasis should have been local:

> We should have got plays out of the locality, and there were plenty of
> stories going about. Old Mother Compton, with a treasure house full
> of fridges and washing machines and six children, so they never put
> her in prison. It was a sort of thieves' den. There were tragic
> incidents too. The kid who got mugged coming home from school –
> his body wasn't found for four days. Had we put these sort of stories
> on the stage, I think it would have worked.

It is far from certain that this would have been the answer. A play by a
local writer, Anthony Nicholson, set in Stratford, wasn't well supported.
Peggy Soundy said:

In *Van Call* you were trying to put across a line and you could feel
it. If it doesn't come from somebody's gut, in a real sort of way, it
shows, and I think the locals saw this. On the other hand, they loved
The Good Soldier Schweik. I used to travel home to East Ham on
the bus, and I'd be sitting there with the theatre audience. I could
hear them talking about the show and they felt *Schweik* was,
somehow, part of them.

The people of Stratford who provided us with cheap food and lent us
props became our friends, and they came along, curious to see what we
were up to. They expressed no preference for plays about local events or
characters and, indeed, preferred *Richard II* to *Van Call*. They
represented, of course, a small minority of the local population. The
majority had no views on the matter, because they just didn't want to see
anything. Theatre played no part in their lives and we were now engaged in
the uphill task of trying to change that situation.

We had some success with the schoolchildren of the area. With the help
of the local Education Authorities, they packed the theatre for
performances of *Richard II* and other classics, and for Christmas shows
like *Treasure Island* and *Christmas Carol* and the Company experimented
with Saturday morning shows.

Interesting and exciting productions like *The Alchemist*, *Dutch
Courtesan* and O'Casey's *Red Roses for Me* came and went, playing to
small but enthusiastic audiences, but unseen by the national critics. When
they did begin to make the journey to Stratford, around the time of the
revival of *Richard II* in January 1955, it was only to be expected that Joan
would be singled out for praise. As a group theatre we had never, in the
past, sought personal publicity, but as Harry Corbett recalled, we were
now in a new situation:

> I think it began with *Arden of Faversham*, the first time the play had
> been done for three hundred years, and gradually our popularity
> increased. The notices all started – 'Joan Littlewood this that and the
> other.' We had all been inculcated with the non-personality cult and
> we felt, rightly or wrongly, that Joan was being forced into a situation
> she didn't really want, that for publicity purposes, she was being put
> through the screws. Then came massive Sunday coverage. They tried
> to single out the actors, and eventually they got to know them and
> that, quite rightly, caused a certain amount of dissension.

In the past we'd had plenty of local publicity in the places we visited,
the occasional article in a national magazine, and acclaim from the foreign
press on our trips abroad. But now, for the first time, we were under the
constant scrutiny of the national critics. It wasn't something to avoid, even

if that had been possible, and when notices were good it brought in the audiences. It did mean, however, that as actors began to be singled out for their performances, offers of work would sometimes follow and they were tempted away to bigger, if not better, things. Also, as Ewan had predicted, we were now becoming increasingly dependent on the goodwill of the critics. Eventually their favourable response to a particular show would lead to offers of transfer to the West End which, in the absence of a subsidy, we were in no position to refuse, but which also ultimately led to the break-up of the Company.

Richard II which had just been produced by the Company in January 1954 was revived in January 1955 to coincide with Michael Benthall's production at the Old Vic, and with the intention of inviting comparison between the two productions. They had a cast of forty-five, we had fourteen, and a great deal of doubling and trebling. (I finished up with four parts.) The differences in approach were predictable. At the Old Vic all was pomp and ceremony. On a stage full of light, coloured pennants flew, fanfares played, and the attendant Lords and spear-carriers manoeuvred into position, while everyone waited for the scenes to begin. The actors were elegantly dressed and beautifully spoken. John Neville's Richard, as befitted an actor who had been compared to the young Gielgud, was a truly regal figure, always aware of his bearing and the poetry of the lines, even when chained to the floor of his cell. While not pretending to be objective in our judgement, we didn't feel that anyone on the stage was really involved in the events taking place. In John Bury's stark setting, conceived to emphasise fear and oppression, we aimed to bring out the hatred and cruelty of the period. Light was used to break up the stage, scenes were able to merge swiftly one into another, and there was no pause for spectacle. Our concern always was for the inner action behind the lines – what they meant, rather than the poetry of the words. Harry Corbett's Richard was a less noble figure, slightly unbalanced, and with an effeminate streak. An unorthodox interpretation certainly, but consistent with the arrogance, cruelty and ultimate self-pity of the man. He may have lacked some of the poetry of John Neville, but the lines were alive and their meaning unmistakable. It was all rather more than the critics could take, and we probably just lost the contest by a few points. The general feeling was that we needed some of the Old Vic regard for poetry and they could profit from some of our energy and conviction. However, our vindication was the approval and enthusiasm of the Stratford audience, and the run had to be extended.

Highly praised also was Joan's modern dress production of Ben Jonson's *Volpone* in March 1955. Without needing to alter or cut, it transposed to modern day Italy, as a satire on spivs and hangers-on; Mosca rode a bicycle laden with pineapples and champagne, Corbaccio wheeled himself around in an invalid chair and Sir Politic Would-Be, the Englishman abroad, wore swimming trunks and carried a snorkel. This production took the Paris Festival by storm when it played there with another successful production, *Arden of Faversham*.

Despite these successes abroad no subsidy was forthcoming and we were still wholly dependent on the Box Office for our wages which, if receipts permitted, were now £4 per week. A substantial nucleus had now been working together for some time, Harry Corbett, Joby Blanshard, George Cooper, Gerard Dynevor, Marjorie Lawrence, George Luscombe, Maxwell Shaw and myself. The measure of understanding between the actors and the complete trust in each other was reflected in the productions of this period. It was group theatre in its truest sense and, with Joan as its catalyst, was at the peak of its achievement.

Thanks to the good offices of Oscar Lewenstein, Theatre Workshop had obtained the British rights of *Mother Courage* from Bertolt Brecht, and Oscar suggested we present it with *Richard II* at the Devon Festival in Barnstaple in the summer of 1955. Lewenstein:

> I went to Berlin, saw Brecht and said I thought Joan would make a perfect Mother Courage and that Theatre Workshop was a company that ought to have his sympathy. He was very co-operative, and said we could use any of the designs, music and so on and he'd send a young assistant called Karl Weber to assist in the production. The next thing I heard from Karl was that he'd been refused admission to rehearsals and that Joan had decided to put another actress in the part of Mother Courage. This development had to be reported to Brecht who threatened to bring an injunction to stop the play going on unless Joan played the part. So, rather late in the day, Joan put herself back in the part and the play opened at the Tor and Torridge Festival at Barnstaple. The first professional performance of a Brecht play in Britain, but it wasn't a very wonderful performance, it was bit of a shambles. Neither Brecht nor Theatre Workshop wanted to transfer it to London.

As it transpires, it might have been more fruitful if Joan, or even someone else, had followed Brecht's own production script that Karl Weber had brought with him to London so as to leave Joan with more time to concentrate on the difficult role of Mother Courage. As it was, her energies were divided, to the ultimate detriment of her performance and the production. It failed to make the anticipated impact, and there was a general feeling that it had not succeeded in bringing out the real merits of the play.

There followed, though not as a direct consequence of the adverse reaction to *Mother Courage*, the most significant changes that were to take place in the composition of the Group. After the Devon Festival, Harry Corbett, Joby (John) Blanshard and George Cooper left to take up other work in the theatre. They were followed shortly afterwards by George Luscombe who returned to Canada to form his own company. The nucleus of the company built up over years was now split. Those that remained, including Maxwell Shaw, Gerard Dynevor, Avis Bunnage and myself, were joined by Brian Murphy, Dudley Foster, Glynn Edwards and others. Though some were to remain with the company for a long time, there was far less stability from this time on, and many actors were to come and go over the succeeding years.

There was also to be less emphasis on the training and discussion which formed an integral part of the work over the first ten years – a trend that was hastened in 1958 by the switch from classics and revivals to contemporary plays and the resulting West End transfers. Dance and movement ability and social awareness essential to an actor playing in MacColl's *Uranium 235* or *The Other Animals* were hardly necessary when appearing in *Fings* or *A Taste of Honey*. The attracting of new writers to the Company also became a necessary part of the struggle to achieve critical recognition and financial stability in the face of continued lack of subsidy.

The influx of new actors, some of whom had had conventional theatre training or experience, resulted in a change in working relationships. Much had to be re-learned, and the emphasis was now on learning from Joan rather than on learning together as previously. Consequently, her role, always a key one, now became predominant. So the focus from 1955 onwards tended towards Joan's work in the Company, without, I hope, minimising the contributions of those who worked with her.

Harry Corbett returned in 1960 to play in *Ned Kelly* and George Cooper in 1964 to play Falstaff in *Henry IV*, but none of those who left at this time were in the West End successes that followed the policy of new plays. But that is looking ahead. Those who were left returned from the Devon Festival to the Theatre Royal in the autumn of 1955, and the re-formed company opened its new season with *The Sheepwell* by Lope de Vega. It was followed by a re-production of *The Good Soldier Schweik* from the Czech novel of Jaroslav Hasek which had been first staged by the Company the year before. Maxwell Shaw replaced George Cooper in the title role. It received good notices and was followed by *An Italian Straw Hat* by Labiche. The sets and costumes were beautifully designed by Claude Marks, and this was one of the rare occasions when a designer was brought in from outside the Company. *Schweik* was revived for the West End and transferred to the Duke of York's Theatre in March 1956. The opening night was a glossy affair with many stars in attendance, but the West End audience proved less appreciative than the Stratford one. Unlike the audiences at the Paris Festival, they were more used to naturalistic acting and set. In style and presentation *Schweik* didn't follow the tradition of British theatre, which had always managed to insulate itself from the influence of theatrical movements on the Continent. The stylised acting was not to West End taste, and the decor of black and white cartoons on revolving screens was too avant-garde.

Harold Hobson gave it one of the few good notices, and it ran for only a few weeks. It would have been wiser to have resisted the temptation of the transfer and extended the successful run at Stratford, but we underestimated the insularity of the West End audiences.

Our brief visit to the West End was followed by another notable Elizabethan production, Marlowe's *Edward II*, in which Peter Smallwood gave a most moving performance as the tragic King. John Bury created a rich evocative setting of a vast map of England covering the tilted floor of the stage, across which Edward dies. Jean Vilar and the T.N.P. Company, who had seen the Company at the Paris Festival, were our guests at a performance, and enlivened the curtain call with loud 'Bravos'. Jean Vilar said after the performance — 'We shall never stop hailing your theatre as being the most vital in England.' The subsidy for his company at the time was the equivalent of £54,000. We were receiving £100 from the West Ham Council.

Then came *The Quare Fellow*. I recall Joan's enthusiasm for a script she had received from a Dublin playwright called Brendan Behan, and which had been rejected by the Abbey Theatre. Set in a prison, it was a rambling story of the last twenty-four hours in a condemned man's life, seen through the eyes of the wardens and his fellow prisoners. It would need cutting and shaping, but was full of wonderful characters and humour. I knew a lot of hard work was involved and I was tired and couldn't face it. So I opted out for a few weeks and, feeling rather pleased with myself, went to do a special week at St. Helens Rep. in a well-tried Lancashire comedy. All I had to do was more or less learn the lines. Then on to a broadcast in Manchester where I didn't need to learn them at all. However, it was clear from the reviews on the Sunday after *The Quare Fellow* opened that Joan's enthusiasm had been well founded, and I felt less pleased with myself. The critics were unanimous and fulsome in their praise. Bernard Levin had this to say:

Brendan Behan is the most exciting new talent to enrich our theatre since the war, and his play is a marvellous combination of passion and humour which dwarfs anything else to be seen at present in London, West or East. It is not in mortals to command success. Brendan Behan has done more, at one bound, he has achieved immortality.

During the run of *The Quare Fellow* the Company received £10 a week – the first time wages at Stratford reached double figures.

The achievement was the result of a great deal of hard work, even more than I had imagined. Rehearsals were well under way before the cast were given scripts or told what parts they were playing. They had just to set about creating the atmosphere of prison life, marching round and round the flat roof of the Theatre Royal as prisoners on exercise. The day to day routines were improvised, cleaning out cells, the quick smoke, the furtive conversation, trading tobacco and the boredom and meanness of prison life were explored. The improvisations had, of course, been selected by Joan with the script in mind, and when it was finally introduced, the situation and the relationships had been well explored. The bulk of the work had been done and the groundwork laid for any cutting and shaping that was necessary. Brendan welcomed this way of working and commented on the finished play – 'Christ, I'm a bloody genius' and in his curtain speech on the first night – 'Miss Littlewood's company has performed a better play than I wrote.'

Brendan was well supported by his fellow countrymen on the first night at Stratford. In the audience were three I.R.A. men who had been barred from the country, more than fifteen recognised leaders of the Republican Movement, men whose prison sentences totalled three hundred years, and two Special Branch detectives. When the Irish National Anthem was played in the course of the action, half the audience stood to attention. This, of course, was in 1956, long before the terrorist campaign of the I.R.A. had begun. Brendan became overnight the darling of the media, and his fondness for drink, which was to eventually kill him, made good copy for the popular press. One unfortunate result, amongst several, was a completely incoherent interview on television with Malcolm Muggeridge, which led to scores of outraged viewers ringing in to protest at the spectacle and the language.

Brendan was not spurred on by the success of *The Quare Fellow*. On the contrary, it rather overwhelmed him, and getting a second play, *The Hostage*, out of him was to prove a long and painful process. Despite the good notices it had received, *Quare Fellow* only ran for a couple of months in the West End followed by a short tour.

There followed a season of plays produced by John Bury, who had been left in charge of the theatre for a few months. It consisted of *Captain Brassbound's Conversion, Treasure Island, The Playboy of the Western World, The Duchess of Malfi* and *School for Wives*. If not reaching the heights of some of the earlier classical productions, they certainly maintained the standard which was now expected from the Company and provided the necessary continuity of production.

Joan returned to produce her modern dress version of *Macbeth* which was taken to Moscow and is described in the chapter on 'Foreign Tours'. *You Won't Always Be On Top*, which followed, was by Henry Chapman, a building worker, and one of Theatre Workshop's rare incursions into naturalism. The theme was a day in the life of a building site, and John Bury's setting reproduced in every detail a three-storey building in the course of construction, including a working concrete mixer. During each performance an entire brick wall was actually constructed, the cast having learnt the art of bricklaying from builders working on a new post office in Stratford. The plot was a series of everyday incidents bound together by the job in hand, each incident developing easily into the next. Harold Hobson objected to the detail, describing it as 'Seen through the eyes of Zola and not Chekhov.' Ken Tynan disagreed with him, as he often did in those days, and gave it a very good notice. However, what attracted the public interest was not the notices, good or bad, but the Court proceedings which arose out of the performances and which became something of a 'cause célèbre'. The exchanges that arise naturally between men working on a building sight lent themselves readily to improvisation, and as the cast became more familiar with the situation and their relationships developed, the language became less restrained. The Lord Chamberlain sent two of his minions with their notebooks to a performance and, as a result of their visit, the Management were summoned to West Ham Magistrates Court and charged that they had 'Unlawfully for hire presented parts of a new stage play ... before such parts had been allowed by the Lord Chamberlain contrary to Section 15 of the Theatres Act 1843.'

Gerry Raffles as General Manager, John Bury as licensee of the theatre, Joan Littlewood as producer, Henry Chapman, playwright and Richard Harris, actor, appeared in court. Richard Harris was accused of imitating Winston Churchill's voice at the official opening of a public lavatory, to which particular charge he pleaded guilty. The wider implications of the case were immediately recognised. It was seen as part of the fight against censorship in the theatre generally, and the proceedings aroused a great deal of interest and publicity. A fund was set up to ensure that the case for the defence was conducted as well as possible and the sponsors included the Earl of Harewood, Kenneth Tynan, George Devine, Peter Hall and Henry Sherek, the West End impresario. Gerald Gardiner Q.C. and Harold Lever M.P., now Lord Lever, who had been Business Manager of Theatre Union in 1938, conducted the defence, making no charge for their services.

The accused naturally pleaded guilty, a plea that was upheld by the Court, but it was a hollow victory for the Lord Chamberlain. The fines imposed were minimal, less than £15 in total, including costs, and the case against censorship in the theatre had been given a good airing. The Censorship Reform Committee was set up soon afterwards. This speeded the eventual demise of the Lord Chamberlain's office in 1968.

A week of *Macbeth* at the Oxford Playhouse was followed by *And The Wind Blew* by Edgard da Rocha Miranda at the Theatre Royal, a contemporary play set in a small village in Brazil. The next production, *Man, Beast and Virtue* by Pirandello, was produced by Franci Jamnik, a director of the National Theatre Slovenia. It ran for six weeks at Stratford, followed by three weeks at the Lyric Theatre, Hammersmith. During those three weeks *Celestina* was produced at Stratford. In March 1958, Joan made one of her periodic acting appearances as Amanda Wingfield in *The Glass Menagerie* by Tennessee Williams. It was directed by Clifford Williams who had worked as an actor in Theatre Workshop in the pre-Stratford period. John Bury then directed Shaw's *Man of Destiny* and *Love and Lectures* – a selection of the correspondence between Ellen Terry and Bernard Shaw – followed by Sartre's *The Respectable Prostitute*.

All these played to reasonable houses, but it was now evident that a realistic subsidy was necessary if the overheads of the theatre were to be covered. The Arts Council had doubled its grant, but it still only amounted to £1,000 and Local Authority grants totalled around £950. There was little hope of any substantial increase from these sources, and the Company was forced to look to West End transfers for its financial salvation. With the arrival of the script of *A Taste of Honey* by Shelagh Delaney, the first of these successful transfers was less than a year ahead.

THEATRE ROYAL
and PALACE OF VARIETIES
STRATFORD, E.15

Sole Lessees—Theatres and Music Halls (South) Ltd.
Licensee and Managing Director— J. Roland Sales, F.V.A.
GENERAL MANAGER — HARRY LOSS

By arrangement with Theatres and Music Halls (South) Ltd.

THEATRE WORKSHOP
PRESENT
A SEASON OF GREAT PLAYS

FIRST PRODUCTION

TWELFTH NIGHT
By Shakespeare

PRODUCED BY JOAN LITTLEWOOD

PROGRAMME THREEPENCE

FOR ADVERTISING ON THE
PROGRAMME OR SCREEN
AT THIS THEATRE, APPLY:
THE "EXPERT" ADVERTISING CO. LTD.
GLENWOOD HOUSE, ALLERTON HILL,
LEEDS 7.

THEATRE ROYAL
AND
PALACE OF VARIETIES
STRATFORD, E.15.

GRAND THEATRE SEASON
OF
GREAT PLAYS

PRESENTED BY

THEATRE WORKSHOP
(BY ARRANGEMENT WITH THEATRES AND MUSIC HALLS (SOUTH) LTD)

THE INTERNATIONALLY FAMOUS
COMPANY THAT HAS PLAYED IN
THE MOST IMPORTANT CAPITALS
OF EUROPE.

"THE MOST EXCITING THEATRE COMPANY
I HAVE EVER SEEN."   —Sam Wanamaker.

"A MODEL OF WHAT A THEATRE GROUP
SHOULD BE."   —The Times.

OPENING PRODUCTION

TWELFTH NIGHT
By SHAKESPEARE.

COMMENCING MONDAY, FEBRUARY 2nd, 1953
NIGHTLY at 7-30.   SATURDAYS 6-0 and 8-30 p.m.
BOX OFFICE OPEN FROM 10 a.m.   Telephone: MARYLAND 1075
POPULAR PRICES.

Eight

1958–1961
The Price of Success

The West End transfers

During the three years from 1959 to 1961, there were five successful transfers of plays from the Theatre Royal, Stratford, to the West End. Theatre Workshop's share of the resulting profits kept the Theatre Royal going and provided the actors involved with a much needed improvement in their standard of living. But the ultimate result was far from beneficial: the disintegration of the Company and Joan's departure in 1961 to work in Nigeria. And two years were to elapse before there was another Theatre Workshop production.

On 27 May 1958 Shelagh Delaney's *A Taste of Honey* had its opening night at the Theatre Royal. The author was nineteen and had worked in an engineering factory and as a cinema usherette in Salford. After seeing Terence Rattigan's *Variations on a Theme* at the Opera House in Manchester, she decided she could do better.

Her play is set in a sparsely furnished, sordid bed-sitting room in Salford, the lodgings, for the time being, of a teenage schoolgirl and her mother, a brassy tart who contrives to live off a series of boy friends. She goes off with the intention of marrying her current beau, and the girl, left alone, has an affair with a coloured sailor, who leaves her pregnant. She is befriended by an effeminate art student, who wishes to look after her, but is turned out when her mother returns, her marriage in ruins. With the mother talking directly to the audience and taking them into her confidence, Joan's production gave the play a theatrical quality which brought out the richness of the humour and the very real development in the characters of the student and the girl. The language is full of idiomatic catchphrases, a rich expressive dialect, and it came as a welcome relief from the rigid, stereotyped dialogue which had, over the years, become the hallmark of traditional character acting.

I asked Frances Cuka about rehearsals of *A Taste Of Honey*:

The first read-through lasted about four and a half hours. There were a lot of people there and they took it in turns to read the parts, but I was the only one reading Jo. The next day it was whittled down to Avis Bunnage and someone else reading the mother, and Murray Melvin and Jimmy Booth reading Geoffrey. It wasn't finally cast until the day we started rehearsals. There was a considerable amount of re-writing but most of the best bits were Shelagh's. We did a lot of improvisation using the original dialogue. It was too long, of course, but I think Shelagh just wrote down what she felt without editing or cutting. Peter, the mother's boy-friend, came in for the most re-writing. Some outrageous speeches of his were kept in because Joan said it was a young girl's play and we musn't wreck the flavour of it …

Avis Bunnage, initially at least, didn't share Joan's tremendous enthusiasm for the play:

My first reaction was that whoever wrote this needed a swift kick up the arse. We did a lot of improvisation. When we came to bits that didn't seem to work we ad-libbed round the ideas, made it up as we went along. We used things that were around, an aspidistra that someone had left on the stage became incorporated into the production. I said some of my lines to it. Joan gave us hell during rehearsals. She had us running from the stage to the paint bay and back over and over again, to give us a feeling of real tiredness …

The critics were divided. Some praised it highly, others found it too sordid for their tastes and were unable to accept the situation or the characters as plausible. They were unanimous in their praise of the performances of Avis Bunnage as the mother, Frances Cuka as the girl and Murray Melvin as the art student. Shelagh won the Henry Foyle new play award. Graham Greene described the play as: 'Having all the freshness of John Osborne's *Look Back in Anger* and a greater maturity.' The film rights were sold, and a year later it was to transfer to the West End.

A financial crisis hit the Company in June 1958 when the Arts Council withdrew their grant on the grounds of lack of support from local councils and audience. There followed a correspondence in the columns of *The Times* between Joan and the Arts Council, in which she denounced their attitude, pointing out that total grants over a period of four years had only been £2,350. Graham Greene joined in, offering to contribute £100 if nine others would do so, thus replacing the £1,000 withdrawn by the Arts Council.

A note in the *Taste of Honey* programme read: – 'Provided we are allowed by economic circumstances, by the goodwill of the landlord, and by a change of heart on the part of the Arts Council, we will re-open this theatre in the Autumn of 1958 with another series of new or forgotten plays which help to interpret the modern world in exciting dramatic terms.'

As a result of increased support from local councils, the Arts Council restored their grant, and the theatre did re-open, after a three months' closure, on 14 October 1958 with Brendan Behan's *The Hostage*. The play the audience finally saw on the first night had been built up over the rehearsal period in a way that was unique to Brendan Behan. Surrounded by bottles of Guinness, he regaled the cast for hours with anecdotes, songs, imitations of the lead fiddle at the Dublin Gaiety Theatre, and his idea of how actors behaved at the Royal Court. Out of all this wealth of meandering entertainment would emerge material which could be incorporated into the script. Tremendously helpful to the actors were his true stories about the people on whom his characters were based. Miss Gilchrist, the social worker in the play, emerged during a pub session. When actual written material was needed, desperate measures had, sometimes, to be taken, as Avis Bunnage recalled:

> Brendan was going round the Covent Garden pubs in the morning, taking a kip in the afternoon and drinking again at night, so he wasn't taking too much notice of rehearsals. The actors were improvising a second act and Joan was getting desperate, so one night, Gerry sat Brendan down, pointed a gun at him and told him to write. It probably wasn't loaded, but it did the trick.

Re-writing went on until the very last minute, and the afternoon before we opened some of us were in a state of confusion and quite sure we had a flop on our hands. We could no longer see the wood for the trees, and weren't sure what it all added up to. A Dublin brothel full of eccentrics, a young English soldier held as hostage to prevent the execution of a young Irishman, a mock air raid, a few songs and dances and 'taking the mickey' out of an I.R.A. officer. It all seemed a mess, if a glorious one, and quite lacking in form. But we had underestimated Joan's overall vision and imagination. From the first moment, it worked, and it filled the theatre night after night. At the end of two months, it was decided the local audiences should have a change of programme, and as the Christmas season was now on us, Joan's adaptation of *A Christmas Carol* was put on.

The Saturday night of the first week of *The Hostage* was the first completely full house the Company had ever had. A search was made for the 'Full House' board, which was eventually found, tattered and motheaten, underneath the stage. It was to stand outside the theatre many times during the next few years. A black market in tickets sprang up and spivs sold them outside the theatre at double the price. It was one of those rare occasions when the critics were unanimous in their prasie – even Harold Hobson and Ken Tynan were in agreement. Tynan described the show as 'A prophetic and joyously exciting evening,' and Hobson as 'An honour to our theatre'. A transfer to the West End was a forgone conclusion.

Following *A Christmas Carol*, *A Taste of Honey* was revived at Stratford as a run-in for its transfer to the West End; this being brought about by the good offices of the impresario Oscar Lewenstein – a man with genuine love of theatre and great insight. He had been a friend of Theatre Workshop for many years, and though he had doubts about the commercial viability of *A Taste of Honey* he felt it important that it should be shown to a wider audience in the West End. He brought Donald Albery down to Stratford, and the two of them took it into Albery's theatre, the Wyndham's, on 10 February 1959, with the original cast, after Joan had resisted demands that she re-cast with star names. It transfered from there to the Criterion (to make way for *The Hostage*) and ran in the West End for almost a year without the benefit of star names, though Joan as director was of course now something of an attraction and Shelagh had received a tremendous amount of publicity when the play had been first produced.

Awards came thick and fast from *Variety* in the U.S.A. – Frances Cuka was named the Most Promising Actress of 1959; Murray Melvin was runner-up as Most Promising Actor; Joan as director came second to Jerome Robbins for his production of *West Side Story*; and Shelagh Delaney came third after Peter Shaffer and Willis Hall.

A week after the West End opening of *A Taste of Honey*, Frank Norman's *Fings Ain't Wot They Used T'Be* had its first performance at the Theatre Royal. Frank had written forty-eight pages of dialogue in 1958, put it away and forgotten about it. Later he mentioned it to Penelope Gilliat, who read it, liked it and showed it to Joan. Some time later, he was asked to go and see Joan and Gerry. In his book *Why Fings Went West*, Frank recalls this meeting:

My impression of Joan Littlewood, when I met her for the first time backstage after the show, was of a solidly built, sympathetic woman in a woolly hat, chain-smoking Gauloises. She greeted me warmly, then we piled into Gerry Raffles' flashy American car and sped off to eat at a Chinese restaurant in dockland. Over the meal Joan talked as though *Fings Ain't Wot They Used T'Be* was going into production the following morning, i.e. 'What you've written is marvellous, but I don't think we ought to do it as a straight play, like all that old rubbish those West End managements put on. It should be a musical, or anyway have a few songs in it. I've met this wonderful nutcase called Lionel Bart, I've already talked to him about it and he's agreed to write some songs. What do you think, Frank?' – 'It's a great idea.'

It was Oscar Lewenstein, who had known Lionel Bart from the days when they had worked together in Unity Theatre, who had introduced him to Joan. The rehearsal period that followed turned out to be a somewhat traumatic experience for Frank, as he explains in the same book:

Rehearsals of the first production of *Fings* commenced in January of the following year. Lionel had already written a few songs, or what he called 'top line and chord symbols' for the show. On the first morning the cast forgathered on stage and the peculiar process began. The famous extemporising of the actors that had been infused into the text of *The Hostage* and *A Taste of Honey* was now permitted to run riot in 'Fings'. With every day that passed my original conception of the play seemed to drift further and further away, until eventually I was hardly able to identify with the antics on the stage at all. As the weeks went by more songs were added and once in a while I was called upon to write a few more pages of bad language. Then on Tuesday 17 February 1959 the show opened and the rest is *innacurate* history. In the books about the English theatre of this period that have come my way, there have been any number of discrepancies about exactly how many pages of *Fings Ain't Wot They Used T'Be* there were for Joan Littlewood and her company to elaborate upon. They have ranged from less than a dozen to a 'scruffy' eighteen and one ungenerous columnist put it as low as five. As mentioned earlier, the true figure was forty-eight, and I wrote many more during rehearsals as well as a number of synopsis ideas for the songs. Like Brendan Behan and Shelagh Delaney, I had provided enough meat for a feast.

Brendan Behan had a much more easy going attitude towards what happened in rehearsals, thanks perhaps to a difference in temperament. Like Frank, he supplied plenty of 'meat' but he didn't mind seeing it altered, re-shaped or even cut. If the result worked in theatrical terms then, however it was arrived at, he was more than happy to go along with it. He believed that Joan would remain faithful to what the author wanted to say, and tended to leave her to get on with it, while he attended to the more serious business of socialising in the pub, though occasions did arise, of course, when it would have been more useful to have had him around.

John Wells also welcomed Joan's methods, but he worked more closely with the Company in rehearsals:

> Working on *Mrs. Wilson's Diary*, I was immediately impressed by Joan's gift of being able to catch the joy of the moment and actually fix it, incoporating anything good that came up in rehearsal into the production. She talked about 'taking the arse out of it' by which she meant changing, when necessary, what had been written sitting down at a typewriter, into the same ideas and emotions expressed by someone running about on their feet. She takes a rather sedentary, heavy sentiment that might have crossed the writer's mind one morning in April and, with the actors, she transfers it into something which is actually dramatic and which had its own conflict, which is the essence of theatre.

Wolf Mankovitz shared Frank Norman's view that the author was not always given the respect he deserved. Mankovitz was far from happy during rehearsals of his *Make Me an Offer*. In a radio feature broadcast in 1961 he said:

> I knew from the start I would have great difficulties with her at the writing level. I'd come back after having worked on a scene with her the day before, having seen it set and seeing it work to apparently everybody's satisfaction, to find that she'd been up all night, worrying herself into writing a completely new scene, which was so irrelevant and so bad, that one could hardly believe it was worth the loss of a night's sleep. There she was rehearsing the new scene. The actors were confused and I was utterly infuriated by the impossibility of getting to grips with her intentions. I think Joan doesn't know what her intentions are until she acts them out on the stage.

The last sentence hits the nail on the head. It has to work in action, not on paper. One can only assume that Joan rewrote the scene in question because in her view (which may have been a minority view) it didn't work. As to the actors' confusion, one needs to bear in mind that most of the cast of *Make Me An Offer* were unused to Joan's way of working, having been brought in to replace the company who were now working in the West End. It was easier for Stephen Lewis, author of *Sparrers Can't Sing*, to understand and appreciate what went on in rehearsals because he was also an actor in the Company. In the same broadcast in 1961 he said:

> Actors don't go out of their way to write lines for an author, they try to get at the truth of the character. Sometimes it's found that lines

impede the play and don't contribute to the story. They might be good lines in themselves, and, by ad-libbing and working round them, you can find out whether or not what the author has written is true, whether he needs to rewrite the lines or eliminate them.

In fact the author was simply expected to work along with the actors in making the play come alive. After all, they had to live with it night after night. Joan put her view in a radio interview in 1959:

I believe very much in a theatre of actor-artists, and I think the trust that comes out of team work on what is often a new script, cleaning up points in production, or contact between actors, is essential to the development of the craft of acting and playwriting. I feel that the playwrights have got to be in the theatre. If they are there, working with the fabric and problem of theatre every day, then perhaps out of our type of play, which has a great deal of improvisation in them, we shall get better plays.

Nevertheless, whatever misgivings Frank Norman may have had about what went on in rehearsals, the first night of *Fings Ain't Wot They Used T'Be* at the Theatre Royal was a great success. It went on to pack the theatre for six weeks and wages rose to £20 a week. Frank's own experience of two years in jail for bouncing cheques, and his first-hand knowledge of the seamier side of Soho life, had been used to good advantage. He set his play in a small, tatty gambling den, inhabited by ex-members of a razor gang, small-time thieves, prostitutes and ponces. The lyrics and music of Lionel Bart contributed a great deal to the success of the show. It was all rather larger than life, but with a basic authenticity that served to shock and upset some of the audience and critics. Complaints were made at a meeting of the Theatre Royal Supporters' Club that it was all too outspoken and sordid. Bernard Levin welcomed it as 'A play of brilliant, bawdy irreverence'. Others were less happy, seeing it as yet another example of the 'kitchen sink' genre that, since *Look Back in Anger* in 1956, seemed to be threatening to take over British theatre. One worried critic wrote 'Love with no tattered strings, kindness, hope, faith and common decency are no longer the thing. Banished are the musicals such as came from the Lehars and the Novellos who gave us such wonderful shows.'

Their fears, very real at the time, were to turn out to be groundless. Though the theatre was never to be quite the same again, escapist entertainment survived, and not many years were to elapse before the New Wave was to recede, certainly as far as the West End was concerned. Perhaps a more valid criticism of *Fings* was expressed by those who questioned the morality of using razor gangs, crooks and, in particular,

Mother Courage, 1959. 36: Harry Corbett (Parson), Joan (Mother Courage), George Cooper (Cook). 37: Barbara Brown (on roof) as Kattrin. 38: The morning after the premiere.

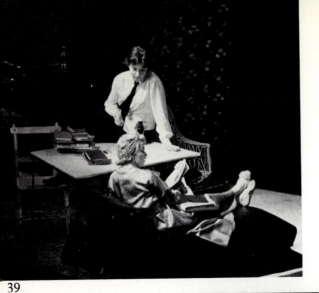

A Taste of Honey, 1958: (39) Frances Cuka (left), Avis Bunnage.
The Hostage, 1958: (40) The Company; (41) Murray Melvin (centre) and Company.

39

40

41

42

Sparrers Can't Sing, 1960: (42)
A Kayf Up West, 1964: (43)
Barry Humphries, Edward Roscoe.
Joan with John Bury (right) and
Gerry Raffles in the Cafe L'Ange,
Angel Lane, Stratford, 1959
(44).

Oh What A Lovely War, 1963: (45) Judy Cornwell, Victor Spinetti (left) and John Gower; (46) Brian Murphy (left) and Murray Melvin; (47) Avis Bunnage.

46

prostitutes and their ponces, as subjects for humour and comic songs, an issue that went deeper than good or bad taste. In some people's minds, it wasn't far removed from poking fun at physical deformities.

Apart from *A Christmas Carol*, three new modern plays had occupied the Company for a year, and it was very satisfying to return to the classics with a revival of John Marston's satiric comedy *The Dutch Courtesan* of 1605. Marston's extravagant characters and vocabulary and his wonderful sense of theatre provided the actors with something they could really get their teeth into. Though press notices were usually good for these classical productions, they were not, of course, considered 'commercial' and never found their way into the West End. They were probably seen by more people abroad than in this country, through the Company's foreign tours and visits to the Paris Festival.

The Hostage was then revived at Stratford in May 1959 prior to its transfer to Wyndham's Theatre on 11 June 1959 by Oscar Lewenstein and Donald Albery. Eileen Kennally replaced Avis Bunnage in the part of Meg, and the part of the soldier was played by Alfred Lynch, taking over from Murray Melvin – both Murray and Avis being now in the West End with *A Taste of Honey*. Ann Beach took over the part of Miss Gilchrist, the social worker. The publicity and acclaim that *The Hostage* had received when it first opened seven months previously made its success certain and it ran for over a year, enlivened by occasional visits from Brendan. He had been resting in Connemara and missed the opening night, but his unexpected – and noisy – appearances in the front of house every couple of months made up for that!

I was playing Pat, the landlord of the lodging house cum brothel with the fairly impossible task of keeping the inmates in some sort of order, so it naturally fell to me to cope with Brendan on these occasions. When he was only moderately drunk, it wasn't difficult; he was expansive and witty, and our exchanges over the footlights all added to the fun of the evening, providing the audience with a unique form of author participation. At the end of the show he would join us in the curtain call, and dance his celebrated Irish jig. There was no 'fourth wall' between the actors and the audience, and the music hall style of production made it easy to involve anything untoward that happened in the auditorium. Latecomers were given short shrift; as they struggled to their seats in the stalls, comments were made on their unpunctuality. The odd ones who were spotted walking out got a very rough time. We reckoned that while they had a perfect right to leave, we also had a right to make them wish they'd at least waited for the interval.

In the earlier part of the run, Brendan's interruptions were positive, and made a contribution to the general chaotic enjoyment of the evening. They were in no way intended as such, but proved a great boost to the box office; they provided a lot of free publicity in the Press the following day. Later in the run, however, he would turn up really drunk, and then it was a different story. His interruptions were destructive, and it was impossible to get through to him. One awful night he started bellowing out the lines before the cast could speak them and then started on an interminable, mournful Irish ballad. That he nearly ruined the entire performance was bad enough, but the real tragedy, of course, was that this brilliant man, now sick, was on a path that, five years later, was to lead him to his grave.

A part in one of the shows that transferred to the West End, around 1959, meant a rise in wages of course. But a differential scale now operated, with salaries ranging from £20 to £40, according to the size of the part. Although we were now 'commercial', there were those who argued that, as it was still a group venture, equal salaries should have been maintained, and that a principle of some importance had been destroyed. Even at Stratford in the latter years, a differential scale operated to attract back ex-members of the Company who had become established actors. Both in the West End and at Stratford, of course, salaries were always less than for similar work elsewhere. The subsidy for the Theatre Royal continued to come from the actors.

Theatre Workshop now had two shows running in the West End, and it was estimated that if they ran for a year £9,000 would accrue to the Company. On the strength of this in October 1959 much-needed improvements to the Theatre Royal costing £4,000 were carried out with the help of Company members and volunteers. The exterior was repainted dark blue and white, the interior blue, grey and gold; new heating was installed plus extensive recarpeting. A new chandelier, a replica of the one in Wyndham's Theatre, was presented to the Theatre by Donald Albery, and installed in the auditorium. It was all completed just in time for the opening, on 17 October 1959, of *Make Me An Offer*, a musical set in the Portobello Market, by Wolf Mankovitz with music and lyrics by Monty Norman and David Heneker.

The cast of *Make Me An Offer* had in it very few Theatre Workshop actors and it was chosen with the possibility of a West End transfer very much in mind. Daniel Massey, Diana Copeland, Dilys Laye and Meir Tzelniker played the leading parts, and the show was to set Sheila Hancock, in a supporting role, on the road to stardom. Though it was produced at Stratford by Joan, it is difficult to regard it as a Theatre Workshop Production, as it was in no way a product of the continuing work of the Company, and those brought in never worked with Joan again. It achieved its purpose and transferred directly from Stratford to the New Theatre, now the Albery, adjacent to the Wyndham's, where *The Hostage* was playing to packed houses. It ran for six months. Harold

Hobson considered it to be the best musical running in London, and as it was competing with *My Fair Lady* and *West Side Story* that was praise indeed. The story of the conversion of an honest young market dealer in antiques to the more devious and profitable practices of his competitors, and whether it is possible for a poor man to make an honest but exciting living, raised some interesting moral questions. Speaking on radio in 1961, Wolf Mankovitz was critical of Joan's production:

> I thought it lacked heart. Littlewood is very bad, in my opinion, on husband and wife material, and *Make Me An Offer* was a husband and wife story. It was also a 'metier' story about street markets, on this second element Littlewood is very good, but on the first element, I think she hardened and overpaced this, and lost the heart.

In the same programme, Meier Tzelniker disagreed:

> She was cleaning it like a diamond, sharpening and polishing. She even did invisible mending in certain scenes. The alarm goes at six o'clock in the morning and the young couple have to get up to feed the baby. I went wild the opening night watching it from the wings – it was so beautiful. This is her art.

For the first time Joan was working with a company of established actors, trained and experienced in the conventional theatre and unused to improvisation. There were the inevitable difficulties of communication at first, and differing approaches to problems that arose. Miriam Karlin had been in a similar situation when she took over from Avis Bunnage in *Fings* and, in the same radio programme in 1961, said:

> One was just told to improvise, and, for the first few days, I really was dead scared, but Joan had the most marvellous way of breaking down all that. The trouble is, she is always bloody well right. I have had a hell of a lot of arguments with her, and then it transpired she was kind of right.

Meir Tzelniker was also new to working with Joan:

> She is an intellectual. She is a very intelligent woman; and she's well read, she knows theatre from the top to the bottom, inside and outside. You can trust her with a performance. I wouldn't say that for every play – but certain plays. I really enjoyed working with her – I respect that woman very much indeed.

As many of the original cast of *Fings* were now playing in the West End, it had to be re-cast for its revival at Stratford in December 1959, and it transferred to the Garrick Theatre in February 1960 where it ran for just over two years. Lionel Bart's contribution to the success of the

production, as composer and lyricist, was acknowledged when *Fings* won
the Evening Standard Award for the Best Musical of 1960.

The street offences act dealing with prostitution had become law since
the first production, and re-writing was necessary to bring it up to date.
The Lord Chamberlain had also laid his constraining hand on the script,
and various expletives had been eliminated, cutting down the number of
'piss-offs', 'sod-offs' and 'bugger-offs' to what, in his view, was
acceptable. His minions kept their eye on the show, and after it had been
playing for a year, the following letter was received from him:

The Lord Chamberlain's Office,
St. James's Palace, S.W.1.   7th February 1961

Dear Sir,
    The Lord Chamberlain has received numerous complaints against
the play *Fings Ain't Wot They Used T'Be* in consequence of which
he arranged for an inspection of the Garrick Theatre to be made on
1st of February last.
    It is reported to his Lordship that numerous unauthorised
amendments to the allowed manuscript have been made, and I am to
require you to revert to it at once, submitting for approval any
alteration which you wish to make before continuing them in use.
    In particular I am to draw your attention to the undernoted, none
of which would have been allowed had they been submitted, and
which I am to ask you to confirm by return of post have been
removed from the play.

Act I
    Indecent business of Rosie putting her hand up Red Hot's
bottom.
    The dialogue between Rosie and Bettie. 'You've got a cast iron
stomach.' 'You've got to have in our business.'
    The interior decorator is not to be played as a homosexual and his
remark '... Excuse me dear, red plush, that's very camp, that is,' is
to be omitted, as is the remark, 'I've strained meself.'
    The builder's labourer is not to carry the plank of wood in the
erotic place and at the erotic angle that he does, and the Lord
Chamberlain wishes to be informed of the manner in which the plank
is in future to be carried.

Act II
    The reference to the Duchess of Argyll is to be omitted. Tosher,

when examining Red Hot's bag, is not to put his hand on Rosie's bottom with finger aligned as he does at the moment.

The remark, 'Don't drink that stuff, it will rot your drawers,' is to be omitted.

Tosher is not to push Rosie backwards against the table when dancing in such a manner that her legs appear through his open legs in a manner indicative of copulation.

Yours faithfully,

It is difficult to believe that this letter was actually written by Colonel Penn, the Lord Chamberlain, and was intended to be taken seriously. Indeed it had to be, and there was no appeal against his decisions.

William Saroyan, the noted American writer, had phoned Gerry Raffles to tell him how much he had enjoyed *The Hostage* and Gerry took the opportunity to ask him if he would like to write and direct a play for the Company. The result was *Sam, the Highest Jumper of Them All* which opened on 6 April 1960.

Saroyan believed in the inherent goodness of man. An optimistic note ran through all his plays and stories, and this one was to be no exception. It told the story of Sam, played by Murray Melvin, a bank clerk, overwhelmed by a sense of failure, who decided to escape by jumping higher than anyone else. The play was peopled by characters who bore names like Sam Hark A Lark, Wally Wailer and Daisy Dimple.

The author's intention was to write a play in every capital of Europe, with the aim of paying off tax arrears of £20,000, but it was clear that he didn't really believe this would happen or that *Sam* would transfer to the West End, or be a commercial success:

I have no financial interest. I'll get royalties but they won't cover my bill at the Savoy Hotel. But all I ever wanted was a theatre and some people.

He got what he wanted, and when rehearsals started they turned out to be a revelation, even for Theatre Workshop actors. Improvising around a script was something they were used to, but now they were engaged, with the author, in putting a script together as they went along. He would outline the situation, think of possible appropriate lines, mutter them over to himself and offer them to the cast for their opinion, and they were free to make alternative suggestions. On his arrival at the Savoy Hotel, Saroyan had been handed a London Underground map and he decided that this would make a good background for the setting. Against this John Bury designed a very effective expressionistic set, on different planes and with stylised furniture. As might have been expected the majority of the critics found it all too whimsical for their tastes, and the lack of sophistication and worldliness bothered them. Many of the audience, however, found this almost innocent quality a welcome change from the earthiness of *Taste of Honey* and *Fings*.

After *Sam* the theatre was dark for a few weeks, apart from Sunday evening performances by visiting companies, until the opening, on 23 May 1960 of *Ned Kelly* by James Clancy, produced by Joan. Harry Corbett played Kelly, the Australian outlaw and folk hero who was hanged in 1880. Harry Corbett recalls rehearsals:

> Something always pulled you back, things were always going to be 'like they were'. After the West End transfers, the seasons at Stratford were going to start again. Joan started off with *Ned Kelly* to free the actors she'd got together – 'get away from your old habits, improvise'. In the process, she sacrificed completely the character of Ned. 'These two policemen are being marvellous, let's have more of them.' One didn't get uptight, we were trying to 'do what we'd done before'. The Keystone Cops did rather take over the production, which decided the critics as to its merits.

Harold Hobson made the point, particularly valid in Joan's case, that work would continue on the play after the first night and this should be taken into account. The idea of several preview performances, giving time to get things right before the Press were invited, had not been thought of, and in those days a first night was actually the first time a play was presented to an audience. Harold Hobson also made the point that the Company seemed to be relying, for their support, on the bourgeoisie and intellectuals, and that we had not yet succeeded in attracting a working-class audience. Though we *had* built up a local following, it was not sufficient to fill the theatre for any length of time, and we had to rely on the support of regular theatregoers from a wide area of London. Stratford tube station was a very busy place during the runs of our most successful productions. None the less, Hobson's point was less valid than the composition of a first night audience would indicate, since the occasion would inevitably attract those who wanted to be seen as well as a leavening of critics, agents, actors and showbiz people generally.

After playing at the Paris Festival, Ben Jonson's *Every Man in His Humour* opened on 2 July 1960 at the Theatre Royal to a mixed reception, though it included several of the Theatre Workshop regulars now released from the West End. Topical allusions had been included, and Joan's production carried it along at great speed and with a wealth of slapstick – which was not how some people felt Ben Jonson ought to be treated.

August saw the very successful opening of *Sparrers Can't Sing*. It was the story of an East End street and had little plot, but the humour of the characters had all the veracity of an author who was drawing on a background he really knew. Stephen Lewis, then thirty years old, had lived in the East End all his life and had been a bricklayer before joining the Company as an actor. The critic Alan Brien described the show as 'Thirties music hall, preserved and pickled by Joan Littlewood, but with a genuine emotion which just runs underground.'

Joan, on holiday in France, had left John Bury in charge of the theatre and he invited Harry Corbett to direct a play of his choice. He chose *Progress to The Park*, Alun Owen's play about racial and religious conflict in Liverpool, and the relationship between a Protestant boy and a Catholic girl. It opened on 24 August 1960 with Billie Whitelaw playing the girl and was revived in May 1961 for the West End, directed by Ted Kotcheff. Alun Owen was quite emphatic he did not want Joan to direct it, though she had never expressed any desire to do so. 'With her ideas about actors improvising lines, she kills an author's words. Kotcheff protects my lines from the actors. If they change a word, he yells, "So we are all writers now!" I like that.'

At least Alun Owen was clear as to what the consequences might be if he entrusted a play to Joan, and he preferred to take no risks. Marvin Kane, an American writer living in London, was not so clear, with unfortunate results. His play *We're Just Not Practical*, produced in January 1961, had originally been written as a T.V. play and an attempt was made to adapt it for the theatre. Kane had difficulty in going along with Joan's way of working, and was finally excluded from rehearsals, and the actors made the necessary changes. The play, dealing with the misfortunes of a young couple who take on the job of housekeepers in a boarding house, was not a success either with actors or with audience. The author blamed the failure on the Company and on Joan and offered through the press to give the audience their money back without actually explaining how he would do this. It is sheer speculation whether the play would have been more successful had the author been left to his own devices. Perhaps there just was not enough of the 'meat' that writers like Brendan and Shelagh had provided.

In March 1961 *Sparrers* was revived at Stratford prior to transferring to Wyndham's Theatre. Stephen Lewis's characters were too deeply rooted in the East End to survive the journey up West and their down-to-earth humour didn't appeal to the more sophisticated taste of West End audiences. It ran for only just over two months.

On the 28 June 1961 *They Might Be Giants* by James Goldman, also
an American playwright, opened at the Theatre Royal. It was a whimsical
satire, a comment on affluent American society, about a former judge, now
a paranoiac, who imagines he is Sherlock Holmes. Played by Harry
Corbett, he set off on the track of Dr. Moriarty, assisted by a female Dr.
Watson, played by Avis Bunnage, and harassed by his brother who is
trying to get him committed to an asylum.

All eyes were now on first nights at the Theatre Royal, the critics came
down in full force, and the onus was on the Company to have the shows
'ready'. This conception was, of course, quite alien to Joan whose
productions changed and developed over the period of playing. There was
now created a pressure for longer periods of rehearsal than the Company
could afford. John Bury, who designed the sets for 'They Might Be
Giants', takes up this point:

> Hal Prince, the American impresario, was backing *Giants*. He had
> Princess Margaret coming down for the opening night and Joan
> wanted to postpone it. It wasn't a problem particular to that piece. In
> the early days when we were a repertory theatre it didn't matter so
> much. No-one came on Monday, and by Thursday it would be quite
> good, and by that time we were rehearsing the next one. Now we
> were transferring shows and so everything had to be on the boil for
> the first night. Of course Joan was always late and she wanted to
> postpone the opening night of *Giants*. Gerry said, 'You can't, I've
> got the Press coming.' Joan's answer was 'I don't want the sodding
> press.' Then he said, 'We've got Princess Margaret coming.' She
> said 'And we don't want Princess Margaret either.' Hal Prince
> didn't want to postpone either. I think he'd come to the stage where
> he thought he wouldn't get a better show even if he gave Joan
> another month. I think he'd written it off. He realised he wasn't
> going to have a viable London and New York success.

Apart from a general enthusiasm for John Bury's settings, most of the
critics had little to say in its favour. An exception was Alun Owen who
reviewed the production in *Encore*. He highly praised the Company, the
author and Joan's presentation of his 'world of words and ideas'. This was
to be her last production for some time and Owen used Moriarty, a
character in the play, to express his feelings:

> It's a worthy farewell present and thank you. You can hear Moriarty
> minions rationalising, 'she's been corrupted by success' ... 'She's
> not to be trusted with public money' ... 'She's mad and she uses
> *those words* and she wears funny hats.' Well, they don't fool me and
> most of the other people who've learned from you and argued with

you up and down Angel Lane. The minions are glad you're going because you refused to be corrupted, idealism might be contagious and they fear to be exposed to it.

Despite a succession of successful transfers, by July 1961 there was very little in the kitty. £16,500 had been spent in keeping the Theatre Royal open and on its re-decoration, and the Arts Council grant was only £1,000 a year, though there was now on hand an offer of £2,000. Six trade unions had donated £335, ten local authorities grants totalled £1,500 and the London County Council had matched this with a further £1,500. Wages at Stratford at this time were £15 per week. The grants were quite inadequate for the needs of the Company, and the efforts to subsidise from West End profits had simply destroyed the continuity of work. As Joan said at the time:

I think the theatre should be as important as public libraries, art galleries and education. We are forced to export our shows to the West End and are always losing our companies. We are hamstrung by the money grubbing commercialism of the West End.

Joan's bitterness was understandable. The fault, of course, did not lie with the commercial managements but in the absence of adequate subsidies making the transfers necessary. Many of the Company now had domestic responsibilities, and without the extra wages from the West End contracts they would have been unable to meet them and would probably have had to leave anyway.

I asked Bill Bryden, while I was working at the National's Cottesloe Theatre under his direction, what he thought about this problem.

I suppose if Joan and the Workshop had been properly funded it may have been possible to have a bigger company, some playing in the West End, the more experienced playing in Stratford East and touring. I think the necessity to give up touring and become a London playhouse was a real tragedy. Perhaps if Joan had been reasonably subsidised she would have been frightened of becoming a bourgeois institution, so it's something of a Catch 22 situation. I can only say that the productions were the pride of the West End, the most interesting work at that time and that has got to be something. It showed the potential of good work being popular.

John Bury's view was, as always, down to earth:

We'd burned ourselves out. We'd lost about three companies in the West End, and Joan was having to come back to Stratford after every West End show and put together an ad hoc company and do it again. Now everyone who was coming to work for her was working on the theory that the easiest way to get into the West End was to work at Stratford East! You and me and the rest of us had got to the stage when we needed a bit more than we could ever get at Stratford. After all, we had earned £40 or £60 a week in the West End for several months. We couldn't actually go back to where we were before the transfers started, we had run a circle and we needed somewhere else, and Joan wanted to try it somewhere else. She wanted to go off to Nigeria, she was well into her forties by now and she wanted to find another area of work.

Some of the Company would not have agreed with John and would have been willing to work again at Stratford for a living wage in an effort to rebuild the Group. Joan, however, was tired and in need of fresh stimulation, and in July 1961 she did go off to Nigeria, and nearly two years was to elapse before Theatre Workshop was again to occupy the Theatre Royal. Following a season of visiting companies, Oscar Lewenstein took over the lease of the theatre in November 1961.

Joan believed in *They Might Be Giants* and resented the pressure that had been put on her to open before she thought it was ready. Its failure may have been the immediate reason for her departure, but it was never more than the last straw. In a television interview with Malcolm Muggeridge before she left, she spoke nostalgically of the early days of Theatre Workshop, and summed up her present position:

For the past few years I have had dozens of West End managers breathing down my neck. The money from the West End was put into Stratford but we can pack the Theatre Royal to the roof and still cannot make it pay. I cannot accept any more a situation where I am unable to work with a company freely.

Nine

1963–1974
The Beginning of the End
Oh What a Lovely War

Joan celebrated her return to Stratford in March 1963 with the enormously successful production *Oh What a Lovely War*. Charles Chilton had written a radio programme called *A Long Long Trail* based on songs of the First World War, and Gerry Raffles had the idea of building a stage show around this theme. Advice was sought from those with first-hand knowledge of the war and Charles Chilton contributed research material. Both Gwyn Thomas and Ted Allan submitted scripts but they didn't fit in with Joan's conception of how the subject should be treated. The final version was based on factual data from official records and war memoirs, threaded through with popular songs of the period. *Lovely War* was regarded by some as the most memorable of Theatre Workshop productions. However, it's as well to bear in mind that one can only compare with what one has seen. The Company had been producing plays for eighteen years, and many of the audience had not seen earlier shows like *Volpone* and *Arden of Faversham*, let alone pre-Stratford productions like *Uranium 235*.

Joan rejected from the outset the notion that the actors should dress up as khaki-clad soldiers, imitating the appearance of those who had gone through the First World War. She thought khaki an ugly colour anyway. Instead she conceived the idea of presenting the Company as a pierrot troupe called 'The Merry Roosters' who had actually been performing at that time. Some of the Company still had qualms about being paid for portraying men who had actually died in the war, and Brian Murphy recalled Joan's answer:

She said we are not doing a show about the First World War. We are finding a background for the songs, and these trace a period of history which can be presented without the realistic background that you would need in a film. Here we are, on the stage, The Clowns, and never in the course of the evening are we going to forget that the audience are out there. Tonight we are going to present to you 'The War Game'. We've got songs, dances, a few battles, a few jokes, and we start to put on Sam Browne belts and helmets. Some of the scenes were dealt with very realistically, we had to work for hours and hours pretending to be in the trenches, getting the feeling of real boredom.

The cast were completely involved in building up the script. We improvised lots of different scenes, read books and came up with ideas. I read one of the few books written about the Great War by a Private, and out of it came the scene of the French Cavalry retreating in full glory with trumpets blowing.

A real inspiration was to use, behind the actors, a screen which ran the width of the stage and on which were picked out in moving lights the terrifying facts, ten thousand men lost, a hundred yards gained, and so on. It was based on a similar principle to that used in advertising or for news flashes and, juxtaposed against the scenes on the stage, it made a tremendous impact.

The creation of an anti-war play was never in the minds of those connected with the production. *Lovely War* was a piece of social history showing the behaviour of men under certain conditions. Clive Barker takes up this point:

> The presumption was, you could reasonably expect everyone going into the theatre to think that war was horrible, there was no point in telling them that. That's why Joan rejected those realistic scripts that showed what life was really like in the trenches. Having been in the production, it's quite clear to me that *Lovely War* is a celebration of human resourcefulness in the face of the most appalling catastrophic conditions. So Joan celebrates courage, humour, comradeship, the triumph of life over death and the international solidarity between soldiers.

Refreshed and inspired by her work during the break, Joan had brought together for *Lovely War* a group who were full of enthusiasm for the job in hand and who were ready and able to work closely together. There can be no doubting the part they played in its success and, in acknowledging this, Joan, as always, minimised her own contribution:

> Part of the good that has come out of this show is the way which a group of young people have worked together. Each brought a different point of view. They hated some of those songs. They didn't want to do propaganda, so they argued their way through each scene, and you've got, in the piece, the points of view of many people. This has been splendid. What you see is not a piece of direction by a

producer. There were no rehearsals as they are known. There was a collection of individuals, more of an anti-group than a group, working on ideas, on songs, on settings, on facts. And if you get a few people with a sense of humour and brains together, you'll get theatre.

The critics were unanimous in their praise, no fewer than fifteen managements offered a transfer to the West End, and in June 1963, *Oh What a Lovely War* transferred to Wyndham's Theatre.

There were some who were less enthusiastic. George Harvey Webb, who had worked on research for *Lovely War*, said:

It was a cop-out. It played down the war and made it seem as if it were great fun. I thought it would tell the world that men shelled their own troops in no-man's-land in Christmas 1915 so that the war would go on. This was how we conceived the play would end, but it wasn't even brought out.

Frances Cuka recalled the change in the ending of *Lovely War* when it went into the West End.

When I saw it at Stratford Victor Spinetti made the closing speech, which went something like 'The war game is being played all over the world, by all ages, there's a pack for all the family. It's been going on for a long time and it's still going on. Goodnight.' This cynical speech, which followed the charge of the French soldiers, was quite frightening and you were left crying your heart out. When I saw it again in the West End, I was shocked by the change of ending. After Victor's speech the entire cast came on singing 'Oh What a Lovely War' followed by a reprise of the songs. All frightfully hearty and calculated to send the audience home happy. I think it was George Sewell who said 'The Management didn't take kindly to a down ending'. As far as I knew Joan and Gerry were the Management, having rented the theatre from Donald Albery ...

Whether Joan instigated the changes or agreed to them under pressure seems to be a matter for conjecture.

Ewan MacColl's objections were more basic. Far from *Lovely War* being a triumph, it represented, in his view, the climax of a long period of betrayal of the original aim of Theatre Workshop to create a theatre for working people:

The wrong kind of good write-up from the critics produced a situation where you couldn't get near the Theatre Royal for Bentleys and Mercedes, with the result that working-class people in the area felt 'This is not for us'. They felt uncomfortable in that sort of society and just didn't come. It is sometimes said that shows like *Fings Ain't Wot They Used T'Be* and *Lovely War* were the high point of Theatre Workshop's existence. I think they were the nadir, the low point. They symbolised the ultimate failure of Theatre Workshop. Here was a show, *Oh What a Lovely War*, which was ostensibly an anti-war show. Yet it was running in the West End. You had, for example, a retired general in the audience saying 'Good show, damn good show, that is the real thing'. I maintain that a theatre which sets out to deal with a social and human problem like war and which leaves the audience feeling nice and comfy, in a rosy glow of nostalgia, is not doing its job, it has failed. Theatre, when it is dealing with social issues, should hurt; you should leave the theatre feeling furious. It was at this point we could say farewell to the dream of creating a working-class theatre.

Some of those who saw *Lovely War* would quarrel with Ewan's assessment of the impression it made. There can be no doubt, however, that it was easy to be overcome by the nostalgic nature of the songs and, in the process, lose sight of their implications and the conditions in which they had originally been sung. One could also argue that most of the audience who flocked to Stratford came by tube, not in Bentleys, but that wouldn't in itself destroy the basic validity of Ewan's argument. Harold Hobson's comments on the bourgeois composition of the audience are referred to in the previous chapter. From 1961 onwards there were only short seasons of sporadic performances, and long periods in between when the theatre was leased to outside managements. It was just not possible, in that situation, to build on the limited local following that had been built up in the previous eight years.

Lovely War had been preceded in January 1963 by a production of *High Street, China* by Robin Chapman, an actor in the Company, and Richard Kane. Produced by Brian Murphy and designed by John Bury, it told the story of twelve hours in the life of a young amateur boxer. A full year after *Lovely War*, in March 1964, Frank Norman's *Kayf Up West* opened at the Theatre Royal. Written while *Fings* was still running, *Kayf Up West* was set in the post-war years and told the story of a young innocent corrupted by the layabouts he meets in a seedy cafe. His travels take him to Soho, Kew Gardens, Hyde Park, a flat in Mayfair and finally to prison. The cast of thirteen, some working with Joan for the first time, had to play over forty characters ranging from prison warders to guests at a Mayfair party. The play sprawled over space and time, had no music to help it, and though it had its moments, as no production by Joan could fail to have, it received a bad press and, consequently, poor audiences. Frank Norman in his book *Why Fings Went West* put the view that whereas

Fings in 1959 had been accepted as part of the 'New Wave' drama that followed *Look Back In Anger*, tastes had changed by 1961, and *Kayf Up West* was too late. That may well have been a contributory factor, and it was certainly the last play of this genre to be seen at the Theatre Royal.

On 20 March news came through during the performance that Brendan Behan had died that evening in Dublin, and I was asked to inform our audience in a curtain speech. Though not totally unexpected − Brendan had been ill for some time − his death was a deep personal shock. I didn't share Brendan's enthusiasm for the social life of the public house, so I was not as close to him as some, but working with him on *The Hostage* had given me an insight into and a deep appreciation of his brilliance and warmth. Tributes to Brendan were many and from all quarters. For Joan, the loss was profound:

Brendan was caught between love for, and mockery of, obsolete myths. His personal suffering and loneliness gave the world some of the finest laughter medicine of the century. Already in his last notices the greatness of the man was undervalued. He was a fine scholar as well as a glorious clown, a man who translated Marlowe's verse into Irish and improvised his first ballads for the street sweepers and lonely vagrants of every city in the world. He squandered his life and his genius, but he took the world out on a spree with him.

Despite the success of *Lovely War* the Company were in yet another financial crisis. Total grants, local and national in the year 1963/64, amounted to only £6,500 and a note in the *Kayf Up West* programme read: 'Unless an adequate grant from the local borough council or the Arts Council is forthcoming in the next financial year, this will be the last production that the Company have the financial resources to mount at the Theatre Royal.'

It became clear that any future grant would be in line with those received in the past and, therefore, quite inadequate. Consequently, none was applied for and, for the next seven years, no money was received from the Arts Council.

After housing only three productions in fifteen months, the theatre was leased to David Thompson and his company 'Newstage' in December 1964 for three years. During those years they lost a great deal of money and, ironically, had to be bailed out by the Arts Council.

After appearing, with great success, on the 'fringe' in the early years of the Edinburgh Festival, we were invited to participate in the 1964 Festival as part of the official programme. Joan condensed and combined the two parts of Shakespeare's *Henry IV*, and it was produced for an open stage

48′ × 15′ that stretched across the Assembly Hall from north to south. The critics attacked it bitterly and almost unanimously. They objected to the way it was cut, the lack of poetry, most of the acting, and the mixture of modern and period in the costumes – Poins, for example, wore Italian slacks, a bowler hat and a leather jerkin. Bernard Levin said 'There is virtually nothing in this production but gabble and shuffle, ill-executed horseplay and unimaginative characterisation.' Philip Hope-Wallace had hoped for 'A fresh and cheerfully irreverent approach ... at first it promised to run true to form. The King wore trousers under his robes. Prince Hal had a cockney accent and the props had a Brechtian quality about them. But, in the end, radical staging and an inability to hear properly had disappointed.'

However, despite the combined displeasure of the critics, or perhaps because of it, long queues formed in the rain for seats, and it played to capacity for most of the three weeks. The manager of the Assembly Hall said 'It sold more unreserved seats than I can remember for any first week.'

Joan usually took a philosophical attitude to the views of the critics, but in this instance she issued a statement defending her approach to the production:

> ... I have never had any ambition to be known as a theatre character. I decided to take my theories outside the theatre set-up three years ago and *Henry IV* is the result of a promise made at that time.
>
> I find the accents of Leeds, East London and Manchester as acceptable as those of St. John's Wood, Eton, Oxford or hangovers from Edwardian dressing rooms. It is easier to attack the Royal Family than attempt to scrape off the patina of age and the dreary respect which stifles Elizabethan verse. Shakespeare's company was made up of leary misfits, anarchists, out of work soldiers and wits who worked at their ideas in pubs and performed them as throwaways to an uninhibited pre-Puritan audience.
>
> My Company works without the assistance of smart direction, fancy dress, beards and greasepaint and was prepared for the wave of opposition which we knew would come. I hope the audience will enjoy our work as much as we do.

Having whetted their appetite, Joan decided to confront the critics personally by calling a Press Conference under the Chairmanship of Lord Harewood, Artistic Director of the Festival. The Hall was packed to the doors. Members of the Company entertained by 'guying' the conventional approach to Shakespearian acting, and Joan went into the attack:

We have no respect for Shakespeare. In Scotland, England, the whole world they are bogged down with art and respect for the past. We are not. You can attack the poor Queen Mum but don't attack art. Ever since Queen Victoria, you lot have been so artistic. I don't know what we are doing here supporting Lord Harewood in his old rubbish. Let's have something of meaning to people.

When Lord Harewood saw the show a few days later he said:

It was absolutely stunning and very exciting. I think half the critics would change their minds if they could see it again. Theatre Workshop are now succeeding in Miss Littlewood's aim of getting through to an audience.

Though Joan took great pains, on this occasion, to defend her approach to Shakespeare, she was fully aware of the gap between the concept and how far the actors were able to achieve it. This point was made by one of the critics, and work continued throughout most of the run of *Henry IV* in an effort to narrow this gap.

In October 1964 *Lovely War* went to America and on their return, the Company, for the time being, disbanded. It was not re-formed again until March 1967 when rehearsals commenced on *MacBird*. During the long break, Joan had been involved in the disastrous Lionel Bart musical *Twang*, absorbed in her 'Fun Palace' projects and working with students from many countries at Hammamet, the cultural centre of Tunis.

After the initial few years of repertory work at Stratford, the Company had gradually dispersed over the years, culminating in the eighteen month break after July 1961, and had joined the rest of the overcrowded profession in their struggle for a living in films, television and theatre. It now became a question of who was available rather than who Joan wanted when seasons started up again, so that casts varied from play to play. Actors usually found it more exciting working with Joan than anyone else, and though it often meant earning less, they tried to make themselves available. Obviously Joan always aimed for a leavening in the Company of those who had worked with her before. This made it easier to absorb comparative newcomers.

No money was made available from any source to enable the Company to plan ahead, and before the end of 1967 the theatre was to be again leased to an outside management.

MacBird by Barbara Garson was an American satire on the assassination of Kennedy and the alleged implication in it of Lyndon Johnson. It was written as a take-off of Shakespearean verse and caused a tremendous stir when played in Greenwich Village, New York. It was banned public performance by the Lord Chamberlain's office because the play portrayed the head of a friendly state, so the device of Club Membership was resorted to, though this was no guarantee against prosecution. In January 1966, the English Stage Company at the Royal Court Theatre had fallen foul of the law over Edward Bond's *Saved* even though it had been presented as a 'club' performance.

As *MacBird* featured other less well-known public figures than Kennedy or Johnson, it was necessary for the cast to master the intricacies of American politics, and reference books littered the Green Room during rehearsals. There was a great deal of improvisation, and parts were swapped around, expanded or eliminated. Toni Palmer, a member of the cast, commented at the time: 'If Joan likes what you're doing, she may fill out your part, but if you dared go down with flu, there might be no part left when you got back.'

In the view of many of the critics, the anticipation was not fulfilled. Those conversant with the original script felt that replacing some of the Shakespearian-type verse with song and dance was not an improvement – a view incidentally that was shared by Barbara Garson.

Intrigues and Amours based on Vanbrugh's *The Provok'd Wife* was the next production in May 1967, and a note in the programme read: 'This season of Theatre Workshop owes nothing in the way of support, co-operation or even sympathy to the Arts Council of Great Britain or Newham Council.'

Intrigues was an updated, vigorous production with plenty of slapstick. Most of the critics, however, were unprepared to accept the cutting of the original play, its down to earth quality and the absence of the stylised acting normally associated with Restoration Comedy. But Harold Hobson welcomed it as being 'free from uneasy affectation'.

Lack of continuity in production had made it difficult to build up a substantial local following, and consequently, the Company became increasingly dependent on favourable notices from the national critics to induce theatregoers to make the journey to Stratford from other parts of London. However, those that defied the unfavourable notice and came anyway seemed less inclined than the critics to allow pre-conceived ideas to come between them and their enjoyment of the shows.

It was estimated at this time that, even playing to full houses, a £50,000 subsidy was needed to keep the theatre open all the time. As there was no subsidy at all, there were no productions during the summer months, but there was a great deal of activity in and around the theatre. Drama sessions and workshop instruction for teenagers went on inside the building. A group of teenagers formed a supporters section, with the aim of furthering the idea of a community theatre. They persuaded a local firm to give them forty gallons of paint, and they painted the exteriors of all the shops in Angel Lane in different colours. In eighteen months' time Angel Lane was to be demolished, along with the whole area around the theatre. Between 1968 and 1975, as sites were cleared of buildings and were awaiting redevelopment, a group from the theatre moved in to make them usable as playgrounds for local children. The children were consulted as to what should be done and were involved in the actual work. In all, five sites were worked on, gardens planted, crazy paving laid, maths games played on chequerboard floors, and at Easter 1974 a zoological garden was set up. Local people and organisations became more and more involved, and the children were given the responsibility of organising a grand Easter Fair. In 1969, a disused factory was taken over and, led by Christine Jackson, children, teachers and helpers cleaned and redecorated it, and it became a venue for classes and games and drama therapy. All these projects were organised under the auspices of the Fun Palace Trust and subsidised largely by Gerry Raffles and Joan. In 1974, however, the Arts Council granted £700 towards this work, rising in 1975 to £1,000 plus £1,600 from other bodies. Newham Council came up with £12 a week towards Youth Leaders' salaries.

As a prelude to all this, in July 1967, in the face of opposition from the Local Authority, eighty tons of rubble and waste were bulldozed from a nearby bomb-site to provide a playground for local children throughout the school holidays. Over the years Joan had been increasingly aware of the limitations of working with actors in theatre buildings:

> Theatre is not just the putting on of plays. It is everywhere; the transformation scene, in the markets, processions, meetings, partings, in the clothes we wear, our manners and mores and the front we put on. At its best it is the great educator, keeping our language alive, giving us the music and poetry which seem to identify us and add some value to our brief journey. Theatre knows no boundaries and only withers when it is confined.

Joan had set up the Fun Palace Trust with Buckminster Fuller, the Earl of Harewood, Lord Ritchie Calder and Yehudi Menuhin and herself as trustees. Plans were drawn up by the architect Cedric Price, the most ambitious being a project for a Fun Palace in the Lea Valley. An enormous space framework would enclose many leisure pursuits and experiences. Included would be warm air curtains, vapour zones, optical barriers and a variety of new and exciting gadgets. Joan's own description was: 'A place of toys for adults, a place to waste time without guilt or discomfort, to develop unused talents, to discover the fund of joy and fun and sadness within us.'

It was an imaginative concept requiring a great deal of money, but backed by the resources of, say, the G.L.C. it might well have come to fruition. However, the G.L.C. decided that the proposed site was required for an extension to the sewage works. A smaller scheme in Camden Town was opposed by local residents and also had to be abandoned. These and similar projects, her work with children in Stratford and with students abroad, left Joan less time and inclination for theatre production, and from 1968 onwards she directed only five plays at Stratford.

Joan's faith in the viability of the Fun Palace was not shared by her closest colleagues in the theatre, and they offered no support. John Bury saw no future in it: ... 'The concept was fine, but from a building point of view it was cloud-cuckoo land. No G.L.C. could have licensed a thing like that. The actual practical experiment was those girls in that muddy hut outside the theatre. Gerry couldn't see it coming to anything. Where was the money to come from? Joan accused Gerry of sabotaging it because he wasn't actually promoting it. You can't promote something you don't think is viable.'

Despite Joan's lessening involvement the theatre kept open, albeit sporadically, and in September 1967, rehearsals commenced on *Mrs. Wilson's Diary*. This was a current serial in the satirical journal *Private Eye*, based on the imagined jottings of Mary Wilson, the then Prime Minister's wife. Earlier in the year, Joan had discussed with the authors, John Wells and Richard Ingrams, the possibility of adapting it for a stage show. John Wells thought the idea fairly implausible, but began working on it with Joan, and was present throughout rehearsals:

> I was immediately impressed by the way she snatched ideas out of the air, developed them with the writer and actors and incorporated them into the production, sometimes into whole scenes, sometimes just the odd line. She would set up situations and characters that paralleled those in the play, and the cast would act them out. She would then go back to the original scene in the play and it would be now enriched and animated by the work on the parallel situation.

The events, many and varied, spanned a crowded day in the life of the Wilson household at No. 10 Downing Street. They hinged on schemes devised by Harold Wilson and Gerald Kaufman, who was responsible for public relations, to halt Wilson's falling popularity in the polls and included a threatened American nuclear attack on London, an interview on the David Frost programme and a plan to parachute George Brown, the Foreign Secretary, into North Vietnam. Songs were written by John Wells and put to music by Jeremy Taylor, and the show was described in the programme as a 'Political Lampoon'. It was necessary, of course, to adapt the show after it opened so as to keep pace with changing political events. On one occasion, we did even better than that. George Brown's resignation as Foreign Secretary was accepted on stage by Harold Wilson half an hour before it was officially announced. But George Brown, as played by Bob Grant, was a colourful character and we wanted to keep him in the show, so we allowed him to stay on, supposedly under the impression that he was still Foreign Secretary.

There were the inevitable long discussions with the Lord Chamberlain on what could and what could not go into the script. He cut some of the anecdotes about Government Ministers and ruled that a yellow duster draped over a statue of Lyndon Johnson was not sufficiently decorous, insisting that the figure be fully clothed.

Bill Wallis played Harold Wilson:

I probably got the part because Joan had never had anyone so solidly and boringly middle-class audition for her. I had that particular attribute without any problem, but I lacked real political knowledge, and I was scared of what I thought would be the political content, but it turned out to be immensely enjoyable. I think my impersonation of Harold Wilson owed more to the goodwill of the audience than any accuracy on my part. I remember Joan saying that if you are doing any sort of caricature impersonation, and you come on and amuse the audience enough on your first entrance, they'll like you so much they'll accept your impersonation from then on. The technique we used for devising the script was to take wads of material supplied by John Wells and Richard Ingrams, pick out the sequences we wanted and improvise around them. This seemed to me to be a good way of working, because you never got out of character, you'd grown up with it, and in the same way, the show grew with you. There is no way you can be caught out, by anything that happens, because you're right there, it's part of your life.

The show was an immediate success, transferring to the Criterion Theatre and running there for 255 performances.

The Marie Lloyd Story by Daniel Farson and Harry Moore (with lyrics by Daniel Farson and music by Norman Kay) opened in November 1967 with Avis Bunnage playing the name part. Marie Lloyd is shown at the age of forty, her second marriage as disastrous as her first, her private life unhappy and frustrated. Subjected to harassment and scandalous gossip, she was made to appear before a 'Purity Committee' who vetted her songs. On her arrival in America, she was detained on Ellis Island accused of moral turpitude. In a series of realistic scenes, these events were juxtaposed with the more familiar figure of Marie Lloyd, the darling of the

Music Hall, putting over her songs to her admiring public with all the confidence and vitality they expected.

Avis Bunnage received high praise for her performance, but negotiations for a West End transfer fell through, and in December 1967 the Theatre Royal was again leased to a new management who opened their season with a traditional pantomime, *Aladdin*.

During the break in production that followed, energies were devoted to alleviating the havoc caused by demolition and development. Gerry appealed to the local council:

> If the people of Stratford do not make their voices heard, the planners and commercial developers will face us with a generation of vandalism caused by young people with nowhere to go and nothing to do ... For very little effort on the part of the London Borough of Newham an entertainment complex could be created around the Theatre Royal, housing not only the theatre but a cinema, dance hall cum discotheque, youth theatre, public meeting hall, coffee bar and restaurants – catering for people of all ages.
>
> The theatre would be the focal point, but the space surrounding it should be designed for changing use, for the entertainments of the future ... There is space now, there won't be again for a hundred years ...

Gerry's plea was, as might be expected, rejected; and the theatre was to be left isolated, surrounded by office blocks and new development. His own plans for an extension to the theatre to include a discotheque and an experimental theatre for young people could not be implemented because of the high cost of land and the lack of financial support.

Though still without subsidy, it was felt imperative that the theatre should re-open if it was to have any place at all in future plans for the area. When it did so in September 1970 much of the neighbourhood had already gone, including the street of small houses familiar to thousands who had made their way in the past from the tube station to the theatre. £2,000 was raised to repaint the theatre and install new seating in time for opening of the first production of the new decade: *Forward Up Your End* by Ken Hill, produced by Joan in a cartoon setting by Larry of Punch and with music by Len Newberry. It was a satiric comedy aimed at exposing bureaucracy and corruption in local government. It was set in Birmingham, as the author had worked there as a clerk for the council for four years. It aroused a great deal of indignation amongst councillors in that city, who objected to its being used as an example of maladministration, suggesting that the author look nearer to his new-found home. Certainly ample evidence of bureaucratic disregard for the value of art and leisure to the community was on the doorstep, considering the very existence of the theatre was threatened by the re-development of the area taking place at that time.

In 1968 Ronan Point, a tower block of flats in the East End, had partially collapsed, making headline news. Joan wanted to produce a play which would expose the real causes of this disaster. Risk of libel made it impossible to do this directly, so in December 1970 she produced *The Projector*. Ostensibly, it was adapted by John Wells from a little known ballad opera by the eighteenth-century playwright William Rufus Chetwood first produced in 1733. No trace of this play could be found, and a few critics began to express doubts as to whether, in fact, it had ever existed. John Wells maintained that his copy had been taken to America by a scholar with the unlikely name of Emil Potbohm, who had since disappeared. Chetwood himself was genuine enough of course and had written many plays, but there can be little doubt that John Wells had succeeded in emulating his style in a completely original play on the theme of a Dutch builder who built houses that fell down. Discussion on the merits of the play and the production were somewhat obscured by the controversy over its origins, but it was generally considered an improvement on *Forward Up Your End*.

There was by now a tendency, on the part of some of the critics, to compare a current production with what they had seen at Stratford in the immediate past, or even some years previously, rather than to judge it on its own merits. Understandable, given the distinctive Theatre Workshop style, but in the long run, unhelpful. They failed to take into account the particular circumstances that surrounded past successes, the resources, actors, writers and the changing political and social climate.

In December 1970 the theatre was threatened by a plan by Newham Council to demolish part of the offices, two dressing rooms and the Long Bar as part of the development schemes. Letters poured in to the local paper demanding not only that the theatre should be left intact but that financial help be forthcoming from the council. The fight to save the theatre, led by Gerry Raffles, was at least for the time being won, but the threat remained. It wasn't until 28 June 1972 that the Theatre Royal was declared a listed building by the Historic Buildings Council, preserving the physical structure from future threats. A request to the Arts Council for a subsidy of £53,000 was turned down, and the theatre was again forced to close.

A grant of £35,000, subsequently raised to £41,000, was finally offered to Theatre Workshop in January 1972 by the Arts Council with no reference to support from local councils. The L.C.C. offered a further £17,000 and Newham £3,000. So, nineteen years after coming to

Stratford and twenty-seven years since its foundation, Theatre Workshop was at last being offered grants that bore some relation to its needs, though still less than those being offered to comparable companies. In the same period, the grant to the English Stage Company was £120,000.

Suggested explanations for this long delay differ widely. John Bury seems to feel that lack of planning worried the Arts Council:

> In the early days, we were regarded as a bunch of Reds. Moscow Gold and all that stuff. At Stratford East, I think it was the lack of accountability that worried them. There was a lot of fuss about the books and keeping it together, programming and playing. Joan would always be rude to them. We didn't play their game and they weren't going to play ours. They felt if we wanted to behave like that we could run our own theatre. Then they gave us a bit, but we were always well below the Royal Court. We never had a forward moving programme – shows went to the West End – the theatre would be closed. Joan expected money from the Arts Council on trust, but she didn't get it.

A plausible explanation – though many would argue that the quality of Joan's work did give her a right to expect money from the Arts Council. Clive Barker puts forward the interesting view, that, in fact, it was Joan herself who was suspect:

> Joan is, for my money, the finest theatre scholar in this country, but because she worked in a seemingly unstructured way, she created in some people's eyes, the picture of an irresponsible dilettante, playing at theatre, a brilliant amateur, which she is not. I think this image acted against the subsidy, against her getting money. It was a totally blind and philistine view, insensitive to the quality, knowledge and understanding that that woman had.

Oscar Lewenstein, on the other hand, believes that, in this country, individuals are not taken into account:

> Whereas in France they will back a particular artist because he or she is considered to be brilliant, for instance, Peter Brook, in England, if you had a genius running the Bristol Old Vic, it would get the same subsidy as if there was an idiot running it. So if you're Joan Littlewood, it doesn't mean anything, they simply say Stratford East has a population of so much, the theatre's potential is such and such...

A group of students from West Ham Technical College cleaned out the theatre, which had been closed for almost a year, and Larry (the Punch cartoonist) brightened up the stairways with cartoons. Well-wishers 'adopted' the dressing rooms to pay for their redecorating. *Sparrers Can't Sing* had been re-written and turned into a musical by Lionel Bart, re-titled *The Londoners*. It opened in March 1972. The story of three cockney families living in a slum mirrored what had happened around the theatre building itself. It now stood alone in a wasteland awaiting the builders, and the audience stumbled through stone and rubble, left by the destruction of the streets of small houses, to get to the theatre. No formal invitation was sent to the critics, but they came as 'friends' and all welcomed Joan back to her besieged theatre. Despite the sheer physical discomfort of getting to the theatre, the show was successful enough to extend its run, but didn't transfer. Perhaps, as Frank Norman said of *Kayf Up West*, the 'New Wave' had receded and the West End no longer regarded this short of show as a commercial proposition.

In any case the subsidy provided the possibility of building up a company at Stratford in preference to transferring to the West End. In an article in July 1972 by Judith Cook in the Birmingham Post, Joan is quoted as saying: 'A series of packaged replicas of the living work were sold to the West End; the consequence was the exhaustion of the nucleus who trained and directed the experiment, a dissipation of talent and a sense of direction lost.'

Brendan Behan's *The Hostage* was revived in May 1972. Since the original production in 1958, the I.R.A. had become a day to day reality rather than merely a part of Irish history, and re-writing was necessary to take this into account. Patience Collier, who had gone to America with the production in 1960, regretted the up-dating:

> I thought it would be nice to have a refresher with Joan, but I did not know she'd decided to re-write it, to de-Brendanise it a lot, many of the things I had treasured went. We were always experimenting with the words and making them up, and I thought what happened was a nightmare. Some people loved it, but I didn't.

The actors who loved it were those more used to working with Joan, and who knew that a complete re-working of the script would take place anyway regardless of the alterations demanded by the changes in the political situation. Never would Joan repeat what she had done before in an attempt to emulate a previous success. Understandably, Patience Collier, a well established character actress, had mastered the part of Miss Gilchrist, enjoyed playing it and wanted to be left in peace to continue to do so.

Joan was by now too tired and disillusioned to take advantage of the increased Arts Council grant and the belated recognition of her work that this implied. There were only six productions in the eighteen month period to November 1973 and four of these were not directed by Joan. The first was in July 1972 when Henry Livings directed his own play *The Ffinest Ffamily in the Land* with a cast that included Griffith Davies, Eileen Kennally, Brian Murphy and Maxwell Shaw. The second, directed by Joan, was *Costa Packet*, a musical by Frank Norman about a package holiday in Spain, with songs by Lionel Bart and Alan Klein. It opened in October 1972 and ran for ten weeks. Frank had to go away during rehearsals and in his absence, extensive re-writing took place. He complained on his return that the show now lacked the polemic he had put into it and had deteriorated into a romp. After a row with Joan he virtually disowned the script.

Then followed a revival of *Big Rock Candy Mountain* by Alan Lomax, produced by Avis Bunnage, with Long John Baldry as the cowboy narrator.

Is Your Doctor Really Necessary? written and directed by Ken Hill with music by Tony Macaulay opened on 17 February. It took a look at the drugs industry. The cast included Maxwell Shaw, Brian Murphy, Avis Bunnage and Toni Palmer and it ran for nearly three months.

As the Theatre Royal had now become obscured from view by the office blocks around it a seventeen foot silver balloon was launched in April, two hundred feet above the theatre, to serve as a landmark. Unfortunately, it only survived a week. As it was being lowered at the week-end it was punctured beyond repair by an over enthusiastic child. There followed in April a successful production by Maxwell Shaw of C. G. Bond's version of *Sweeney Todd* with Brian Murphy and Avis Bunnage in the leading parts.

An entertainment called *Nuts*, devised by the Company, was produced in June.

Joan's last production at the Theatre Royal was *So You Want To Be in Pictures* by Peter Rankin in November 1973. It had very few of the old members of the Company in the cast. The setting was the shooting of a film on the rooftops of Rome and the play was a send-up of the lunacies of film making. It received good notices, Harold Hobson described it as having 'an atmosphere of carefree joyousness'. It was followed by Philip Hedley's revival of *A Christmas Carol*. In February 1974, Ken Hill's *Gentlemen Prefer Anything* was the last production before the theatre was swamped by redevelopment of the surrounding site. A financial crisis also threatened to close the theatre. The then Minister for the Arts, Norman St. John Stevas, promised to try and help, and when he visited the theatre a four point plan was put to him:

(1) Adequate subsidy to form a permanent company of actors and technicians.

(2) Sufficient storage space for sets and costumes.
(3) Improvement of area outside the theatre.
(4) Provision of more leisure facilities adjacent to the theatre.

A great deal of publicity attended his visit, with pictures in the Press of him and Joan picking their way through the rubble outside the theatre, but very little more. The Arts Council made the provision of more money conditional on increased help from local authorities.

In March 1974, the Minister for the Arts in the new Labour government, Hugh Jenkins, supported the Arts Council view that it was up to local authorities to rally to support their own theatre. Gerry Raffles had estimated that the theatre needed a subsidy of £110,000 a year, and the Arts Council offered a half if the other half could be raised elsewhere. There seemed little chance of this as the only other grants were £3,000 from Newham, £5,000 from Waltham Forest and £17,000 from the G.L.C. Ten years previously, nine local authorities made grants to the theatre, albeit small ones. However, the Arts Council did agree to make a grant of £60,500 without the condition of a matching sum from other sources. Gerry resigned at what he considered the inadequacy of the grant and handed over the administration of the theatre to Ken Hill, remarking that 'Newham value the ground at £750,000 but will only give £3,000, less than 1/10th. of a penny rate'. A year later, on 11 April 1975, a week before his fifty-second birthday, Gerry Raffles, who had been in poor health for some time, collapsed and died in Vienne, France.

Ten

Foreign Tours

Not without honour save at home

Our first opportunity to play abroad arose, rather surprisingly, through an invitation to tour West Germany playing to the British Army of Occupation. It came from the organisation that had replaced E.N.S.A., the Combined Services Entertainment Unit; and the contract covered the period from 27 January to 30 March 1947. The Company were to be accommodated in hostels, taken from place to place, paid expenses and wages, and accorded the status of British Army Officers. Our only responsibility would be to play the shows. Naturally we had no hesitation in accepting the offer, though Joan decided to stay at home and try to sort out some of our problems. She placed me in charge of the Company with the title of Artistic Director – this in addition to taking part in the productions. We took two programmes; *Uranium 235* and a double bill of *Johnny Noble* and Chekhov's *The Proposal*, and on 28 January we left Hull in the 'Empire Cutlass' in bitterly cold weather. As we approached Cuxhaven an ice-breaker was needed to clear a way for us into the bombed and ruined harbour. The War had been over for less than two years, and rebuilding had scarcely begun. The ravages of the bombing were everywhere to be seen, as Bill Davidson recalled:

> It was unbelievable; the destruction in all the big cities – it blew one's mind. It was difficult to find streets. There were just neat piles of rubble, and occasionally you would see a tin pipe with some smoke coming out – the smell of wood smoke and poor quality petrol is what I remember – and you would find the smoke was coming from a ladies' hairdresser – one of the first necessities of life!

The Company were insulated from all this discomfort; we lived in centrally heated hostels and ate and drank well, whilst being surrounded by people who were cold and hungry. Though we kept reminding ourselves of the misery the Germans had inflicted all over Europe, it was impossible not to feel acutely uncomfortable and even guilty, faced with the immediate reality of children demanding bread and seeing their hungry faces pressed against the windows of restaurants, watching us while we ate. In a sense we were part of the occupation army, reaping the rewards of victory, though we were rarely aware of any actual hostility towards us. The Company were well looked after in the hostels and restaurants, and stage staff at all the theatres we visited were always co-operative. There was a curious feeling of sharing in a tremendous relief that at last the horror of the war was over. We also sensed an underlying confidence, which we now know was not misplaced, in the resilience of the German people, and in their capacity to overcome their present difficulties.

In fact the only really unpleasant experience was an outburst of anti-Semitism, not from Germans but from British officers in their own club in Wuppertal. Less unpleasant perhaps, because less unexpected, was a demonstration of organised clapping after a performance of *The Magic Flute* at the Hamburg State Opera House. It was led by a group of former Nazi Party members and directed against the presence of British officers in the audience.

Uranium appealed particularly to those who had been on active service during the war, and who were better able to relate its warnings of the dangers of nuclear war to their own war-time experiences. We were always able to rely on the support of those who had been habitual theatre-goers in civilian life – usually officers, as might be expected. Many of them came round after the performance to congratulate us. The real appreciation and understanding, however, came from the Germans in the audience. They were able to recognise, in our productions, the affinity with the mainstream tradition of European theatre, in which their own theatre had played such an important part. Friedrich Wolf, a leading figure in German theatre at that time, wrote: 'Theatre Workshop might well serve as a model for the new German theatre.' German impresarios invited us to play in their own theatres, but this, unfortunately, was not possible to organise.

We returned to England with the feeling that if the tour had been less than a success in terms of size of audiences, the discussions we had had with German theatre workers, and the opportunity to play to them, had been a most valuable experience for us. It had come at just the right time, providing the Company with a more critical and knowledgeable appraisal of its work than it had received so far – appreciation that was to be a source of great encouragement in the difficult days that lay ahead.

Our second trip abroad was in September and October 1948 when, through the good offices of Tom Driberg M.P., we were invited to tour Czechoslovakia under the auspices of the Ministry of Culture. We took Ewan's new play *The Other Animals* and a double bill, *Johnny Noble* and

The Flying Doctor. We left Paris by train at 7.50 in the evening and at 9.30 the following morning crossed the Czech border at Cheb to be greeted with flowers and speeches. Here we met our interpreters, Vladimir, Zoe and Beatrice, and went on by coach to Karlovy Vary, formerly the spa of Karlsbad. Here we sat down to a splendid four-course lunch. A large helping of fish followed the hors d'oeuvre, and assuming this to be the main course, we tucked in heartily, to be confronted by an even larger meat course, followed by dessert. These lavish meals were to become a feature of our daily lives. They were attended by the civic leaders of the town we were visiting with speeches and toasts to 'Peace and Friendship' and always went on for a long time. There was no way in which they could be hurried, and when they took place before a show, getting the curtain up on time could become quite a problem. When we tried to explain our dilemma to our hosts, they took the view that the time to start the show was when we were ready, and that everyone must be perfectly happy to wait. It was not easy, but gradually we ceased to panic as the half hour call was given while the veg. was still being passed round; we adopted a more philosophical attitude to time and concentrated on enjoying the meal. The only dish that defeated most of the Company was Czech dumplings. As it was a national dish and a source of great pride, it was difficult to refuse them, so we ate what we could and furtively slid the rest on to George Cooper's plate, who actually seemed to like them. As guests we were exempt from food rationing, and whatever was available was given to us with tremendous generosity. Some shortages could not be avoided, an egg for breakfast was a rare treat, coffee was a luxury and milk in very short supply.

We were to experience the Czechs' easy-going attitude to time on several occasions. In Krnov, the safety curtain stuck halfway, apparently a not unusual occurrence, and no-one was at all bothered. The little Jewish mayor took the opportunity to harangue the audience on the latest Party line, the stage hands leisurely set about the problem, and eventually the show proceeded. On one occasion, our gear was being moved by horse and cart from the theatre to the railway station in the charge of two men who were paralytic with drink. They sat swaying on the top of the cart, while the horse plodded gently along. There was no way we could get through to them that at the speed we were going, we were in grave danger of missing the train.

This Czech visit took place only a few months after the Communist Party had taken power in a 'bloodless revolution'; but to interpret the invitation and the warmth of reception as purely politically motivated would be a mistake. In those early days of Communism in 1948, there was an unmistakable feeling of hope and confidence, a genuine longing for friendship and a more just society, and, above all, a very real desire for peace. Talking freely to Party members all over the country, we found no feeling of bitterness against us, only a desire to know why Britain had turned against Czechoslovakia at the time of Munich. The horrors of German occupation were still fresh in people's minds, and during our visit to Opava we began to get some inkling of what it had been like. This town had been in Sudeten territory, and all the Party leaders who welcomed us had been for years in Concentration Camps. As they showed us the numbers tatooed on their arms, we wondered how they were still able to smile and sing. We also began to understand the source of their political strength and their violent reaction against a system that had caused such misery, and which they were determined would never return. Looking back on those days, the tragedy of what has happened since seems even more poignant.

During our stay in Prague we were able to see something of the work of Burian and his theatre, D.49. He was directing his energies towards Socialist Realism, the sort of plays, in fact, that Joan and Ewan had rejected in the pre-war years. Burian's productions were, of course, of a much higher standard than the left-wing groups of that time. A leading Party critic, Zadek, described *The Other Animals* as existentialist and 'Pre-War Burian' in its form, which is an indication that we would have found Burian's earlier productions more interesting than the ones we saw. Zadek was a lone voice, expressing the orthodox Party line, for wherever we went, the other critics were full of enthusiasm. The leading dramatic critic of *Rude Pravo* wrote: 'Here is a theatre in the great tradition, ensemble playing at a particularly high level, production which is flawless.'

A week or so after our visit to the D.49 theatre, we saw a production of *Twelfth Night* at the Brno National Theatre. It had all the ingredients of a traditional Shakespearian production. The costumes and settings were heavy and in 'period', the action, such as there was, slow and unimaginative. The audience, who appeared to enjoy it, received it with all the respect due to Shakespeare. Whatever Party directives Burian's theatre may have received in the past or might receive in the future, it was clear that the National Theatres would be left to pursue their traditional way. After an evening at *Twelfth Night* one had the feeling that any directive from whatever source could only result in an improvement. We discussed our ideas of a People's Theatre with actors all over the country and the reaction was similar to what we might have expected at home. Some were really interested; those who worked in the National Theatres seemed satisfied with the conventional theatre they were working in; and those working in Socialist Realism felt the emphasis should be on involvement in the political struggle. We felt we were at least able to show, with our productions, that this involvement did not need to be at the expense of interesting, exciting theatre.

The tour was extended for eight days with a break for a short holiday high up in the Tatra mountains. On 11 October, after playing twenty towns in five weeks, we made our farewells at a large meeting in the magnificent Miners' Hall in Ostrava, which was packed to capacity. The Company sat on the platform while questions were put to us from the body of the hall, not about theatre, but about war and peace, the atom bomb, and fears and hopes for the future. It was a meeting charged with emotion. They knew we wished the Czech people well, and we knew that despite the Iron Curtain their desire for friendship with the English people was deep and genuine.

We made our way to the station, sang the 'Internationale' with our friends, said goodbye to Carl, our driver, now in his best suit, to Zoe and Beatrice, our interpreters, got on to the train and waved our very sad farewells. We were not heading for home, we were on our way to Sweden, via East Berlin and the Polish corridor. After a very uncomfortable night in a crowded Polish train, a pleasant ferry journey from Odreport to Telleborg, and another night in a train, this time a comfortable Swedish one, we arrived in Norrkoping.

The origin of this Swedish tour went back to April 1947 at the end of the German tour. During a short break, Kristin Lind had decided to go back home to Sweden with the aim of planning a visit for the Company. She recalled how she went about it:

> Sweden had been isolated during the war from the rest of Europe and this may be one of the reasons why everyone I contacted showed great interest in this group of actors from London, although, at that time, no-one had heard anything about Theatre Workshop. Every municipal theatre wanted to be the first to sponsor this new experimental Group theatre from England. I started with the manager and producer of the theatre in Gothenburg, he was very helpful and contacted his colleague in Norrkoping, and so I went from town to town. Everywhere there was sympathy for our ideas and our way of working. We would not have empty houses, I was assured. Unlike in England, here we were unknown, but very welcome. In the meantime, the struggle for survival went on. Letters of despair reached me from Joan: 'We need the tour desperately. We are trying to raise money to get on our feet, so far – £5. 10. 0. We shall have to live Youth Hostel fashion, and eat oats and oil. We are making a silk screen so we can print our own posters, and John Bury is trying to get three pounds to buy a small printing press, so that we can print our own leaflets. We will get a brochure and leaflet

of this style through to you soon if it is any use.' I badly needed publicity material, but of course, Theatre Workshop could not afford photos of a professional standard. Despite these difficulties, I was managing to sell *Johnny Noble* and *The Flying Doctor* to the municipal theatres. They would pay for publicity, and not charge for rent and staff; and 'Riksteater' – a body that organised tours – would pay the travelling, recoup 50 % of the net takings and pay our expenses. The biggest headache now was money to get the Company to Sweden and home again. I suddenly had an idea. The president of the Co-operative movement was known for his idealism, and his belief that the arts should be subsidised. This elderly working-class man listened politely and sympathetically to my long story. He then said that he felt a great understanding for our struggle to create a people's theatre, and our fight against commercialism in art. He lifted a telephone, then told me: 'Go downstairs to the cashier. We will be glad to help your comrades to get here.' I received an envelope from the cashier with 5000 Swedish kronor in it. I had never held so much money in my hands before. I rushed to the nearest bank to put it away safely.

To travel directly from Czechoslovakia to Sweden was a revealing and somewhat disturbing experience. The Company had left behind them a country whose people had suffered all the privations of war and enemy occupation, and arrived in a country of affluence and stability, that for centuries had been free from war and revolution. Here, everything was in abundance, the shops were well stocked, the people well fed and clothed. On the table, at our first reception, stood large jugs of milk, the first we had seen for six weeks. We were now reliant on private hospitality, and this was never lacking. Most of it was very luxurious indeed. The Company were wined and dined in well appointed flats, magnificent old farmhouses and chateaus and even in the official residence of the Lord Lieutenant of the county. Each morning we outvied each other with tales of splendour, reporting on the social gaffes we had committed, the butlers and maids who resented us because we weren't posh enough and, of course, the inevitable amorous intrigues.

There were official receptions with all the Swedish love of formality, the toasts, the flowers for the ladies and the speeches; and there were less inhibited theatrical parties into the early hours. We enjoyed it to the full while it lasted, for though the austerities of communal living in the Parrot House in Manchester seemed very far away, we knew the stuggle to survive was, in reality, only round the corner.

The shows were even more acclaimed than they had been in Czechoslovakia, particularly taking into account the hostility of the

Swedish Press to left-wing ideas, and the conservatism of theatre audiences.

Following the success of our performances in Norrkoping, Kristin obtained an invitation for the Company to play a special matinee of *The Other Animals* at the Royal Opera House in Stockholm – never before made available to a foreign company. At twenty-four hours' notice, the theatre was packed, and the Company received a standing ovation from an audience that included all the leading figures of film and theatre, Swedish and Belgian royalty and the Swedish Prime Minister. It was ironic that a company that had yet to achieve recognition in its own country and that had rehearsed *The Other Animals* in a cellar in Manchester should be acclaimed by a discerning audience in one of Europe's stateliest theatres. Though most of the Swedish critics did not take to the politics of *The Other Animals*, Ewan MacColl was described as 'a brilliant new star in the dramatic firmament', and Joan's work was compared to that of Reinhardt and Piscator. Everywhere they were united in their praise of the Company. The critic of the *Svenska Dageblatt* wrote: 'British theatre makes a revolt at the Opera House! The storm of applause for Theatre Workshop yesterday was fully justified. It was an exciting experience. It is not very often that we see such high standards in Sweden.'

We played sixteen performances in ten towns. On 16 November we loaded our gear, bought ham, bacon, butter, honey and mayonnaise in anticipation of shortages at home, and at seven p.m. sailed for England. The tour had not only been a triumph for the Company, it had also been a tribute to the hard work and determination of Kristin Lind who, starting from scratch, had organised a tour which normally would have utilised all the resources of the British Council. We returned home to a very uncertain future and it was not until March 1949 that we were able to give our next performance. It was the first in a schools tour of *Twelfth Night*, and on that day we received our first wages since arriving home – a pound note. Nothing had changed!

In February 1951 the Company paid a second visit to Scandinavia. This time Kristin, with the assistance of the Swedish equivalent of the Arts Council, had put together a tour of *Uranium 235* for Norway and Sweden. It was rather like a fairy tale. We had just completed a one-night stand tour of South Wales, a hand-to-mouth existence dependent on homely working-class hospitality; and overnight, as it were, we were transported to the solid bourgeois homes of Norway with money to spend in our pockets – back to the gracious living we had enjoyed in 1948. George Cooper fondly recalls:

My favourite memory is of staying with a kindly old gentleman in a magnificent house with his own lift. There was a music room, an aquarium room full of tropical fish, a splendid set-up with silver salvers, butler and the lot! A very polished style of life.

We played eight towns in Norway and covered longer distances in Sweden than on our previous visit; from Goteborg in the West to Stockholm in the East, from Malmo in the South to Ustersund in the North.

There was more than praise for our work from the Swedish critics. There was a genuine interest in what the Company was trying to do, and more understanding of the sources of its inspiration than we had found in England. Erwin Leiser wrote: 'It is the dream of a People's Theatre that Theatre Workshop realises in a hard struggle against the theatrical industry and commercialism. Ewan MacColl finds his inspiration in the hard reality of the lives of the working class. The Group has unity – there are no stars. And so it should be when you not only work together, but live together until the theatre becomes your life.'

During this tour, the critic Sven Stahl in a long review in praise of the Company also analysed where its roots lay: 'Kurt Jooss has preached the same evangelism, and Erwin Piscator has, with Ernst Toller's help, made visual the same thoughts and ideas. Nothing under the sun is new – and yet, in spite of this, there is about this young English group a quality of magnificent freshness, a novelty that thrills ...'

Of Joan he had this to say:

What a woman this must be who handles all the different media of the stage with such brilliant touch. She is a woman of real greatness, worthy of our admiration and reverence, a woman of importance of whom the English theatre can be proud. As an artist she is worth the entire Old Vic. Her name should be written in letters of fire until the blinkers are burned off the eyes of the English theatre public.

It was to be quite a long time before this passionate appeal for general recognition of Joan's work was to be answered.

In May 1955, still without any form of subsidy, and struggling to keep the Theatre Royal, Stratford, over our heads, the Company received an invitation from the Director General of the International Theatre Festival in Paris to represent Great Britain at the Théâtre des Nations with *Arden of Faversham* and *Volpone*. The theatrical establishment was quite outraged that this invitation should have been extended to an 'unknown' company, and after a great deal of hesitation, 'Under the patronage of the British Ambassador' was reluctantly allowed to be printed on the programmes. This was the total extent of official support for our visit. No message of greetings from the Ambassador appeared in the Festival brochure, though there were messages from the mayors of some of the East End boroughs. We received no financial help, of course, and we were so hard up we had great difficulty in getting to Paris at all, as Harry Corbett recalls:

> It was quite hysterical. We had no money to pay freight charges, and we had to take all the set over as personal hand luggage. Gerry held the ferry up for two hours while he argued with the crew and the Customs. We had masses of stuff including cheese-shaped rostra and two pillars, about twelve feet high and three feet wide. I carried one of these up the gang plank as personal luggage! We all carried a piece of the bloody set. Somehow, we got there and took Paris by storm.'

The reception by the audience on the first night of *Volpone* was tremendous, and we lost count of the number of curtain calls. The effect was compared to that created by the Compagnie des Quinze who had taken London by storm in 1932.

Shirley Dynevor remembers Joan's reaction to our success:

> We woke up the morning after our opening performance to find that the whole Company was being celebrated and applauded. Suddenly, Theatre Workshop was famous, and I remember Joan coming into the auditorium, where we were all gathered, with her hat squashed down on her head, and she looked so miserable, so fed up about the whole thing. And I remember her saying 'Ah well, now that we're a success, the whole thing will fall apart.' One felt that success was the last thing she wanted and that we could only really survive with struggle, there had to be something to fight against.

Certainly it could be said that the West End transfers from Stratford that were to come later did contribute to the eventual break-up of the Company. To that extent, Joan's fears of success were well founded, but there was nothing to fear from the effects of the visit to Paris. Like the tour of Sweden, it went quite unregarded at home. Indeed, if the powers that be had had their way, we wouldn't have been there at all, as Morvan Lebesque explained to his French readers in *Carrefour*:

> *The Miracle of the Workshop.*
>   This story resembles a fairy tale: once upon a time there was in London a company of actors who ran a people's theatre. I repeat, a people's theatre, the like of which no-one has done in this country as yet, in a small theatre in a working-class quarter of East London (translated that means playing not in Chaillot but in Belleville).

Then see what happens: one day the organisers of the Festival of Paris hear news of Theatre Workshop and decide to invite it. They asked the officials who immediately cried out loudly 'You want an English company? Very well. Take X. or Y., famous companies, of noted worth, the glories of our national stage, but, by God, not this Workshop. They have no renown and no splendour, and their productions are not fit to represent the British theatre abroad.'

Fortunately the French organisers held firm. Against wind and tide, against the indignant cultural attachés, against the British Council which refused a subsidy, against Her Majesty's Government which would not deign to write a word of introduction in the programme, against the Ambassador himself who, right up to the last moment, could not make up his mind to be present at the opening night, Theatre Workshop came, installed themselves in the Herbertot Theatre, and carried off the biggest, the most unexpected, the most extraordinary success that a British company has known in France: in that same Paris where, not long ago, a very official British company bored us so implacably during a whole evening.

My admiration for Theatre Workshop can be expressed in a few words: we do not possess a single company in France comparable to this one. Nothing which resembles its ardour, its generosity, and, to say all, its youth.

The last paragraph of his review sums up the reaction of all the Paris critics who, without exception, were full of praise for the productions:

There were incomparable moments. And what diction: what spirit: what discoveries.
Dear friends of the Workshop, I will not take up space to list your names which would not mean anything yet to French readers. Besides, do you really care? You form a company which is very obviously the pride of the contemporary English theatre. You have set the Festival of Paris alight in its first week. We salute you with joy as being the purest, the simplest, and the greatest artists. We hope to see you again and to applaud you once more.

There was some wishful thinking on the part of this critic, for far from being 'the pride of the contemporary English theatre' we had yet to receive a single penny of public subsidy. No doubt the theatrical establishment would have preferred to ignore the whole episode, but a column in *The Times* of 24 May from the Paris correspondent headed 'A popular success' made it impossible for them to do so:

Theatre Workshop, with its playing of *Arden of Faversham* and *Volpone* has had a success at the Paris Drama Festival far exceeding that accorded to any other British company in France since the war. Apart from the intrinsic merit of the Company's performances and choice of plays, French audiences and critics seem to derive much satisfaction from the fact that Theatre Workshop is a popular theatre, which they compare with the Theatre National Populaire – not, alas, a fair comparison, for the T.N.P. is heavily subsidised by the State. There is also something attractive about the idea of a theatre group, in which individual performances count for less than does the joint effort ... As those connected with the Company themselves observe, this is a triumph that they never knew in their own country – but none the less pleasant for that.

It was Harold Hobson's view that 'Theatre Workshop has done more to raise the international reputation of Britain on the Continent than any of our most famous or chauvinistic actors or companies.'

It is not difficult to understand why the official arbiters of English theatre did not look kindly on Theatre Workshop. In its style and with the content of its productions it owed nothing to contemporary English theatre and, indeed, came into being as a reaction against it. Its roots lay in left-wing political theatre and it had later drawn its inspiration from European theatrical forms that had quite by-passed this country. We just did not fit in to the accepted pattern. Also, as a group theatre with a political conscience it was naturally viewed with extreme suspicion. There was no 'fringe' at this time, and it was only ten years or so later that fringe companies were to spring up and gradually become accepted, if somewhat reluctantly, by the public funding bodies, as a part of the British theatrical scene.

The Company's third and last visit to Sweden took place in January and February 1956 with *Arden of Faversham* and this time the tour was not only artistically successful but also financially profitable. It helped to pay off the debts in England, pay the rent of the Theatre Royal, and send the Company home with a couple of hundred kronor each in their pockets. Kristin summed up the result of our visits to her country:

> Today it would not be as sensational to meet a group like Theatre Workshop in Sweden as it was when we only knew established, traditional theatre. Now in Sweden, as in the rest of Europe, there are dozens of groups fighting for the same ideals, and it is very possible that some of these were inspired by Theatre Workshop.

In 1956, the Company returned to Paris to play in the Third International Theatre Festival, this time with *The Good Soldier Schweik* adapted from the Czech of Jaroslav Hasek by Ewan MacColl. Because it wasn't an English play, the British Council refused us financial support and, once again, Theatre Workshop was the only company in the Festival which had to rely on their own resources and the generosity of the French organisers of the Festival. *Schweik* was singled out as one of the highlights of the Festival, but, as might be expected, did not provide the sensation of *Volpone* and *Arden of Faversham* had done the previous year. The vulgarity of the production which had upset some of the West End audience was singled out by Pierre Marcabru in the souvenir book of the Festival:

> This is its strength and there is no compromise. It is popular theatre in the best sense of the term, and it has a sharp reality ... in a sense, 'slang'. ... The courage of Theatre Workshop is in its espousal of the vulgar. It is a very human comedy ... The acting is miraculous, near perfection. ... there is a devilish coarseness ..., the characters came straight off the street without having been made theatrical by the tradition of dramatic art ... magnificent work.

Harold Hobson also pinpointed the difference in approach:

> It is easy to see what captivated the Parisians. Theatre Workshop throws out of the window the naturalistic acting which is the staple of the British Theatre, and which seems to French audiences indistinguishable from immobility. Its style is caricatural, charade-like, simplified and exaggerated.

In July 1957 the Company took Joan's modern dress version of *Macbeth* to Zurich and then on to the International Youth Festival in Moscow. I was living it up in the West End on temporary leave from the Company, playing in *Free as Air* and so missed this trip. What should have been a straightforward, if long, journey to Zurich turned out quite differently, as Brian Murphy recalled:

> Glyn Edwards, Richard Harris, the photographer Alan Vines, and myself got off the train at Lille to go to the buffet, leaving in the compartment, our jackets and passports. We got back ten minutes later just as the train was leaving. We all tried to dive into the guard's van, he wasn't having any and pushed us back onto the platform. We tried to explain our plight in bad French to anyone who would listen, and Richard Harris did an elaborate mime, chasing up and down the platform to represent the train leaving, but we couldn't get anyone to understand. We weren't able to make contact with the British Consul because it was Sunday and he was playing golf. So, eventually, we filled in some cards at the nearest police station and they put us in a taxi to take us to a hostel. It turned out to be a fleapit,

so we didn't stay there. Instead we went to the pictures with the few francs we had and then went to sleep in a field. The next day, the Consul fixed us up with some sort of substitute passport, and we got to Zurich a couple of hours before the curtain was due to go up. Apparently, most of the Company had got onto the wrong train, and only Avis Bunnage, Joan and Gerry arrived in time to be met at the station by a brass band and flowers. It was all very embarrassing for them.

The journey from Zurich to Moscow was also not without its hitches, with Gerry at one point hanging onto a train that was about to depart, shouting wildly in French that on no account was it going to leave till all the Company was aboard. There was no food on the train during the sixteen-hour journey, but once in Moscow, the Company were given tremendous hospitality and, indeed, respect. They were not only shown all the treasures of the Moscow Art Theatre, Stanislavsky's study and the seat in the auditorium from with he directed, but they actually played *Macbeth* in the theatre. It is not surprising that, in those surroundings, some of the audience and critics didn't approve of Joan's conception of the play. She had set it in the period between 1914 and 1945. Macbeth is a General who becomes a dictator, finally killed by a firing squad. The events of the play all take place as a flash back in the mind of the General just before he is shot, and re-arrangement of scenes and cutting were, of course, necessary to accommodate this idea. The critics in Moscow didn't approve. They felt that the modernisation of the play undermined the belief of the audience in the truth of what was happening on the stage, and the need to abandon the mysticism destroyed Shakespeare's conception of the play as well as his poetry. Joan defended her approach:

In presenting Shakespeare in modern dress we are not trying to be clever or experimental; the fundamental truth of a great work of art needs no decoration to make it acceptable. We try to wipe away the dust of three hundred years, to strip off the 'poetical' interpretation which the nineteenth-century sentimentalists put on these plays and which are still current today. The poetry of Shakespeare's day was a muscular, active, forward-moving poetry, in that it was like the people to whom it belonged. If Shakespeare has any significance today, a production of his work must not be regarded as a historical reconstruction, but as an instrument still sharp enough to provoke thought, to extend man's awareness of his problems, and to strengthen his belief in his kind.

In the course of a long reply, a Moscow director, A. Solodovnikov, wrote:

The crux of the matter is that in Art ideas do not exist except in a concrete setting created by the author. The ideas and content are inseparable from their setting, characters and epoch. Arbitrary violation of the author's conception and separation of content from form inevitably lead to eclectics, to weakening the impact of a work of art.

He condeded, however, that in provoking thought and discussion, the production had served a useful purpose.

An invitation to play in a festival in Leipzig had to be turned down as there was no money for the fares. All the other companies attending were state aided.

In 1959, the Company returned to Paris again to the Théâtre des Nations, to represent Great Britain with *The Hostage* by Brendan Behan, this time with recognition and support from the British Council. It would have been difficult for them to withhold it in the light of our success at previous Festivals and at the Theatre Royal, and in view of the belated support we were now receiving from the Arts Council. On this occasion, the Company travelled in comfort, flying over, accompanied by Shelagh Delaney, Frank Norman and, of course, Brendan. The opening performance at the Sarah Bernhardt Theatre was a splendid occasion, red carpets in the foyer, blazing chandeliers and a guard of honour in full dress uniform. The British Ambassador managed to arrive late and missed the National Anthem. The applause on the final curtain was loud and long, and Brendan stood up in the circle to acknowledge the cries of 'Auteur' – declaring in French that he was 'the best writer in the English language' and the French public were 'the most civilised in the world'. The more erudite sections of the Press went into a very detailed analysis of the philosophy behind the writing of *The Hostage* revealing a depth of meaning that was quite a revelation to those of us who had been rehearsing and playing it for months. The historical allusions to the Irish struggle for independence and the role of the I.R.A. must have been bewildering to a large section of the audience, but it did not seem to prevent them enjoying it, and Joan received an award for her production. *Le Figaro* commented:

Ten minutes after the curtain had gone up, everyone was laughing, the bilinguals, the unsophisticated, diplomats, officials, critics ... those who usually go to sleep when the theatre goes dark, those who didn't understand it, those who didn't want to understand it, the hilarity was general.

The following year, 1969, *Everyman in His Humour* by Ben Jonson was taken to the Festival in Paris. The set failed to arrive and a new one had to be built in Paris at very short notice. Compromises had to be made on the construction, which meant last minute changes in the production. Despite these setbacks, it was well received, and Bob Grant, playing Kitely, won a prize for his performance from the 'Young Critics Circle'.

In September 1960 *The Hostage* went to America. As some of the original cast, including myself, didn't want to go, and some of the parts had to be played by American actors, to fulfil Union requirements, there was a great deal of re-rehearsing to be done. Patience Collier, who had taken over the part of Miss Gilchrist, described a rather remarkable dress rehearsal, when the parts of the young lovers were played by a middle-aged actor and actress:

> One night before we opened at the Cort Theatre, we were having a dress rehearsal that the audience had paid to see – it was a full house and Joan brought Victor Spinetti to my dressing room and said – 'Now listen you two, I want you to do something for me and I don't want any argument. Celia and Alfie are getting a bit fly, a little bit stale. They think they're good, they think they're being funny and they're going to ruin themselves. I want you two to take your books and play their parts tonight – don't change your costumes.' – I was dressed as Miss Gilchrist, funny black boots, Salvation Army clothes and a hideous wig. I looked dreadful. Victor was dressed as the I.R.A. officer. – 'Just read the parts, you know the moves, if you don't it doesn't matter, and the other two will play your parts.' Before the curtain went up, she simply announced to the audience: 'I've asked these people to do this because it's good for them, and I think they're good enough actors for you to understand what's going on.' – I was entirely uninhibited and I've never played so well. I felt I was seventeen, with beautiful red hair like Celia. The applause was enormous. Now Joan could do that with people. Who else could be so daring?

The show opened to good reviews but, as far as the Press was concerned, Brendan was the main attraction. He was in his element, inundated with offers to appear on T.V. and to write articles. In fact New York gave him the attention and respect he felt a writer was entitled to, and Brendan loved every minute of it. He held court in the Edwardian lounge of the famous Algonquin Hotel, where so many eminent writers had done before him, and regaled the Press for hours. Their only disappointment was that Brendan was not drinking at this time. They felt he would put on an even better show if he was drunk. The fact that drink, for Brendan, was a killer, was no concern of theirs. He was finally persuaded to take up drink again, and after an altercation with a group of reporters, stormed down the aisle of the theatre as the Company were lined up for the curtain call, singing 'The Red Flag' and creating an uproar in the theatre.

After six months on Broadway, *The Hostage* went on to play to good houses in Toronto, Montreal and San Francisco before returning home.

In 1963 *Oh What a Lovely War* went to the Paris Festival and made a tremendous impression. That the carnage and killing actually took place on French soil must have brought the horror of the First World War very close to the French audiences, and during the scene when the French soldiers are depicted as sheep going to the slaughter, the audience rose in their seats and cheered. They threw flowers and programmes onto the stage at the curtain call and gave the Company a standing ovation. Joan shared the prize for the best production at the Festival with Peter Brook's *King Lear* for the Royal Shakespeare Company.

In 1964 *Oh What a Lovely War* went to Philadelphia for three weeks, and then to Broadway, where it played for six months. It received some critical acclaim, but failed to make a great deal of impact. Since it dealt with the period of the First World War prior to American involvement, it was of less interest to Americans than it had been to English and French audiences. Changes had to be made in the production to make it more understandable to an American audience. It was generally regarded as a play that ought to be seen rather than one that must be seen. One critic asked 'Do we have to think when we laugh?' This was not an untypical reaction.

In December 1965 *Oh What a Lovely War* was taken to East and West Germany. This was the first time a tour had been organised by a British company which covered visits to both countries, and special visas had to be obtained to go back and forth through Checkpoint Charlie in Berlin. The production received a most enthusiastic reception in East Berlin, and the visit was extended; but at a press conference in West Berlin, questions were asked as to why the Company had gone to East Germany first, and strong exception was taken to this. The play opened in West Berlin in a large concert hall holding two thousand, and the Press attended unofficially. The hall was only half full, but after the first performance and the publicity that followed, it was packed to capacity. This was to be the last visit abroad by Theatre Workshop. They had been of tremendous value to the Company. The enthusiasm with which we were received confirmed our belief in our work and helped to offset the effect of years of lack of recognition in our own country. They enormously enriched the lives of those taking part as well as providing welcome periods of material comfort. It is arguable that the Company could not have survived as long as it did without them.

Eleven
Rudolf Laban and Nelson Illingworth

The demands made on an actor in street theatre were specific and limited; and it was clear that from the moment the Group moved indoors in 1933, a radical new approach to the whole style of acting was needed. The techniques of the conventional theatre were geared to a static drama of mannerisms and behaviour and had nothing to offer. The achievement of a deeper understanding, and the flexibility of voice and movement required, was in the earliest days largely an intuitive process, a period of experimentation and trial and error – there were no guidelines to follow.

So since the days of Theatre in Action in the early thirties, through to the late fifties, training formed an integral part of the work of the Group, often but not always linked to rehearsals. The importance of daily practice to improve one's skill has always been accepted by musicians, dancers and singers. It is a concept which more and more actors are beginning to accept.

The most significant influence on the form this training should take was the movement theory of Rudolf Laban, known as 'The Father of Modern Dance'. Jean Baptiste Atilla Von Laban was born in 1879 in Bratislava into an aristocratic family, and from a very early age he had been interested in the potential for free movement in the human body, leading the revolution against the formalism of classical ballet. In 1924 he had his own dance group and went on to work with movement choirs all over Europe, influencing teachers, dancers and choreographers in many parts of the world. He evolved a system of dance notation that was able to record precisely and in great detail any form of choreography, folk dance or ritual. His work influenced the use of movement in education, and he in his turn studied the movements used by workers on factory machines. In Manchester the 'Art of Movement Studio' was founded by Lisa Ullman and Sylvia Bodmer, and it was there that the Group were able to work with Rudolf Laban for a brief period before his death in 1958.

His theories were known to Ewan and Joan before the war, and they began to try and adapt them, at that time, to the work of the actor. After the formation of Theatre Workshop in 1945, they realised that if the Group were to benefit fully from Laban's work, it was necessary to have someone in the Company who was fully trained in his methods. As a result of contacting Laban himself, Jean Newlove, who had been one of Laban's first pupils in this country and his assistant during the war, joined the Company in 1948. Her experience as a teacher and a dancer were to prove invaluable. She not only put us through gruelling exercises over a long period of time, but was able to show us how Laban movement could be applied to specific parts, and help overcome acting problems. So we became aware of a much wider range of movement in the space around us. Jean described her work:

All living matter conforms to certain basic principles. They have always existed, but Laban was the first to tabulate them. He discovered there was a certain crystal shape from which all living matter developed, called the Icosohedron. He was able to give us exercises to make us aware of the space in which we move, based on this Icosohedron and the three dimensions in which all life moves. Now all this was totally different from any series of gymnastic exercises, or even meditation exercises. So far we've got the structure of movement and we know where we are moving in space. How do we move? How can we analyse? We are now concerned with observation and analysis of movement, and this is where my training came in. Laban divided all movement into eight basic efforts (see page 163). When you move, you use not only three dimensions, but also three elements; Space, Time and Energy; and a variation in one of the elements will change the effort. For instance, if you say, 'I am Direct in Space, Quick in Time and Strong in Energy, that is a punch or a thrust. If I change the Time to Slow, we have a press. So one works on these efforts, not just punching with one's fist, but with every part of the body – and not just in front of you. Actors work creatively and their working area is all around them, unlike most people, whose working area is just in front of them, in the kitchen, at a desk, in a car.'

So with Jean's help we were able to extend our range of efforts, rather than always falling back on those which came most naturally and easily to us, and which may have been quite wrong for the character we happened to be playing. This involved not only physical exercises, but a real mental effort to overcome an inbuilt resistance we all have to using our bodies in a different way.

Before each show, during the early years at Stratford, Jean would go through a sequence of efforts and movements selected to help the actors not only with the physical aspects of the character they were about to play but also to help set the mood. This was in addition to the general limbering up exercises and relaxation. As part of rehearsals she would help those actors new to the company to cope with difficult settings, balconies, ladders, ramps and so on. They would develop a fluidity and awareness, the set eventually becoming an extension of the actor rather than a series of obstacles to be coped with. Jean recalled how she was able to help me with the part of Sganarelle in *The Flying Doctor*:

> You had to be very mobile, very lively, much of it was flicking and dabbing, there wasn't much heavy effort. Sometimes you had to slow down, perhaps float a bit, so we had to work on that effort. I remember quite clearly getting you to leap up with a flick, which is a fairly hard thing to do. This is where we came to Ewan's work on voice. Voice is an extension of movement, and when you leapt up from the ground with a flick, you got the right intonation in the voice. Now Sganarelle was a light character, and this suited you. Suppose we'd had an actor whose material efforts were pressing and heavy, his voice when he got up would have mirrored this heavy quality. Knowing about efforts an actor can use them for his own development. We don't use pure efforts, we merge one into another. For example, when Joan, playing Marinette, knocked Gorgibus about, she didn't slash him, neither did she flick him, it was in between, and by defining the efforts she should use, we arrived at the essence of the character.

We were also able to break down the barrier between acting and dancing. Even a ballet, though it involved an enormous amount of hard work, was now within our capabilities, as Jean described:

> In *Uranium 235* we had to split the atom, and because our actors were trained as modern dancers, it wasn't much trouble to get them to understand that they had to actually represent the atom in a ballet. The bodies were intertwined and twisted, leaning over in the most difficult, extraordinary positions, legs up in the air. An actor from the ordinary theatre, asked to do this, would probably walk out, saying it was ridiculous, but of course it wasn't. We wanted to show the splitting of an atom, not simply describe it in words. When Sigurd Leeder, co-Director of the Jooss Ballet, came to see us, he said: 'These actors move as some of the best dancers I've ever seen', and coming from him, this was praise indeed.

It would be difficult to overestimate the part the Laban movement theories played in the development of the group. Our opportunity to meet and work with Rudolf Laban in Manchester for a short period enhanced our admiration for him, and his letter to Joan was a great source of encouragement:

I consider your group to be the only one in England which is, in the true sense of the word, experimenting in the use of all those factors which go to the creation of real theatrical art.

For the first time in this country I have met a group who is tackling fundamental problems of movement as affecting the individual actor and the group as a whole in such a way as to affect the rhythm of contemporary life.

Another important influence on the Company during these early years was Nelson Illingworth, an Australian who had been a teacher of voice production at the Metropolitan Opera House in New York. He came to London in the thirties and set up 'Labour Stage' in an old warehouse on the Thames at Battersea. It was a centre for all forms of theatrical training and students paid a percentage of their income to the school. Nelson taught the bel canto method and subjected us to many hours of voice and breathing exercises. The culmination was an intensive week, when we all crowded into his riverside bungalow on the Thames at Penton Hook. Nelson presided, a tall gaunt figure, wrinkled and brown as a berry and always in sandals and shorts. He swam like a fish in the river, cooked very strange meals and did his best with our 'English voices'. He worked on the principle that breath is the fundamental of good voice. The air rises in the form of a column from the diaphragm which fills automatically as it expands. This breath is then sent out straight along the tongue, the vowels are concentrated on and the consonants are 'thrown in'.

The agonies we endured in order to achieve all this to Nelson's satisfaction are well described in Kristin Lind's vivid account:

I remember him as very tall, very thin and very old. Maybe he was not so old. Only life had used him. If he himself thought that he was the world's greatest teacher of human voice, he was not wrong. He *was* a miracle-man in getting 'voice-resources' out of people who had hardly any voice at all. But most of all did he remind us of a tyrannical ballet master of old times. But he was a psychologist as well. He seemed to know exactly how far he could drive us in the hope of getting rid of our complexes, mostly inherited from scared parents from which so called 'well-educated' children suffer. – 'Be quiet! Don't talk so loudly! Shut up! Don't speak until you are spoken to ...' etc. All that poisonous 'education' which already after two years of age kills every individuality and freedom of movement, imagination and voice. He realised all that. What obstacles to pull down. The most important years in children's lives ill-used to destroy and distort our voices. Whispering politely through life.

This irritated Mr. Illingworth. 'You English women, why do you speak like shy little school girls? And YOU, why? You have been born with gold in your throat and what have you done – picked up dirt! You don't even know how to breathe. Inspiration! Do you all know the meaning of that word! Inspire … yes … fill your whole body with air. Feel the blood stream into your veins from feet to head. That is inspiration! Then let your breath softly float through your mouth and lips and make a natural sound AHHHHHHHH! You see there lies your natural voice. Not high up in your little useless head! But down in the very depths of you – if you have some … Say after me: FAR AWAY AND LONG AGO. Again and again! Sing it! Again and again! Inspiration do you feel it? It makes you dizzy. Good! That is because you have never breathed properly before …'

What lessons. We were 'AAHING' and shouting 'FAR AWAY AND LONG AGO' until we could vomit. We felt silly and desperate. We would never become Chaliapins. That was his dream as he had been the teacher of that great Russian singer. And now he had to contend with us 'small-voiced nonentities'. Poor Mr. Illingworth. I think he came from Australia. But his wonderfully trained voice reminded you more of a Russian folk singer. His patience was endless. Especially as he must have known that very few of us would ever find that 'gold' he believed we were born with.

I suppose we did make some progress. We felt different. But the result was that we all went about listening to our own voice and the voices of the others. And not to the meaning of the words. So our acting got worse and worse. We became 'voice-maniacs'. In all the corners of the stage there echoed 'LA-LE-LI-LO-LOO …' coming from unknown voices. We became self-conscious and it took a long time before his training became a natural part of our words and movements.

Dear old Illingworth we owe him a great deal. We learned inspiration. And that you need in all life.

After several months of voice training and pain we felt better and became better. And we stopped listening to our new voices. It had become a part of us. And stayed a part of us. If it was not all pure gold we regained, some of the 'dirt' had fallen off. And I don't think anyone going through this hard school has fallen back into the old ways. Mr. Illingworth's patience was not in vain.

The Laban influence can be seen most clearly in the dance-mime sequences of *Uranium 235* and *The Other Animals* and in the classical productions of the fifties. After this, when the emphasis was on new plays and the company became less integrated, it lost the awareness of the need for movement and voice training and the very distinctive quality of the earlier productions was lost. The influence of Rudolf Laban and Nelson Illingworth had prevailed, however, for several years, and during that period its importance to the Group cannot be overestimated.

The Laban efforts

EFFORT	SPACE	TIME	ENERGY
Thrust	Direct	Quick	Strong
Slash	Indirect	Quick	Strong
Wring	Indirect	Slow	Strong
Flick	Indirect	Quick	Weak
Press	Direct	Slow	Strong
Float	Indirect	Slow	Weak
Dab	Direct	Quick	Weak
Glide	Direct	Slow	Weak

Twelve

Down the Years

The influences

The concepts that formed the basis of Theatre Workshop's approach to production, and its methods of working, had their origin in the studies of the pre-war groups, Theatre of Action and Theatre Union, led by Ewan MacColl and Joan Littlewood. Reacting against the sterility of British Theatre at that time, they explored the great theatres of the past, and also the Continental theatres of Stanislavsky, Meyerhold, Vakhtangov, Reinhardt and others, absorbing ideas and adapting them to the needs of the Company. Common to them all was the ensemble, the group of actors working together over a long period of time; and ideally, attached to the ensemble a school for training actors, which was a concept virtually unknown in the British Theatre at that time. A school of training from which actors could be drawn would have greatly increased the strength and stability of the Company over the years; but the resources were, of course, never available.

Studies were confined to books and photographs, but they revealed a world of theatre almost unknown in this country. Apart from Terence Gray's work at the Cambridge Festival Theatre in the thirties, little had been done to break down the proscenium arch or to explore the relationship between an actor and his audience through the use of three-dimensional and architectural setting. In this country, setting was still regarded as a means of decorating a picture frame stage or as a box providing a background and exits and entrances for the actors. Lighting was still used as simply a means of illuminating the stage and the actor. Its potential for adding to the atmosphere of a play, of breaking the stage up into separate acting areas, and forming an integral part of the production had yet to be realised.

At a time when philosophies of acting were unpopular in this country, the theories of Stanislavsky were intensively studied by the Company and adapted, where necessary, to the needs of a non-naturalistic theatre, as were the constructivist ideas of Meyerhold and his system of bio-mechanics. The work of Rudolf Laban (dealt with more fully in the chapter on Training) was, from the earliest days, a strong influence, and his theories of Modern Dance and Efforts were adapted to the specific problems of the actor and the need to extend his range of speech and movement.

Ewan MacColl's understanding and love of language, which he was able to transmit to the Company through his plays, was another important factor, particularly in the pre-Stratford days. He was the only playwright who wrote from an inside understanding of the Company, and his influence as a writer and artistic director cannot be overestimated. He spoke of the necessity of keeping in touch with 'ordinary' people:

> Staying in the homes of working-class people meant at least one was in touch with the language to start with. Language grows at the place where wealth is created; in an industrial country it's the industrial working class who create language. ... An actor living in that environment is going to protest if what he's asked to speak is too fey, too whimsical or too purely literary. Recording for radio ballads led to the conclusion that educated people use language for the purpose of hiding behind it, non-educated people tend to use the language for expressing both their feelings and their ideas at the same time. That's why Shakespeare and the Elizabethan dramatists were so great. They really had their ear to the ground, they were so close to their audience. In particular Ben Jonson, who I think is the best satiric dramatist the world has ever produced. They were able to take the speech of ordinary people and crystallise it into poetry.

Joan's and Ewan's thirst for knowledge extended far beyond their study of particular theatres and how they functioned, and their combined understanding of world dramaturgy was possibly unique in this country. It was not acquired in an academic sense, for it's own sake, but in order to be able to relate it directly to their own work in the theatre. It influenced much of Ewan's writing: for instance, his twentieth-century comedy *Hell is What You Make It* was based on Ben Jonson, using Jonsonian humour; his *Operation Olive Branch* was adapted from Aristophanes' *Lysistrata*.

Their own working-class background and political awareness provided the mainspring for their whole attitude to their work. Clive Barker describes the effect on Joan, as he sees it:

> She constantly celebrated the resources of the working people, their humour, their intelligence, their sharpness, their ability to cope with enormous problems and dilemmas in life: above all, their ability to survive. That's political, but it arises out of Joan's very deep love of humanity which, when applied to individual cases, could get idealised, even sentimental.

Peter Hall assessed this quality in a different way, when comparing Joan to the other internationally acclaimed director of her generation, Peter Brook:

> Peter is an intellectual to his finger tips. He's economic, he's chic, he's surprising, he illuminates like a laser beam. Joan's theatre was about energy, vitality, blood and sentiment. It could be very common, it could be very vulgar. But it was very very alive. In many respects, Peter is the opposite of all that. The only parallel is in the size of their talents.

Clive Barker has studied the effect of these influences on the repertoire and style of the Company:

> There was a concept of repertoire very much in the humanist tradition and in line with that of Continental theatres at that time. It can be compared with the Berliner Ensemble, Copeau's Vieux-Colombier, Barrault and others, in terms of its concerns and the philosophical basis behind all the plays that were put on. It was not a specific political commitment, it was about people. Another important concept was that of style in production, which was how the actor communicated with the audience. That meant you didn't create pretty pictures on the stage, but you created a live dialogue, and you could use Music Hall styles, you could use Marx Brothers clowning, you could use pastiche, parody and satire, and you could use moments of intense realism within the one production. Or you could use direct contact with the audience, not uncommon in Joan's work. They are all from the Continent and they've all been used before. What Joan did, as did Copeau and Reinhardt, was to take themes, ideas, concepts and bring them together to create the work that was right for that time.

Approach to production

The object of all rehearsals was the exploration of the play by the director and the actors – and out of their discoveries, the production would take shape. The nature of the play broadly determined the overall style, but within this there were no blueprints, nothing was pre-determined and, as Clive Barker has pointed out, there was often scope for variation in style in the production. Complete flexibility ensured that what seemed right one day could easily be rejected the next in the light of fresh discoveries.

Words were rarely the starting point, even when rehearsing a classic;

and in the case of a new play, the script was a long way from being finalised. The approach would usually be through the movement of the characters, exploring their relationships and the atmosphere of the play, moving only gradually towards the dialogue. Joan's reply to an actor's 'I don't feel right' was 'You don't have to bloody well feel right, you just have to do it. – Do it!' Out of the physical action would come the feeling.

The initial rehearsals of *Richard II* were devoted to capturing the feeling of the period in quite basic physical terms. Improvisation exercises aimed at developing the enmity between the characters, the sudden outbreaks of violence, the suspicions, the everpresent fear of the knife in the back. For example, Joan would say, 'You're in a market place and it's full of people. You're getting your shopping and a fight breaks out!' We would fight each other, go berserk, jump on each other. Then she would say; 'Now you're stabbed in the back ... You're on horseback, you're knocked off, you're dragged along, you shout and scream and sweat.'

Jean Newlove, our Laban teacher, would devise specific movements linked to the Laban efforts to help bring out the right feelings, and the emphasis consequently would be on strong, slow movements such as wringing and pressing. She also helped us to cope with John Bury's setting of sloping ramps and low tunnels which was made available to us very early on in rehearsals.

All this work was, of course, slanted towards the characters and situations in the play, but at this stage, we were not concerned with the words. The play had been read initially, but detailed study of the text was to take place later. The emphasis was always on the physical as the key to the relationship between characters and the objects around them: Richard striking Gaunt with his glove as a climax to their confrontation; how the gardener handled his plants; the feel of the texture of materials and so on. Swapping round parts in rehearsal helped us more fully to understand the other characters, and by the time we came to the actual script, the physical problems and relationships had been fully explored. By concentrating on what we were doing and feeling rather than the words themselves, we were in a better position to bring out their meaning. Well-known speeches still seemed to present problems, and Joan was able to help me with Gaunt's 'This England' speech by destroying the feeling of respect and awe with which I approached it. I clowned it, put it into gibberish and generally sent it up. Having in this way broken down the artificial barrier I had erected between myself and the speech, I was able to tackle it, without worry, through the verse and its rhythms. Sometimes physical efforts were used as an antidote to any tendency to be carried away by the beauty of the poetry. A thrusting effort might be applied to an aggressive speech, while actually thrusting with the arms and body; and a floating effort might be applied to lyrical passage. Used for rehearsal purposes they were a great help in bringing out the essential meaning of the verse. As far as Joan was concerned there were no 'spear carriers', and she gave all the attention that was needed to any problem that affected the smallest or largest role.

Another example of the emphasis on the physical was in *A Taste of Honey* rehearsals. To arrive at the state of exhaustion with which the mother and daughter open the play, the actresses dragged heavy suitcases around the stage and down imaginary dark tunnels. Rather than trying to imagine how they would feel after a long and tedious journey, they actually experienced the physical condition from which sprang their irritation with each other. This, in turn, would influence their movement, not only *how* they would move, but *where* in relation to the set and each other. All moves originated in this way, rooted in the character and the situation. No-one was ever given a move for the purpose of getting them from one part of the stage to another, or in order to form interesting groupings. These often occurred, and Joan was highly praised for them, but they had been arrived at organically during rehearsal as a result of interaction between the characters and were not pre-determined.

What Joan was aiming for was a truthful response from an actor in a given situation, not a theatrical cliché nor some preconceived notion of what might fit at that particular moment. It could be arrived at in different ways varying with the actor and the situation, sometimes by sheer elimination. An actor would try different ways of doing something, all of which Joan would reject. In sheer despair and thoroughly fed up, he would come on the stage and do almost nothing, and that would be what Joan was looking for. On other occasions, by stimulating the imagination of a group of actors, she was able to help them improvise a situation which extended the relationship of the characters they were playing and provided dialogue that could perhaps be incorporated into the script, or provide the author with ideas and stimulus. This was the method used in nearly all the new plays put on by the Company. During rehearsals of *Fings*, Frank Norman's knowledge of how the characters would react in a given situation made it possible for him to check on the authenticity of what the actors were doing, and Frank himself took part in improvisations which helped him in any re-writing that was needed. Complex didactic plays like *The Other Animals* and *The Travellers* were analysed and discussed in some detail. They would be divided into acting units in order to fully understand the objectives of each character and their relationships. Even in these cases, where no alterations were required to the script, the play was approached as a whole through improvisation and movement prior to working more closely on the individual units.

The actual text was avoided in the early stages with the aim of opening up the situation and the lives of the characters. This would enable the actor eventually to relate more truthfully to the specific action of the play. In rehearsal, Joan and Laban had a common approach insofar as neither spent time theorising about their work. Laban set about destroying what was false in the dancer, and Joan sought for a truthful response from the actor in a given situation.

Relationship between director and actors

The relationship between director and actors is always important, but in a group theatre it is of the very essence. Joan would say 'Don't let yourself be produced', comparing Theatre Workshop to a jazz ensemble of individual talents, as opposed to a symphony orchestra under the guidance of a conductor. She aimed to stimulate the imagination, thereby creating a chain reaction between herself and the actors themselves, rather than imposing pre-conceived ideas. The extent to which this way of working succeeded varied according to the individual actor and the particular situation. It implied a complete trust in Joan and one's fellow actors, and a readiness to throw overboard one's stock-in-trade of tricks and technique and start again. It is easy to see why Joan preferred untrained actors who were not afraid to risk making fools of themselves, rather than those with experience who could play safe by falling back on their expertise. Patience Collier, an established actress, refused to do this. She had worked with Joan before the war in Manchester, and in 1960 joined the Company in New York to rehearse for the Broadway opening of *The Hostage*. She brought with her a wealth of experience, but also an open mind and a willingness to put her trust in Joan's way of working:

> She said 'Come here Patience. Stand on the stage and tell me how the journey was ... No, you're leaning forward and begging me to listen. I want you to stand back, put your arms behind you, push out those beautiful breasts of yours, love your audience and make them love you'. I hadn't thought about it before, but I did what she asked and I certainly felt better. Then she said 'I hear you told Gerry you can't sing. Thank God, because you're going to sing so beautifully you'll be surprised ... You're Miss Gilchrist, a sexy old Salvation Army lady ... You think you have a seventeen-year-old girl's voice. So you have, Patience Collier, and when you come down to the centre of the stage in a spotlight and sing "Only a Box of Matches", you will sing with such beauty you will bring the house down'. And I simply believed her − 'Don't you dare practise it and don't you dare have lessons. Kate can teach you the tune.' I remember singing this song every night in a gentle, pretty voice to marvellous applause, and

it was Joan's doing. It really was quite magic, it was all in my head, but Joan had put it there, and I became so happy on the stage and so relaxed. I'd never known a play and a stage to be so pleasant.

Joan had a unique capacity for being able to assess an actor's potential and then sparing no effort to help him or her realise it to the full. Once the initial inhibitions were broken down, and understanding grew of what was involved, there were very few who were not prepared to throw in their lot completely. David Scase, a founder member of Theatre Workshop, acknowledged Joan's influence on his work as a theatre director:

> I absorbed an awful lot of Joan's ideas and techniques. Also there still remains with me her contention that actors are important, they must be treated as expansive human beings. She made people extend themselves far beyond that which they thought they could do. When people argue about the shapes of theatres – in the round, thrust or proscenium – Joan bypassed all that in the sense that the attitude she created in the actors themselves transcended any consideration of what shape the theatre should be. In fact, watching one of her finer productions at Stratford, you forgot you were in a theatre, you were part of an event.

Most people who worked with Theatre Workshop found it, on the whole, a satisfying experience. But there can be no-one who did not experience, at the same time, an initial loss of confidence. Joan's capacity to think that much faster than anyone around her could sometimes be unnerving, but perhaps, as Harry Corbett put it: 'You can't destroy confidence that's not begging to be destroyed.'

Actresses tended to have the most reservations. Julia Jones was one:

> There was a love-hate relationship. You could really hate her and yet you were mesmerised by her. It was very difficult to leave her and get her out of your system and look at things in your way. I remember she'd have all these ideas, more in the first hour of rehearsal than I could think of in a lifetime. She used to push ideas onto people. She confused me until I realised I could act without Joan telling me. I went off and did my own thing and Joan was delighted.

Barbara Young expressed a similar feeling:

> I suppose the only thing I discovered for myself was that she never helped to get beyond the point that I was already at. What I did was to go back and start again, maybe in a different way, and arrive at the same point. I wasn't sure I trusted her to get me beyond that point. That's one of the reasons why I left, because I felt I could do it for

myself. While I was there I was prepared to fight. I survived and I enjoyed it.

It was indeed possible to be overwhelmed, and actresses particularly had to be on their guard, as Avis Bunnage soon discovered:

Of the women, I think I survived longer than any of them because I wouldn't always give in to Joan. There was always a girl in tears somewhere because Joan was very hard on women. The men she got on with fabulously. She used to upset me in the first year, but I tried not to show it. She used to hate people saying 'Oh yes, Joan, you're right Joan.' I was the one that used to say 'No, that's stupid, I'm not doing that.' I didn't actually argue with her but I wouldn't do everything she said and I think she liked that. If you had ideas of your own she'd use them and build up on them.

Barbara Young's admitted lack of trust in Joan is a crucial point. If you wanted to explore your potential to the full, you had to go along with her the whole way. If you really thought she was wrong, you argued and questioned, as Avis did, but it was usually more profitable to take a chance. When it came to actors and acting, Joan wasn't often wrong.

Research

The pre-war theatre studies, under the guidance of Joan and Ewan, provided a basis of scholarship that stood Theatre Workshop in good stead over the years. It was always at the disposal of the Company, who were encouraged to extend their own theoretical knowledge and understanding through study and research. Shirley Dynevor recalled her own arrival at Stratford:

It was a most amazing world. You weren't just an actress, going to rehearsal, learning lines. You were made to take much more responsibility. We would sit in Joan's bedroom at the top of the stairs and talk about the play, everyone would be asked to go to the library and do their own research. We were all part of a whole ... Joan was a most marvellous teacher. I never learned from anyone what I learned from her ... She had wonderful images: 'Pretend that stretching out before you is your future, your sons and their sons in a great long line. Behind you is a man with a dagger, about to plunge it into your back.' That's how she described to George Luscombe, a Canadian, what it was like to be an English nobleman in *Richard II*.

For Julia Jones, there came a time when the learning had to stop:

> Joan opened up vistas of theatre and art of which I was totally unaware. She opened your mind to so many possibilities, gave you a standard and you realised there were marvellous things you could do. However, by creating visions, she was also cutting the ground from under your feet, gradually destroying your confidence, and then it was time to leave; but I will always be grateful I met her and for the opportunity to learn from her.

Keeping productions fresh

Productions were never regarded as finished products, brought to as near perfection as possible for the first night and then repeated throughout the run. The aim was to improve with playing and keep each performance alive and fresh – a difficult thing to achieve, particularly during West End runs, but at least the method of rehearsal made it possible. All the aspects of the situation and characters had been thoroughly explored and the actors were not attuned to giving or receiving stock responses. They were able to react to changes in mood or expression, and performances could vary whilst still remaining true to the basic intentions of the play and its characters. Sometimes Joan felt an external jolt could be helpful, as Bill Wallis recalled:

> In *Mrs. Wilson's Diary* totally unexpected characters would appear on the stage. In more formal shows, people would be given a private note from Joan and come on stage with an entirely different attitude, and this created a most marvellous freshness. So many actors and directors are brought up to believe that you get this beautifully finished product and you then turn it out night after night, filing off any little burrs, till you finish off with icy perfection. I think if theatre isn't some sort of event, then it's dead.

Joan didn't always rely on other people to stir things up, as Frances Cuka recalled:

> I was at the first night of *Fings*. Streamers were shooting across the stage, the banners read 'Welcome Home Fred from Prison' and the whole company were doing a jolly knees up. In the middle of the wild dancing, cleverly worked out to look natural and spontaneous, there was Joan, in her woolly hat, jumping up and down. She didn't appear again and she said afterwards: 'It was a first night and the

Press were in so I thought you needed a little shot in the arm, that's all.

Ad-libbing occurred far less than was commonly supposed, and usually in unavoidable circumstances, for instance, coping with Brendan's interruptions of *The Hostage* from the auditorium, or when things really went wrong. It was most important that the ad-libbing wherever possible, should stay in the mood of the play, sensitive to its rhythms and structures, and should stop before the sense of excitement had been dissipated. One of the many wise and perceptive notes I received from Joan over the years was the following:

The clownerie at the warm-up was brilliant ... In performance what do you do? Plan and do marvellous things plus add and add self-abnegating, self-destroying banalities which produce embarrassment. One can destroy illusion once in a performance of that length, in my opinion. With reserve, I might say twice because you were so successful at your debut, but four or five times, climaxing with removal of your wig was to throw turds in our face ... Please play again tonight, but don't deign to play for our approbation.

These notes played a large part in the lives of all Theatre Workshop actors, and though awaited with trepidation, they were usually helpful, the style was never boring and life would have been emptier without them. Joan cultivated a variety of styles, caustic, witty, poetical, and downright abusive to the point of obscenity. They could fill one with indignation at some supposed injustice but, in fact, were rarely off the mark. They greeted an actor in his dressing room, were pinned on the notice board addressed to the Company and, when in Joan's view the show had reached rock bottom, were delivered orally over the tannoy system, with a wealth of abuse worthy of Ben Jonson. Those of us who played to the nearly empty houses in the early days of Stratford will not easily forget the sound, from way up in the gallery, of Joan's pencil moving over paper, the rapid turning over of pages, and the sighs of despair as the performance went from bad to worse. It did nothing to bolster an actor's sense of security, but that wasn't something Joan believed in anyway. Here is the opening of four foolscap pages of roneoed notes, published in July 1960 in an article in *Encore*:

Dear Company,
    As a young actress I was told 'Stick your behind out, dear, it's always good for a laugh.' Well, this show of ours, at the moment, is one big behind.
    We may as well go the whole hog and start throwing whitewash at

the audience and custard pies at the obtruding behinds, only that would need better timing.

Can we stop regarding the audience as morons, cut out the rubbish, get back a bit of tension, pace and atmosphere in Act II. Can we stop wriggling our anatomies all over the script, over-acting, BULLYING laughs out of the audience and playing alone, for approbation. This latter, which looks like selfishness, is mere lack of trust in yourselves and each other. YOU CANNOT play alone, stop wanting the audience to adore you and you only, they do anyway. People love actors and actresses, so relax and let them have a look at a play for a change.

The value of conflict

If these notes had the effect of undermining confidence and creating a sense of insecurity, that was all to the good. As far as Joan was concerned, no good could come from a happy, contented Company and a group of complacent actors, as George Cooper recalls:

> I remember coming off stage once to terrific applause, feeling it had gone well and feeling rather pleased with myself. Joan asked me if I was feeling ill, as that could be the only excuse for my performance. If there was any indication that an actor was getting the slightest bit big-headed she would move in and destroy him. I remember the notes she gave me when I first played Malvolio. The first sentence read: 'Ninety percent of this part is unsolved.' That was her comment on my performance.

If the general atmosphere in the Company was becoming too cosy and settled, Joan was quite capable of engendering conflict between actors in order to create a feeling of tension on the stage. Clive Barker's recollections cover the period of the mid-fifties. The vicissitudes of the earlier touring days provided all the stress and conflict that was needed:

> She used to stir up trouble between actors, so you'd have two actors on stage with real tension between them, but she made sure that these conflicts helped, not hindered the work. When people ask me what it was like working in Theatre Workshop, I say, 'A profoundly depressing experience, but the work was good.' I was never happy because my security was constantly being undermined. I never remember rehearsing Act III of *The Hostage* ... I only remember Joan throwing her script down at four o'clock in the afternoon and

telling us to piss off. We went off asking each other when we were going to rehearse it ... A crafty woman, leaving us floundering. Not that she ever used that to dominate the actor, but she used it creatively all the way through, to make the actor find his response to the situation. In *The Italian Straw Hat* we never had a dress rehearsal ... She put things there at the last minute and this demanded a great deal of courage. It also demanded an incredible technical virtuosity and confidence. She could pull a show together and shape it two days before a production opened ... She never worked on stage images and pictures, she got them from the actors, or if she didn't get them, she sharpened them up in the last few days.

There was no escape from Joan's eagle eye. My own experience during the run of *Mrs. Wilson's Diary* in the West End will be familiar to all Theatre Workshop actors. The scene between Harold Wilson, played by Bill Wallis, and myself as his Guru had settled down into an enjoyable romp. The audience laughed, we were happy playing it, and any other director would have been quite content to leave well alone. As far as Joan was concerned, the scene had got into a rut and needed shaking up. She took me off my perch on the piano and re-rehearsed it completely. As far as I recall, the laughs, if less predictable, were fewer. At these moments, one couldn't help longing for a director who got the show on and went off to do something else.

There was little chance of that, and once a scene or a play had ceased to grow, it had to be broken down completely and built up again on a basis of truthful response to the characters and the situation. It became something different, and whether it was 'better' or 'worse' than the scene it had replaced were subjective criteria that were not applied.

The method of working in Theatre Workshop blurred the accepted distinction between the person and the actor, and aspects of what would usually be regarded as his 'private life' were drawn into the actor's work with Joan. The closeness of this working relationship plus Joan's extraordinary qualities aroused strong feelings and reactions in everyone who worked with her. It is difficult to assess the extent to which this affected the work of individuals, varying as it did, between time, place and person. I myself must have experienced over the years, the whole gamut of emotion, from downright hatred to a very genuine affection. A few random memories, which can only reflect the individual, show even in retrospect no consensus — except in one respect: no-one I have spoken to, even those most critical of Joan, ever regrets having worked with her:

Harry Greene:
She had this quality of taking people under her wing, almost like a mother hen, and sweeping them up with her enthusiasm. When Joan

wasn't around you really missed her, you missed her notes and you missed her sharp tongue.

Rosalie Williams:

We had intense emotional scenes very often, for one reason or another, but I found Joan the most stimulating person to work with, the most co-operative person. She drew out whatever talent you had.

Barbara Young:

You got to the stage when you could have just screamed at her. I had a curious feeling that she didn't really like actors because they always had the last word – they were actually there on the stage.

Julia Jones:

Two years was about the longest that anyone with real acting talent could stay with Joan and not be destroyed. She had a very destructive element – she had to break people down and destroy their confidence.

George Harvey Webb:

What she had was a tremendous compassion for people who weren't represented, who hadn't a voice in society. She wanted them to have a voice. Her Communism was not of the Party kind.

Ben Ellis:

The first time I met her she struck me as a kind of Mother Superior with a group around her that she drove to the limit ... She had an extraordinary power of being able to get out of an individual the one spark they possibly had in them. Wherever it was, she could find it and squeeze it out like a pip.

Clive Barker:

What Joan respected in life was a Rabelaisian quality, which has a very serious, philosophical, humanist core at the heart of it ... The quality she put on the stage was of living life to the full. She once said to me 'Life is a brief walk between two periods of darkness, and anything that helps to cheer that up and brighten it is valuable.' Allowing that she herself is a very serious person, I think that sums up her philosophy and what she tried to achieve in Theatre Workshop.

Harry Corbett:

She worked like nobody I've ever seen, directing during the day, giving out her handwritten notes and disappearing to adapt the next play. An unpredictable woman ... She always retained the feeling that a genius could walk in off the streets. She hurt many people ... Someone at that moment in time was brilliant, then their time was over and they were finished with. I do not know Joan Littlewood, the Director, I think I know Joan the Woman, or did in the past ... She's a marvellous, warm, beautiful person to know, love and be with. .... I feel no sorrow for her, I really do not. She's a millionaire in terms of talent ... I can find no negative qualities in her, not in a thousand years, because she gave people an opportunity to do things they could never have conceivably have done themselves – even if they were ruined in the bloody process. I can really find no fault or criticism of Joan, none whatever.

Financial Pressures

A long period of continuous work, culminating in the years of West End transfers, was followed by recurrent long gaps until 1972, the year of the first sizeable Arts Council grant. At the root of most of the Company's problems was the constant lack of money, and we existed for twelve years, up to 1957, without public subsidy of any kind. This was something of an achievement, even in those pre-inflation days, and quite impossible now. It has never been quite clear why Theatre Workshop was ineligible for a grant over such a long period of time. One can speculate that the plays of the pre-Stratford touring days were too avant-garde, despite the acclamation they received when played abroad and the praise lavished on them by the critics in those countries. Our politics too, were no doubt suspect, and the day when a committed fringe theatre group could qualify for a grant without too much difficulty had not yet arrived. The Arts Council had less money to spend, of course, than they have now, even in relative terms. Our arrival in Stratford created a new situation and different explanations have to be sought for the continual refusal to grant us a subsidy. The initial lack of support from local councils and audience was given as a reason for doubting the viability of theatre in that particular area. We would do better, it was suggested at one point, if we moved to a more 'theatre-conscious area of London'. We were then forced into the vicious circle of needing to transfer plays in order to survive, in the process reducing even further our chances of building up a local following and, at the same time, destroying the Group, a point taken up by Peter Hall:

Theatre Workshop was a close-knit group. I think Joan made it even more concentrated when she demanded loyalty and affection and effort as if she was a schoolmistress-cum-mother-cum-psychiatrist and I don't know what. I think her companies were families in some sense. The group was her particular strength and sometimes her particular weakness. The sadness was that she didn't have sufficient artistic – which actually means financial – help to go on developing her group. Every time she transferred a production, a great cell was torn out of the Company, never to be put back. Once you're a transfer theatre, however you rationalise it, once you need a West End success in order to pay to keep going, you're doomed, because you're looking for something different. She should have had a theatre and a subsidy sufficient to keep working ... I'm not being critical of the Arts Council. I've spent a lot of my time working for it and I believe in it, but by its very nature it doesn't take enormous risks. It tries to be fair, not prejudiced, but if there'd been a Commissar of Culture, he should have given a large sum of money to Joan Littlewood. We mistakenly think there's something called 'The Royal Court', 'The Royal Shakespeare' or 'The National Theatre' or 'Theatre Workshop'. There isn't, it's who is running it. But we don't like to think that artists are that unique. We don't like to think that the individual is that important. If a Joan Littlewood dominates a theatre, it's not fair on the others. We're bloody philistines.

Had the grants been made available during the early years at Stratford when the Group was at the peak of its strength, continuity of work could have been maintained and the audiences built up at the Theatre Royal. As it was they came far too late to benefit Joan or the Company. It was the members of the Company, of course, who subsidised Theatre Workshop over the years. Wages, at worst, were at subsistence level and at best, always less than could be received for similar work elsewhere.

The move to Stratford in 1953 set Theatre Workshop on the path which was to lead to critical recognition. West End success and a long, slow decline punctuated by bursts of recovery like *Mrs. Wilson's Diary* and *Oh What A Lovely War*. It was a progression foreseen, to some extent, by Ewan MacColl when he expressed his opposition to the move. It could be argued that the end had to come sooner or later and may well have been sooner had we attempted to continue the rigours of touring without a subsidy. Not that Ewan denied the possibility of being able to build up working-class audiences at the Theatre Royal. What he feared were the consequences of having to rely on the critics' approval:

The argument put by some was 'You've got to play ball with the critics! This way we will get the carriage trade. We don't really like them, but we need their money and that will subsidise our work for the local people in Stratford.' But it doesn't work like that, life isn't so conveniently organised.

It didn't, of course, work like that. We did, eventually, play to bigger audiences than we'd ever dreamed of, but they weren't the working class we had aspired to bring back to the theatre in 1945. Financial pressures simply forced us to cash in on any success we had, and there's always a ready-made audience waiting to follow the critics. It's a much harder task to create a new audience, to win back the working class to the theatre. It requires resources we simply didn't have, but though we came to rely increasingly on existing theatre audiences, our failure to achieve what we had set out to do was only a partial one. We can claim to have built up some following amongst the working people in the area and certainly introduced hundreds of local children to our sort of theatre.

Harold Hobson, one of the first critics to praise the work of the Company, had, naturally, a different view on the consequences of the move:

We simply don't know what might have happened if Theatre Workshop hadn't come to Stratford. It might have continued touring, going to out of the way places, but even then its energy may have failed. On the other hand, we know that what it did do at Stratford was to revolutionise the British theatre. Going to Stratford may have created a new stimulus. The desire to bring a left-wing theatre into the centre of London, to the very heart of the boulevard and bourgeois theatre is a challenging concept and I think very possibly produced new evidence of strength. I saw no signs of compromise at all, and I think it is more exciting to come to an audience which is not actually hostile, but which is not particularly ready to receive what you are going to say, and has not been brought up against the background of the ideas you are expressing, than to always search out people who are inclined to agree with you anyway. I was a very bourgeois critic, writing for a distinguished newspaper, but what tremendously impressed me was that Joan and Theatre Workshop showed that it was possible to present a left-wing drama that was genial and generous. When we came to Stratford – and I think all my colleagues had the same feeling – we felt we were welcomed as friends. This was very largely due to my old friend Gerry Raffles, who was a magnificent person to have there at the receiving end, and he did spread an atmosphere of sweetness and light, combined with complete loyalty to left-wing principles.

Harold Hobson's description of Theatre Workshop as a left-wing theatre is correct, of course, but it could be argued that some of the plays were *too* 'genial and generous' and would have benefited from a more abrasive quality. Certainly it would have been a mistake to treat a play simply as a vehicle for a political message. Such an approach is completely inhibiting as far as artistic style is concerned and leads inevitably, as in the case of Unity Theatre, to playing to largely converted audiences. There was an overall political and social awareness governing the choice of plays and how they were produced, which gave to all plays, new and classical, a sense of immediacy. The aim was to relate them to the lives of the audience bringing them into contact with the characters and the play, bridging, as far as possible, the gap between stage and auditorium. As a result the Company succeeded in winning a broadly based audience and creating a popular form of theatre rather than one that catered for minority tastes.

Not with a bang ...

Though the title 'Theatre Workshop' was associated with productions at the Theatre Royal until 1978, the Company ceased to exist long before that date. Joan's last production was in November 1973 and in April 1974 Gerry Raffles handed over the running of the theatre to Ken Hill, and this date would appear to define the end of Theatre Workshop. However, insofar as Ken Hill had worked with Joan and the Company and intended to continue the Theatre Workshop style in his direction and choice of plays and actors, it is arguable that his season also forms part of the history. On Gerry's death in April 1975, a steering committee comprising ex-members of the Company and well-wishers was set up by Joan, with the aim of keeping the theatre, now in jeopardy, open and functioning. In July 1975 Maxwell Shaw, formerly an actor in the Company, took over as administrator. In February 1976, Joan left England to make her home in France, and in November of that year, Clare Venables took over the running of the theatre, to be succeeded in November 1979 by Philip Hedley.

The beginning of the end can be traced back to 1961, the year when Joan first left the Company, and also the first substantial break after sixteen years of work. During the next thirteen years there were to be many such breaks, and the Company occupied the theatre for only five years during that period.

Clive Barker felt that, even earlier, changes affecting the way of working had taken place within the Company:

> These impressions are purely subjective, but I felt that from 1955 onwards things had begun to slip. Brian Murphy, Olive MacFarland, myself and others were all brought in at this time, and I think Joan was too tired to begin again creating an ensemble like the one she had kept together through *Arden of Faversham*, *Volpone* and the big breakthrough period. Later, she brought in actors like Victor Spinetti and Roy Kinnear, very fine performers in their own right, but not the ensemble actors she was looking for in the earlier years. In those days, in getting it from an actor, she would be ruthlessly hard, she would only accept what she thought was true. Later, I was conscious of actors getting away with things more and more, as long as they

enjoyed themselves on the stage, and this I think diminished Joan's work considerably. Unlike members of the original Company, people began to see Theatre Workshop in terms of a career.

The peak of Theatre Workshop's achievement was undoubtedly the classical productions of 1954 and 1955 and they were based on the understanding that had been built up between a director and a group of actors over a long period of time. In the late fifties this group dispersed. Actors like Harry Corbett, George Cooper, Joby Blanshard, George Luscombe had to be replaced, and integrating new people into a company takes time. To an extent, this was achieved in productions like *The Quare Fellow* and *Edward II*, only to be followed by the transfers to the West End which again disrupted the work of the Company. Though these successes enhanced the prestige of Theatre Workshop in the eyes of the theatre-going public, it destroyed the continuity of work and the cohesion of the Company. From 1961 onwards there were to be long gaps between seasons, and ad hoc companies were assembled as the occasion demanded. Wherever possible, those who had worked in Theatre Workshop were brought in, but none of the group who had left in the fifties were to return. Would it have been possible to re-constitute a permanent company in the post-West End period? John Bury felt that the circumstances we were then in made this impossible, but Clive Barker disagreed:

After the West End, there was money coming in, no doubt about it. Joan could have taken enough of that loot to set up a company. I think the crucial point was when *The Hostage* came off. I think she could then have offered a salary that was lower than the West End, but enough to live on, and I would have gone back to Stratford, Brian Murphy would have gone back, I'm sure you would have gone, Howard, if you could have got a living wage out of it, and there were others. I think she was just too tired to start again. The interesting thing was that in 1963 she came up with *Lovely War* and after that there was no point in going on – she'd done it. You couldn't do any more in a proscenium arch theatre. You needed a new theatre, and that's when the Fun Palace took off, looking for a new form of theatre. She'd summed up the whole of her work and a great deal of European theatre as well in *Lovely War* and done it brilliantly.

It may well have been possible to re-form the nucleus of a group, but it is doubtful if that would have done more than postpone the evil day. The financial pressures remained, always forcing the Company into a situation of expediency, making any consistent artistic policy impossible, and depriving us of the means of maintaining a regular company. It was not a period of unremitting decline: besides the triumph of *Lovely War* there was also *Mrs. Wilson's Diary*, and at these times one almost felt there was a chance of survival, but the odds were against it. The re-development of the area around the theatre and the battle to preserve the very building itself had sapped the energies of Joan and Gerry, and Gerry's plans for improving the building and constructing music studios, childrens' library and a cinema had all been turned down by Newham Council. The only time they showed interest was when a developer put forward a plan to demolish the theatre and construct an office block with a theatre in the basement.

The tragedy was that Gerry died without ever knowing that his battle for an adequate Arts Council grant for the theatre had been successful.

The influence of Theatre Workshop

The answers I received to the question 'How do you think the work of Theatre Workshop has influenced theatre in this country?' ranged from Peter Hall's view that it was simply not possible to evaluate it, to Harold Hobson's attempt to do so, and the others lay somewhere in between.

Anyone working for any length of time in Theatre Workshop was influenced not only in their approach to work in the theatre but also in their attitude to social and political problems. Hopefully, this remains of positive value when working outside the Group, though in practical terms there would be little scope for adopting the techniques acquired in Group work. In a television and a theatre like ours where, generally speaking, actors are brought together for short periods of time, the result can only be a series of individual performances.

For a designer, the transition is simpler, and John Bury's development can be traced from his early work in Theatre Workshop to his present work at the National Theatre. Peter Hall acknowledged the debt:

> I owe Joan a lot, not only as an inspirer, someone I admire, whose theatre I went to a lot, but because when she came to discuss doing a production at the R.S.C., she brought John Bury with her. The plans didn't materalise but she left him behind. He's been a very important collaborator of mine personally, and I think he did a great deal to make the R.S.C. style of the sixties, and now he's here at the National.

His years in Theatre Workshop have clearly influenced Clive Barker, now a lecturer in Theatre Studies at Warwick University, in his work with students. Similarly, Joan's own work at Hammamet with an international group of students has spread her ideas all over the world.

Singing, dancing and the use of music as an integral part of a production was, before the war, generally confined to 'musicals'. That they are now freely accepted in 'straight' productions could well be attributed to Joan's work. Bill Bryden's promenade productions of *Lark Rise, Candleford* and *The Passion* at the Cottesloe in the National Theatre are examples of this integration of music, song and dance into 'straight' plays, in this case with the creative involvement of the Albion Band.

The extent to which Theatre Workshop influenced other changes that have taken place in British theatre since the war must be, to some extent, a matter of conjecture and opinion. John Wells defines what he sees as part of Joan's contribution:

> She shook people into the realisation that theatre has to be about thinking, what she calls the use of the imagination muscle, the progress by which the actor's imaginings on the stage are transferred to the audience. That is something which I think you will find any person working in the theatre now would agree with. When Joan began working before the war, the idea was to produce beautiful productions in which everything was well oiled and perfect. I think her great contribution was to change the centre of gravity of theatre from what seems to be there to the reality of thinking and the real interpretation of plays.

The last point is particularly important. The aim was to present the *play*, and none of the component parts, costumes, settings, acting and so on were allowed to take precedence. Never were the parts allowed to become more important than the whole. This is now accepted by most directors, in theory at least, though in practice the reliance on star performances or elaborate settings and costumes often comes between the audience and the play itself.

Harold Hobson's view was that certain far-reaching changes in theatre since the war could clearly be attributed to the work of Theatre Workshop:

> The subordination of the voice to physical means of expression, which I saw at the Aldwych by the Royal Shakespeare Company, is a direct result of the methods of production brought about by Joan Littlewood. Also the long discussions between directors and players that now take place everywhere but in certain sections of the commercial theatre. Joan broke up the fabric of the British theatre. She, to a certain extent, disorganised it out of its old forms and began an internal revolution in the theatre in the way that plays were

produced, and the sort of plays that were produced. Also in the way they were written and the way directors and players co-operated with the author. I doubt if there would have been any fringe without Joan ... We now look for our dramatic sustenance elsewhere than in Shaftesbury Avenue, to the fringe, the Repertory Companies and, of course, the National and the R.S.C. I'm convinced this change would never have taken place without the erosion of the bourgeois theatre and its commercial organisation, by Joan.

No-one I spoke to doubted the influence of Joan's productions. Peter Hall saw them as more indirect, through individuals working in the theatre, rather than in any definable specific changes she had helped to bring about:

I doubt whether the leading lights of the fringe know what Joan was, in terms of her work. They know of her reputation. She has a mythical influence, but I think it's so dangerous in the theatre to trace influences, because the theatre changes as we're doing it: you can't refer to the book, it's gone. None of us who were trying to work in the fifties and early sixties could be indifferent to Joan Littlewood, but when you ask 'What has she left?' I doubt if any theatre person can answer that question. I think the theatre is so ephemeral. What anybody leaves is a number of talents that they have influenced. So in a way the tradition goes on.

John Elsom in his book *The Theatre Outside London* suggests that the work of Theatre Workshop encouraged a sense of creative purpose in many provincial theatre companies and played a part in stimulating the interest in regional documentaries. He quotes the Octagon Theatre, Bolton: 'We are intending to appoint a playwright and a musical director so that we can create our own plays in much the same way as Joan Littlewood was doing in Stratford East during the 1950's.' John Elsom also points out that Joan became famous all over the world but that the pub half a mile away from the theatre had never heard of her. To attempt to evaluate individual productions in terms of the influence they may have is an impossible task. Certainly *Oh What A Lovely War* has been and continues to be produced by schools and colleges all over Great Britain and, indeed, all over the world. The work of Peter Cheeseman at the Victoria Theatre, Stoke-on-Trent, John McGrath's 7:84 Theatre Company and Albert Hunt's student and community projects in Bradford offer further examples of the influence of Joan's work, and there are many more.

One thing we know is certain: every aspect of the theatre in Britain has improved beyond measure since the end of the war and there can be no

gainsaying the part Theatre Workshop has played in this revival. The last
words must be given to Joan. They are taken from an article in the
October 1961 issue of *Encore* entitled 'Goodbye Note from Joan'. It
marked the occasion of her first departure from the Company and is as
applicable today as when it was written twenty years ago:

> I do not believe in the supremacy of the director, designer, actor or
> even of the writer. It is through collaboration that this knockabout art
> of theatre survives and kicks. It was true at The Globe, The Curtain,
> The Crown, and in the 'illustrious theatre' of Molière and it can
> work here, today.
>
> No one mind or imagination can foresee what a play will become
> until all physical and intellectual stimuli, which are crystallised in the
> poetry of the author, have been understood by a company, and then
> tried out in terms of mime, discussion and the precise music of
> grammar; words and movement allied and integrated. The smallest
> contact between characters in a remote corner of the stage must
> become objectively true and relevant. The actor must be freed from
> the necessity of making effective generalisations.
>
> I could go on but you too know how the theatre must function if it
> is to reflect the genius of a people, in a complex day and age. Only a
> company of artists can do this. It is no use the critics proclaiming
> overnight the genius of the individual writer; these writers must graft
> in company with other artists if we are to get what we want and what
> our people need, a great theatre.
>
> This does not depend on buildings, nor do we need even a fraction
> of the money they are spending on their bomb. Each community
> should have a theatre; the West End had plundered our talent and
> diluted our ideas; cannot each district afford to support a few artists
> who will give them back some entertainment, laughter and love of
> mankind?

Epilogue

If all the people who have said at one time or another 'I have worked with Joan Littlewood' or 'I have worked with Theatre Workshop at Stratford East' had actually done so, the Company would have been bigger than the Royal Ballet. From the middle fifties and through the sixties the work of the Company was highly regarded in the profession, particularly amongst younger actors and actresses, and Joan became something of a legend. To be able to claim an association with the Company gave one a certain cachet. Over the years there had, of course, been a great deal of coming and going. Some actors stayed for a number of years, forming the basis of the Company. Some came and went over a period of time, others came and left quickly, never to return. Some joined as a result of attending a Summer School, some were auditioned and others were accepted after being recommended by someone who understood the workings of the Company. Choosing people who were able to fit into the work of the Group, and make their own contribution, was obviously more difficult than the usual problem of filling parts to be played in a season. But mistakes were surprisingly rare. It was unusual for an established actor successfully to make the transition into Theatre Workshop. He had his stock-in-trade of well-learned techniques and it took a great deal of courage to jettison these and venture into unknown territory; 'to risk making a fool of yourself' as Joan put it, to start again from scratch, relying, not just on yourself, but being prepared to trust fully the other actors as well. Consequently, recruits usually came from young actors and actresses leaving drama school, like Marjorie (now Marjie) Lawrence:

In 1953, fresh from Drama School in Birmingham, I was doing the rounds of auditions in London. I attended a very crowded audition on New Year's Day 1954. I was told that 112 people were being auditioned in two days. Gerard Dynevor and I were the only two people offered a contract – at £3/10/- per week.

There were those with a few years experience, or with no acting experience or training at all, like David Scase, one of the original Company in 1945:

When we all assembled for the first time I was an odd ball. I mean what the Hell was I doing in a theatre, an ex-sailor? Joan called her untrained people, who had worked in industry, or anywhere else, her industrial cripples, and I was one of these. You set about trying to overcome your deficiencies with voice and movement classes. Joan had been travelling all over the country for the B.B.C. during the war, and I think she had been mentally assembling a company from people she met. I was one, and she brought in Pearl Turner, a beautiful singer. To us, theatre was a totally fresh experience and I think it was that naivety she capitalised on, besides the talent she thought we had, helping to bring a freshness to the Company at that time.

Harry Greene had been a member of his local amateurs and he, too, had had no professional experience:

I was an Art and Crafts teacher in Tredegar in South Wales. I was also in charge of Drama, I'd taken a crowd of kids to see a production of Molière and was thrilled: this was something utterly new to us. After the performance a couple of local amateur people, including myself, stayed behind and helped to load the lorry, and we talked to Joan and Ewan. They wanted a Welshman to play Owen Glendower, a deputy in *The Long Shift*, and someone who could also do stage-management. Joan said 'Have you ever thought of joining a company like this?' I'd never thought about it at all. I thought I'd end up a schoolmaster in South Wales and that was that. My pal was working in the bank, another friend was a police constable – we were destined for that sort of life in the valleys. I don't know why, but as Joan and Ewan talked to me, I could see myself joining the Company. Anyway the next day I gave a month's notice in to the Headmaster. He was astounded, he could not believe it, no-one could believe it: that I was going to pack in a steady fifteen pounds a week as a local Arts and Crafts master. Anyway, I worked a month, left on Friday, and on Saturday.

Without money it was not always easy to think and plan ahead, and newcomers had sometimes to be thrown in at the deep end. Three days after he arrived, Harry was asked, at twelve hours' notice, to take over the part of Duke Theseus in *Midsummer Night's Dream* – curiously enough, a part that Joan had been playing.

Even his experience pales beside the alarming initiation of Benedict Ellis:

I was in my first year at the Central School as a student in Further

Education, and I came up to Ormesby Hall in the summer of 1946 for a week-end. I remember very little about it except movement on the lawn and a lot of crazy eccentric behaviour. Ten days after I'd got back, a telegram arrived which simply said: 'Join us in Leeds, Sunday. You're doing the lighting.' Now I had had nothing to do with lighting whatsoever, and it wasn't until I got up there that I found out what a dimmer was. Alf Smith, who should have been doing what I was supposed suddenly to do, was for some reason or other going to light a pantomime at Manchester Hippodrome. I saw him briefly on the Sunday and he burbled things like 'Remember on so and so, you have to re-plug so and so'. I had never even seen *Johnny Noble* and I had no idea what he was talking about. He gave me a lot of information in the shortest possible time, and it all went in one ear and out the other, because I was in a complete panic about the whole thing. On the script there were notes like 'Spot 2 replug *now*.' But I had no idea where spot 2 was. I was looking at *Johnny Noble* for the first time from twenty feet up, and when the curtain went up, there was supposed to be a spot left and right of the proscenium to light up the narrators. I remember Gerry tearing up the ladder, hissing in a stage whisper 'There are no spots on.' I just didn't know what he was talking about. I didn't know one single scene, and my whole recollection of that night was one of sheer madness. Ewan or Gerry tearing up that ladder and hissing at me 'Kill that on the left' or 'Pull that out, push that in.' I can't imagine what it must have looked like from the Front.

George Cooper, brought in as a replacement in *The Gentle People*, did at least have time to rehearse the part, though he did have to go through the agonies of an audition:

I had been working in a drawing office in Leeds for three years, dreading the exams I'd have to take, so I wrote to Joan, saying I wanted to join the Company. I met Joan, who tried to put me off, saying there was no money, times were difficult, it was a very hard life, and all that sort of thing. I remember trying to impress on her that I'd had a very hard life up to now anyway, and she said she'd contact me when she was holding auditions. This was in October 1949. Then I got a telegram asking me to come over to Manchester, bringing an extract from a modern play, a pair of gym shoes and a pair of shorts, which made my knees tremble somewhat. I got there, said my pieces and stood there, Joan said long afterwards, 'like a fish with a glazed look in my eyes'. Then I had to put on my shorts and gym shoes and do movement with the dreaded Jean Newlove.

Shortly afterwards, I got another telegram which said 'Despite your problems, we have decided to take you for a trial period.'

Harry Corbett had no conventional training as an actor, but had worked in a small repertory company in Manchester for some years:

I wandered into the theatre almost accidentally. No-one said 'You can't go into the theatre', but it wasn't in my social class. The father figure of the district was a tradesman. My ambition was to have a white overall with the name of a garage across the back of it. Then came the war, which shook us all up, and because I'd always fancied a student lady with a scarf on, I thought I'd improve my chances if I went to voice classes. I drifted into repertory; they were desperate for actors in 1947. I worked through rep. for five years with a splendid man called Jimmy Lovell – he later worked with Theatre Workshop. He had good ideas, but we had to give people what they wanted, comic versions of working people, maids with adenoids and so on – it was crap, and together we realised the shoddiness of it all. The highlight of the year was two weeks in Platt Fields doing *Arms and the Man* in the blazing sun with the candles melting.

We were doing a show that needed an outside artist, and David Scase was brought in. As he was leaving, he said 'I've seen you work, listened to you chat, you should work with Joan Littlewood – why don't you go and see her?' You must realise the awful shock this was: to work with a woman – it was unknown in the profession, unbelievable, it was going against the laws of nature. Anyway, I went along to this place in Oxford Road. A very curious house, scrupulously clean in a dirty sort of way. A dirt you can't see, the dirt of all the people who'd lived there and gone away, looking superficially like a slum, but it wasn't, and the people who lived there were all clean. I had just played the repertory actor in *Monday Next*, and I had bought a cheap camel-hair coat for it. It was all I had in the world, this bloody camel-hair coat. I had it belted and slung carelessly round my shoulders. I met Joan and burst out 'Are you a Communist?' And she said 'No, are you a Fascist?' Anyway, I stayed, got chatting, and she offered me Hal in *Henry IV* – no-one in their right mind had ever offered me anything like that. I said 'Yes' little realising that with the nut went the sour outer shell, in this case, Gogol's *The Overcoat*. It was always like that, you never actually agreed to do the two things, but you got on with it – and learned quite a lot, no doubt about that.

Those who had been to drama school tended to find their training of very limited value, as Brian Murphy, who joined in 1955 after an audition, describes:

It was a great shock. Clive Barker and Olive MacFarland, who'd
been at the Old Vic School in Bristol, were also confused, it was an
entirely new technique. Improvisation wasn't taught at R.A.D.A. in
those days. We learned how to cross the stage, how not to make
scissors by crossing each other, feel the seat with the back of your
legs so that you sat down in a gentlemanly manner — this all meant
nothing. Joan threw you back on your own resources, told you to
sing a part, play each other's parts; I didn't know what she was
talking about. There was no way of relating Joan's way of working to
anything you had done in drama school. She put you on the stage and
examined you, not only as an actor, but as an individual; she made
you sing, dance, go through your personal experiences that day, it
was like a third degree.

Others were recommended to the Company. Shirley Dynevor was
brought to Stratford East by her drama school tutor, Brian Way. Barbara
Young worked with Rudolf Laban and he suggested her to Joan. The ten
names mentioned represent, of course, only a fraction of those who
worked, at one time or another, with the Company, but they constitute a
reasonable cross-section. Certainly in the earlier years, no-one joined
because they needed a job, the work was too hard and there was no real
living to be made. They were either attracted by what they had seen or
heard of the work, or were recommended by those who felt that their
particular talent and outlook were best suited to the requirements of
Theatre Workshop. Plays were transferred to the West End with the
Stratford casts, whenever possible. When re-casting had to be done
because members of the original cast were already playing in previous
transfers, established actors or actresses had to be brought in. There were
many who were keen to work with Joan, but they were engaged simply for
a specific part in a specific play. During the later years, some may have
been attracted by the hope of sharing in the successes of the West End
transfers, but by this time, the Group idea was already losing its strength,
and its artistic integrity was weakening.

What happened to all the actors and actresses who came and went over the
years? Many went on to become household names on television and in the
theatre, and they would make up a very starry bill indeed. Rather than
take on the invidious task of drawing up that list I am contenting myself
with a full Cast List in the appendix. Those who wish will find there many
names they will recognise. They will, of course, find even more that mean
nothing at all. Some, perhaps wisely, left the theatre to do other things.
Others swelled the already overcrowded profession and joined in the
struggle for a living. A few went into allied fields of work. Julia Jones and

Henry Livings are now established writers, George Luscombe formed his own theatre in Canada, George Eugeniov established the Teatro Technis for his own Greek-Cypriot community in London, Clive Barker became a University Lecturer in Drama, and John Bury, no longer known as Camel, is head of design at the National Theatre.

What is perhaps more interesting, is the effect that working in Theatre Workshop had on the outlook and attitudes of the individual, and this is not so easy to find out. Some of those I asked were aware of a profound effect. They had developed a greater social and political awareness, which affected their whole attitude to human relationships. Others emphasised discoveries they had made about themselves as individuals and as actors, which had enriched their conception of theatre and their own work as artists. As was to be expected, the closeness of the Group, the hardships, and the greater social and political awareness during the touring days and the early years at Stratford, made a greater impact on the individual than in the later more successful years. Barbara Young did three years of touring:

> When I came out at the end of it, I was a very different person and it affected everything, my attitudes, my way of talking, my opinions and everything I have done since. You benefited from being young. I watched a lot of people get very confused and hurt along the way, but they were older when they came in. In the early days, what I gained was the freedom, a feeling of community, and within that world you lived in, your mind expanded, you discussed politics, and sang folk songs, you did a million things, you actually lived. You didn't just go to work and come back. It was enjoyable and must have been beneficial to you and the people that were watching you, because some of that enjoyment must have been transmitted to the audience.

Brian Murphy was in no doubt that the efforts he had to make to adapt to a complete new concept of theatre were more than worthwhile:

> It was never boring, you learnt a great deal more than just about theatre, you never just talked about the play, you had to know the history, the social, economic and political background. I doubt whether a university could provide what Joan did in Theatre Workshop in those days of 1955. It must have been the richest period any individual could go through, whether interested in theatre or not.

Some struggled to survive, not in the material sense – we all did that – but as an individual in the Group. Harry Corbett, who joined a year before Stratford, did more than survive, he positively flourished:

> We gained a lot, not just the ability to play plays, or to listen to Joan

or read books. I learned about Zionism and Judaism, about politics, about the East German situation. One learned in a curious sort of way, through songs, through meeting all sorts of people. You were educated in food you couldn't afford to buy, we had discussions on food, don't ask me why. One learned different ways of life. I was working-class. I'd never made a fire, my mother had always done it for me. I cleaned the fire out and Camel Bury, who was very middle-class, went berserk, because I hadn't put the cinders back on the fire to burn again. I got an insight into the middle-class way of life. There was Alan Lomax, the American folk singer, enriching one's life with a new set of songs, singing to us right through the night. After leaving Theatre Workshop, the inevitable question was, could I act outside it? Having to work with other people and despising their way of working didn't make for a happy relationship. Also one had to take definitive attitudes e.g. about the way Shakespeare should be played. Not realising that, to a certain extent, it was a passing phase with Joan − quite rightly because she was rediscovering new ways of doing things. However, you were left with an iron-clad attitude, and it took a long time to recover from it and realise there were other ways of doing things.

Like Harry Corbett, we were all enriched by the community life of the Group, but the extent of the involvement was, up to a point, a matter of individual choice. Those who gained a great deal of stimulus from the company of others sought as complete an involvement as possible. Others who needed and valued privacy took a less active part in the social life of the Group, and tended to go their own way, but all were agreed on the benefits of working and training together as closely as possible. As this occupied most of our lives, the practical difference really consisted of cooking for oneself, when finances allowed, rather than communally, and avoiding the chats and singing that sometimes went on into the early hours. One had very little spare time and no financial security, which made for tenuous relations with the outside world, and which perhaps led some of the Group to seek an inner strength, a comfort in each other's company and a drawing together. Curiously enough, it was this interdependence which led many, eventually, to leave. As Harry Corbett put it: 'There comes a time when you can no longer work with Theatre Workshop and Joan. You have to leave or you fall apart − it's sheer self-protection.'

No-one could fail to be enriched by the experience of working with Joan. To what extent depended of course on the individual and the particular period he or she was with the Company. Henry Livings felt his short stay as an actor brought rich rewards:

I joined Theatre Workshop, after an odd audition during which I was required to scythe hay across the stage, at an agreed salary of £8 (I think the current Equity minimum was £12); by some flanker I preferred not to understand, I was paid £4 for rehearsals of *The Quare Fellow*. There was, I think, not a feeling in the business at that time that Stratford E15 was a stepping stone to success and riches that characterised later attitudes. Harry H. Corbett had certainly challenged the Old Vic and John Neville with his simultaneous Richard II, the company had stormed the Paris Festival the previous year with *Arden of Faversham*, a magnificent *Edward II* was to put the lead actor in a psychiatric hospital for a time and out of the theatre permanently. But the company was sinewy and poor. This last was about the only way I fitted.

On mature consideration I should have fitted. Joan's destructive analysis (to Bob Grant: 'I see you're still playing your Edwardian poof'), her steely intelligence (to me, huffing and puffing to represent anger: 'He doesn't want to be angry you know'), and worse, her melting retreats (after she'd demolished a scene in performance by changing all the lines round, in the cause of spontaneity, she offered 'Better wasn't it?' I rejoined that it was the worst fucking seven minutes I'd ever spent onstage. Her eyes softened to clear entrancing blue pools of love, and she murmured 'There has to be a destructive as well as a creative art, you know, they go together'); I was equipped for such battles. I learnt my trade in twice nightly rep., and was used to being thrown in with the script half learnt, gripping the story like a drowning man, busking through, rescuing gags, thinking on my feet. The actors who did best with her at that time (late 50s, early 60s) had a similarly rough theatre background: George A. Cooper, Harry H. Corbett, Eileen Kennally, Dudley Foster, Avis Bunnage, Brian Murphy, Roy Kinnear, Barbara Windsor. Many actors with as much talent, but used to a kinder atmosphere, got no benefit, in some cases were destroyed. The difference, possibly, with me (I make no claim to the acting talent of these giants), was that I was used to improvising through desperation, onstage, in performance. Joan engenders desperation in rehearsal. There's a famous story of Howard Goorney going missing during rehearsals of *Twang*; on his return he started to talk and Joan said no Howard, we've just cut those lines. 'Blimey' said Howard, 'I only went for a pee; it's a good job I didn't go for a shit, I'd a lost my part'. I know such desperation is necessary sometimes, have engineered it myself ... but I'd've thought myself a masochistic fool to *accept* it.

What I did reap, with my imaginary scythe, came to be golden: Joan's punchy, freewheeling stage mechanics (I think of the appalling bowler-hatted bulk of Gerry Raffles in silhouette D.S.L. in

The Quare Fellow calculating the drop, with Brian Murphy as the hangman's assistant singing the hymn 'My brother sit and think/ While yet some time is left to thee' to the concertina ... Myvanwy Jenn dressed as Nurse Cavell in *Oh What a Lovely War*, heartbreakingly alone onstage against blue-lit blacks: breathtaking hokum). Also, and I think most important, her relentless analysis of what is *really* going on: we are on a stage, we are telling a story, now. I remember her rehearsing a charming 'monkey-walk' scene in *Schweik* ... the elegant citizens parading their best clothes to some lovely Smetana (the lull before the storm when Lieutenant Lucash is informed that the pooch he so stylishly walks out was in fact stolen for him from the General by the egregious Schweik); we played it through three times, each time differently. There, said Joan, proud of her Piscator-like mechanistic authority: that's fixed now.

I should like to think one play of mine could catch, just once, the rich texture and the tough purpose she displays again and again. I sent her the script, once, of a play that was currently on at Liverpool Playhouse; 'Good heavens' she replied on one of her baroque runic p/cs, 'What do they do, stand there and recite it?'

Kristin Lind, who came from Sweden to join the Company, expresses, perhaps better than anyone else could, the comfort and help the Group can give to the individual struggling with their own creative problems:

Nothing has meant more to me than the hard working years with Theatre Workshop. Our work and life together articulated the values I had always believed in, and suddenly belonging to a group, fighting together towards the same aim, gave meaning to both theatre and life. This group solidarity is a necessity. Theatre is never one man's work.

It was the togetherness that mattered. To give your best, not only inspired by Joan and Ewan with so much more experience and knowledge, but with the spirit of the Group to urge you on. But in the effort to give your best you often broke down. The road is not an easy one, how many dramas did we not experience side by side with the dramas that we played. The girls in tears, suicidal thoughts, depths of despair. You never seemed to achieve what you expected of yourself.

Then in my most desperate moments, I would get a comforting letter from Joan, which is still an inspiration in all my work ... 'The terrible gulf of despair and fear always appears when you are tackling a creative job. They will grow worse as the years pass. Don't comfort yourself with the thought that they won't. Your work grows in status with each new part you take, so grit your teeth and face the pain of it.

It's always pain, there's no naive joy in creative work ... ' So you grit your teeth, and suddenly one day you get that enormous feeling of having taken a small step forward. Not exactly in becoming an actor, but as a socially and politically conscious person who knows 'which side you're on'. What ups and downs. What patience Joan showed us.

Why then did I leave? How could I leave this world of intense living? Was it the security and protection of a group that made me want to go and test my own wings? Or had the theatre given me such a sense of curiosity that I had to go out into the world to see what experience it had to offer me? Or did I feel a humble longing to try other means of expression that might be more personal? Anyway, leaving the Group, the theatre and England was not easy, but I will always carry on the continuous fight for human rights, the fight for 'All un-named tortured people, all un-named working people' as Joan once wrote.

There can be nothing wrong with a group theatre if all the members work for the same ideals and sincerely dare to express their beliefs in words, song and movement. But every member is also obliged to develop personally and individually and contribute with his ideas and criticism. If you then, as Rudolf Laban wrote, 'are tackling fundamental problems as individual actors and the Group as a whole,' the theatre becomes that true reflection of life it is meant to be. Theatre Workshop has always struggled for that truth.

Appendix

Theatre Workshop and antecedents: a date list

1929   Ewan MacColl (real name: Jimmy Miller) joins Clarion Players in Salford. Left-wing plays conventionally staged.

1931   Ewan forms Salford Red Megaphones. Agitational Propaganda Street Theatre focusing on plight of the unemployed and strikes in the cotton industry.

1934   Joan Littlewood arrives in Manchester. Theatre of Action formed. Theatre moves indoors. Experiments in writing, staging and uses of light and sound, e.g. *John Bullion*.

1936   Theatre Union. Period of intensive training and study. Development of theatrical techniques providing basis for work in Theatre Workshop, e.g. *Last Edition*.

1942   Cessation of active theatre work. Studies continued and contact between individuals maintained.

1945–1953   Theatre Workshop founded. Based successively in Kendal, Ormesby Hall, Manchester and Glasgow. The touring period. Mainly one night stands all over the country, 'taking theatre to the people'. Long rehearsal periods and intensive training. Foreign touring. Work acclaimed abroad but Company relatively unknown in Britain. Ewan MacColl writing for the Company as a member of the Group.

1953   Company moves into Theatre Royal, Stratford East. New production every two or three weeks. Struggle to build a local audience. Very little support from national critics.

1954–1958   Classical productions *Volpone, Arden of Faversham, Richard II* peak of Company achievement, attracted attention of critics leading to build up of non-local audience. Successful visits to the Paris Festival. First small grant from Arts Council in 1956. Several 'old hands' leave the Company during 1955/56.

1958–1961   Period of transfers to West End: *A Taste of Honey, The Hostage* etc. Financial strain eased but Company tied up in long runs leading to Joan's first departure from Company in 1961.

1961–1963   Theatre Royal leased to outside managements.

1963–1964   Joan returns to direct *Oh What a Lovely War*. To official Edinburgh Festival with *Henry IV*.

1964–1967   Theatre Royal leased to outside managements. Joan forms Fun Palace Trust seeking a possible alternative to conventional theatre.

1967   *Mrs. Wilson's Diary* and *The Marie Lloyd Story*.

1967–1970   Theatre Royal leased to outside managements. Re-development of Theatre environs commenced 1968. Joan and Gerry lead efforts to alleviate worst effects through work on playgrounds, workshop instruction etc.

1970   Ken Hill joins the Company. *Forward Up Your End* and *The Projector*.
1970–1972 Theatre closed.
1972–1973 Joan's last productions. Revival of *The Hostage*. *Costa Packet*, *The Londoners* and, finally, *So You Want to be In Pictures*. Ken Hill beginning to take over artistic direction. March 1973: financial crisis.
1974   February: last production before Theatre Royal swamped by re-development of site. Gerry Raffles resigns as General Manager over inadequacy of Arts Council Grant and hands over to Ken Hill.
1975   July: Maxwell Shaw takes over administration of the theatre.
1976   November: Clare Venables takes over from Maxwell Shaw.
1978   The title 'Theatre Workshop' dropped.
1979   November: Philip Hedley takes over from Clare Venables.

Chronology of Plays, Venues and Tours:
1945–1973

1945
August   13–18   Girls' High School. Kendal
            20–25   Victoria Hall. Grange-over-Sands
            28–Sept. 1 Princess Hall. Workington   Repertoire:
September   3–8   Grammar School. Penrith   *Johnny Noble,*
            11–15   St. Michael's Hall. Wigan   *The Flying Doctor*
            18–19   St. John's Hall. Windermere
            20–21   Vicarage Hall. Staveley
            27–29   Masonic Hall. Kirkby Stephen
October   22–24   St. George's Hall. Kendal   Repertoire:
November   1–3   Pavilion. Keswick   *Johnny Noble,*
             8–10   Victoria Hall. Grange-over-Sands   *The Flying*
            31–Dec. 5   Community Hall. Blackburn   *Doctor, Don*
December   27   David Lewis Hall. Liverpool   *Perlimplin*

1946

January	10–12	David Lewis Hall. Liverpool	
	22–23	Community Theatre. Frecheville	
	28–29	Technical College. Bury	
February	4–9	Empire Theatre. Dewsbury	
	18–23	Peoples' Theatre. Newcastle-on-Tyne	
	28–Mar. 2	Miners' Hall. Blyth	
March	4–6	William Newton Hall. Stockton	
	7–9	St. John's Hall. Stockton	
	10–16	B.B.C. House, Gateshead	
	18–20	Folk Hall. New Earswick	
	28–30	Oldenshaw Grammar School. Wallasey	
April	1–6	Miners' Hall. Bolton	Repertoire:
	8–10	Technical College. Bury	*Johnny Noble,*
	22	Community Theatre. Blackburn	*The Flying*
May	2–4	St. John's Hall. Middlesbrough	*Doctor, Don*
	6–8	Y.M.C.A. Stockton-on-Tees	*Perlimplin,*
	13–17	Riley Smith Hall. Leeds	*Uranium 235*
	20–24	Butlin's Camp. Filey	
	27–29	Victoria Hall. Grange-over-Sands	
	30–June 1	Town Hall. Kendal	
June	4–7	Community Centre. Frecheville	
	11–14	Crane Theatre. Liverpool	
September	23–28	Riley Smith Hall. Leeds	
	30–Oct. 10	Little Theatre. Edinburgh	
October	14–26	Queen's Theatre. Glasgow	
November	11–16	Carnegie Hall. Dunfermline	
	18–23	Park Theatre. Hanwell	
	30	St. Pancras Town Hall. London	

1947

January	6–11	St. John's Hall. Middlesbrough	*Operation Olive*
	13–18	Arts Club. Accrington	*Branch*
	27–Mar. 30	Tour of West Germany	*The Proposal,* *Johnny Noble,* *Uranium 235*
June	2–21	Pier Pavilion. Felixstowe	
	23–28	Esplanade Pavilion. Ryde. I.O.W.	*Operation Olive*
July	2–12	Pavilion. Castletown. I.O.M.	*Branch, Johnny*
	14–26	Pavilion. Ramsey. I.O.M.	*Noble, The Flying*
August	4–Sept. 13	Library Theatre. Manchester	*Doctor*
October	7–25	Rudolf Steiner Theatre. London	
December	8–13	Dolphin Theatre. Brighton	*The Gentle People*

1948

July	5–24	Library Theatre. Manchester	*The Other Animals*
September	7–Oct. 12	Tour of Czechoslovakia	*The Other* *Animals, Johnny*
October	13–Nov. 6	Tour of Sweden	*Noble, The Flying* *Doctor*

1949
January–
April   Schools Tour. Manchester   *Twelfth Night*
July   5–24   Library Theatre. Manchester   *Rogues' Gallery*

August   22–Sept. 10   Epworth Hall. Edinburgh   { *The Other Animals, Johnny Noble, The Flying Doctor, Don Perlimplin, The Proposal.*

September   12–24   Library Theatre. Manchester   { *Johnny Noble, The Flying Doctor, Don Perlimplin*

October   4–15   Library Theatre. Manchester   *The Gentle People*
November   Schools Tour. Manchester   *As You Like It*
November   28–Dec. 3   Playhouse. Kidderminster   *The Gentle People*
December   26–31   Theatre Royal. Barnsley

1950
January   2–7   Grand Theatre. Llandudno
               9–14   Theatre Royal. Stratford E.15.
               16–21   White Rock Pavilion. Hastings   *Alice in Wonderland*
               23–28   Alexandra Gardens. Weymouth
               30–Feb. 4   Theatre Royal. Leigh
February   20–25   White Rock Pavilion. Hastings   *The Gentle People*
February   26   Adelphi Theatre. London   } *Johnny Noble,*
               27–Mar. 4   Alexandra. Stoke Newington   } *The Flying*
March   6–11   Kings Theatre. Hammersmith   } *Doctor, Don Perlimplin,*
               12   Adelphi Theatre. London   *The Gentle People*

                               South Wales Tour:
November   27   Fleur De Lis
               28   Rhymney
               29   Ystrad-Mynach
               30   Brithdir
December   1   Bargoed
               2   Deri
               4–5   Aberdare
               6   Cymaman
               7   Wattstown   } *Uranium 235*
               8   Tonypandy
               9   Cymmer Porth
               11   Pentre
               12   Treherbert
               13   Cwmparc
               14   Pontycymer
               15   Bryncethin

1951		*South Wales Tour:*	
January	8	Cwmaman	
	9	Aberdare	
	10	Bedlinog	
	11	Treherbert	
	12	Wattstown	
	13	Cwmparc	
	15	Pentre	
	16	Rhymney	*Landscape with*
	17	Cwmparc	*Chimneys*
	18	Pontycymer	
	19	Bryncethin	
	22	Rhigos	
	23	Colbren	
	24	Resolven	
	25	Gorseinon	
	26	Cwmavon	
	27	Ystradgynlais	
February and March		Tour of Scandinavia	*Uranium 235*
		North East Tour:	
April	17	Remand Home. Aycliffe	
	18	Ferry Hill	
	19	Easington Colliery	
	20	Waterhouses	
	21	Fairfield	
	23	Town Hall. Loftus	
	24–25	Town Hall. Spennymoor	
	26	Miners' Welfare Hall. Crawcrook	
	27	Highfield	
	28	Gosforth	*Uranium 235,*
	30	Welfare Hall. Marley Hill	*Landscape with*
May	1	Miners' Hall. Leadgate	*Chimneys*
	3	Mechanics' Institute. Tow Law	
	4	Spa Pavilion. Saltburn	
	5	Training College. Darlington	
	7–9	Y.M.C.A. Stockton	
	10	Welfare Hall. Wheatley Hill	
	11	Royalty Hall. Sunderland	
	16	Mechanics' Institute. Darlington	
	17	St. Luke's Mental Asylum. Middlesbrough	
	18–19	St. John's Hall. Middlesbrough	
July	16–28	Library Theatre. Manchester	
August	20–25	Oddfellows' Hall. Edinburgh	
	27	Peoples' Festival. Edinburgh	
	28	Town Hall. Tranent	*Uranium 235*
	30	Welfare Hall. Wallyford	
	31	Town Hall. Cowdenbeath	

September	3–15	Oddfellows' Hall. Edinburgh	}	*Johnny Noble,*
	16	Jewish Institute. Glasgow		*The Flying Doctor*

South Wales Tour:

October	1	Ystrad-Mynach	
	2	Rhymney	
	3	Tredegar	
	4	Bargoed	
	5	Blackwood	
	6	Aberdare	
	8	Cwmaman	
	9	Tynewydd	*Johnny Noble,*
	10	Bedlinog	*The Flying Doctor*
	12	Cymmer Porth	
	13	Tonypandy	
	15	Ystrad-Mynach	
	16	Gorseinon	
	17	Resolven	
	18	Ystradgynlais	
	19	Colbren	

	21	Ystrad-Mynach	
	23	Rhymney	
	27	Trecynon	
	29	Cwmaman	
November	1	Cymmer Porth	
	2	Clydach Vale	*Hymn to the*
	6	Gorseinon	*Rising Sun, The*
	7	Resolven	*Long Shift*
	8	Ystradgynlais	
	9	Colbren	
	10	Tonypandy	
	12	Swansea	
	13	Blackwood	

November		Schools Tour	*Henry IV*

1952

North East Tour:

January	14	Loftus	
	15	Bearpark	
	16	Yarm	
	18	Thornaby	
	19	Darlington	
	21	West Hartlepool	
	22	Wheatley Hill	
	23	Horden	*The Long Shift,*
	24	Easington	*Henry IV*
	25	University. Durham	
	26	Durham	
	28	Whiston	
	29	Leadgate	
	30	Marley Hill	
February	1–2	Stockton-on-Tees	

February	4	Darlington	⎫	
	6	Saltburn		*The Long Shift,*
	8—9	Middlesbrough		*Henry IV*
	10	Washington	⎭	
March	24—25	St. Andrews Halls. Glasgow	⎫	
May	12—24	Embassy Theatre. Swiss Cottage, London.		
				Uranium 235
June	2—14	Dolphin Theatre. Brighton		
	18	Comedy Theatre. London	⎭	
August		Oddfellows' Hall. Edinburgh		*The Travellers*
September—November		Schools Tour. Glasgow		*Twelfth Night*

1953

THEATRE ROYAL, STRATFORD

February	2	*Twelfth Night*. Shakespeare	2 weeks
	16	*The Imaginary Invalid*. Molière	2 weeks
March	2	*Paradise Street*. Ewan MacColl.	2 weeks
	16	*Juno and the Paycock*. Sean O'Casey	2 weeks
	30	*Colour Guard*. George Styles	2 weeks
April	13	*Hindle Wakes*. Stanley Houghton	2 weeks
	27	*Arms and the Man*. George Bernard Shaw	2 weeks
May	11	*Lysistrata*. Adapted by Ewan MacColl	2 weeks
	25	*Three Men on a Horse*. George Abbott	2 weeks
June	8	*Anna Christie*. Eugene O'Neill	2 weeks

EDINBURGH FESTIVAL: ODDFELLOWS' HALL

August	24	*The Imaginary Invalid*. Molière	$1\frac{1}{2}$ weeks
September	3	*Uncle Vanya*. Chekhov	$1\frac{1}{2}$ weeks

THEATRE ROYAL, STRATFORD

September	15	*The Imaginary Invalid*. Molière	2 weeks
	29	*Uncle Vanya*. Chekhov	2 weeks
October	13	*The Troublemakers*. George Bellack	2 weeks
	27	*The Alchemist*. Ben Jonson	2 weeks
November	10	*The Government Inspector*. Gogol	2 weeks
	24	*The Travellers*. Ewan MacColl	2 weeks
December	8	*A Christmas Carol*. Adapted by Joan Littlewood	3 weeks
	26	*Treasure Island*. Adapted by Joan Littlewood	3 weeks

1954

January	19	*Richard II*. Shakespeare	2 weeks
February	2	*Van Call*. Anthony Nicholson	3 weeks
	23	*The Dutch Courtesan*. Marston	3 weeks
March	16	*The Devil's Disciple*. George Bernard Shaw	2 weeks
	30	*The Fire Eaters*. Charles Fenn	2 weeks
April	13	*Amphitryon 38*. Giraudoux	3 weeks

May	4	*Red Roses For Me*. Sean O'Casey	3 weeks
	25	*An Enemy Of The People*. Ibsen	3 weeks
June	8	*Johnny Noble* and *The Flying Doctor*. MacColl. Molière	3 weeks
September	7	*Long Voyage Home*. Eugene O'Neill	3 weeks
	28	*Arden Of Faversham*. Anon	3 weeks
October	19	*Cruel Daughters*. Adapted by Joan Littlewood from Balzac	3 weeks
November	9	*The Good Soldier Schweik*. Adapted from Jaroslav Hašek	3 weeks
November	30	*The Chimes*. Adapted by Joan Littlewood from Dickens	4 weeks
December	27	*The Prince And The Pauper*. Adapted from Mark Twain	3 weeks

1955

January	17	*Richard II*. Shakespeare	4 weeks
February	15	*The Other Animals*. Ewan MacColl	2 weeks
March	3	*Volpone*. Ben Jonson	4 weeks
	30	*O'Flaherty V.C.* and *Androcles and the Lion*. George Bernard Shaw	3 weeks
April	19	*The Midwife*. Julius Hay	4 weeks
May	10	*Arden Of Faversham*. Anon.	1 week

PARIS FESTIVAL: THÉÂTRE HÉBERTOT

| May | 19, 20, 21 | *Arden Of Faversham*. Anon. | |
| | 22, 23, 24 | *Volpone*. Ben Jonson | |

DEVON FESTIVAL, BARNSTAPLE

| July | | *Mother Courage*. Bertolt Brecht | |
| | | *Richard II*. Shakespeare | |

THEATRE ROYAL, STRATFORD

September	27	*The Sheepwell*. Lope de Vega	4 weeks
October	25	*The Good Soldier Schweik*. Adapted from Jaroslav Hašek	4 weeks
November	22	*An Italian Straw Hat*. Labiche	5 weeks
December	26	*Big Rock Candy Mountain*. Alan Lomax	2 weeks

SCANDINAVIAN TOUR

1956

| January | 11 | *Arden Of Faversham*. Anon. | 4 weeks |

DUKE OF YORK'S THEATRE, LONDON

| March | 15 | *The Good Soldier Schweik*. Adapted from Jaroslav Hašek | 3 weeks |

THEATRE ROYAL, STRATFORD

| April | 19 | *Edward II*. Marlowe | 4 weeks |
| May | 24 | *The Quare Fellow*. Brendan Behan | 4 weeks |

		THE PLAYHOUSE, OXFORD	
June	25	*The Good Soldier Schweik*. Adapted from Jaroslav Hašek	1 week
		PARIS FESTIVAL: SARAH BERNHARDT THEATRE	
July	7, 8, 9, 10	*The Good Soldier Schweik*. Adapted from Jaroslav Hašek	4 days
		THEATRE ROYAL, BRIGHTON	
July	16	*The Quare Fellow*. Brendan Behan	1 week
		COMEDY THEATRE, LONDON	Closed Sept. 29,
July		*The Quare Fellow*. Behan	1956
		STREATHAM HILL	
October	1	*The Quare Fellow*. Behan	1 week
October	8	PIGALLE, LIVERPOOL	
		The Quare Fellow. Behan	1 week
		ARTS THEATRE, CAMBRIDGE	
October	22	*The Quare Fellow*. Behan	1 week
		THEATRE ROYAL, STRATFORD	
November	27	*Captain Brassbound's Conversion*. George Bernard Shaw	3 weeks
December	24	*Treasure Island*. Adapted by Joan Littlewood	3 weeks
1957 January	16	*The Playboy of the Western World*. J. M. Synge	5 weeks
February	21	*The Duchess Of Malfi*. Webster	3½ weeks
March	20	*School For Wives*. Molière	4 weeks
		ZURICH	
July	2, 3, 4	*Macbeth*. Shakespeare	
		MOSCOW	
		THEATRE ROYAL, STRATFORD	
September	3	*Macbeth*. Shakespeare	5 weeks
October	9	*You Won't Always Be On Top*. Henry Chapman	3½ weeks
		PLAYHOUSE, OXFORD	
November	4	*Macbeth*. Shakespeare	1 week
		THEATRE ROYAL, STRATFORD	
November	12	*And the Wind Blew*. da Rocha Miranda	5 weeks

1958
January 8 — *Man, Beast and Virtue*. Pirandello — 6 weeks

LYRIC THEATRE, HAMMERSMITH
February 17 — *Man, Beast and Virtue*. Pirandello — 3 weeks

THEATRE ROYAL, STRATFORD
February 21 — *Celestina*. Adapted from Fernando de Rojas — $3^1/_2$ weeks
March 20 — *The Glass Menagerie*. Tennessee Williams — $3^1/_2$ weeks
April 15 — *The Man Of Destiny* and *Love And Lectures*. George Bernard Shaw — 2 weeks
29 — *Unto Such Glory* and *The Respectable Prostitute*. Sartre — 4 weeks
May 27 — *A Taste Of Honey*. Shelagh Delaney — 4 weeks
October 14 — *The Hostage*. Brendan Behan — 8 weeks
December 16 — *A Christmas Carol*. Adapted by Joan Littlewood — $2^1/_2$ weeks

1959
January 20 — *A Taste Of Honey*. Shelagh Delaney — 3 weeks

WYNDHAM'S THEATRE, LONDON
February 10 — *A Taste Of Honey* Shelagh Delaney — (Transferred to Criterion on 8 June)

THEATRE ROYAL, STRATFORD
February 17 — *Fings Ain't Wot They Used T'Be*. Frank Norman — 7 weeks

PARIS FESTIVAL: SARAH BERNHARDT THEATRE
April 3, 4, 5, 6 — *The Hostage*. Brendan Behan

THEATRE ROYAL, STRATFORD
April 7 — *Fings Ain't Wot They Used T'Be*. Frank Norman — 2 weeks
24 — *The Dutch Courtesan*. Marston — 3 weeks
May 14 — *The Hostage*. Brendan Behan — $3^1/_2$ weeks

CRITERION THEATRE, LONDON
June 8 — *A Taste Of Honey*. Shelagh Delaney

WYNDHAM'S THEATRE, LONDON
June 11 — *The Hostage*. Brendan Behan — closed 18 July 1960

THEATRE ROYAL, STRATFORD
October 17 — *Make Me An Offer*. Wolf Mankovitz — 8 weeks

NEW THEATRE, LONDON
December 16 — *Make Me An Offer*. Wolf Mankovitz — closed 25 June 1960

		THEATRE ROYAL, STRATFORD	
December	22	*Fings Ain't Wot They Used T'Be.* Frank Norman	7 weeks

1960

		GARRICK THEATRE, LONDON	
February	11	*Fings Ain't Wot They Used T'Be.* Frank Norman	closed 18 Feb. 1962

		THEATRE ROYAL, STRATFORD	
April	6	*Sam, the Highest Jumper of Them All.* William Saroyan	$3^{1}/_{2}$ weeks
May	23	*Ned Kelly.* James Clancy	4 weeks

		PARIS FESTIVAL : SARAH BERNHARDT THEATRE	
June	27, 28, 29, 30	*Every Man in His Humour.* Ben Jonson	

		THEATRE ROYAL, STRATFORD	
July	2	*Every Man in His Humour.* Ben Jonson	4 weeks
August	24	*Sparrers Can't Sing.* Stephen Lewis	10 weeks
November	16	*Progress to the Park.* Alun Owen	9 weeks

1961

January	23	*We're Just Not Practical.* Marvin Kane	3 weeks
March	1	*Sparrers Can't Sing.* Stephen Lewis	$3^{1}/_{2}$ weeks

		WYNDHAM'S THEATRE, LONDON	
March	29	*Sparrers Can't Sing.* Stephen Lewis	closed 6 May 1961

		THEATRE ROYAL, STRATFORD	
June	28	*They Might Be Giants.* James Goldman	4 weeks

1963

January	17	*High Street, China.* Robin Chapman and Richard Kane	$6^{1}/_{2}$ weeks
March	19	*Oh What A Lovely War.* The Company	4 weeks

		WYNDHAM'S THEATRE, LONDON	
June	20	*Oh What A Lovely War.* The Company	closed June 1964
December		*Merry Roosters Pantomime*	

		THEATRE ROYAL, STRATFORD	

1964

March	10	*A Kayf Up West.* Frank Norman	

EDINBURGH FESTIVAL: ASSEMBLY HALL

August	17	*Henry IV*. Shakespeare, adapted by Joan Littlewood from parts I and II	3 weeks
Oct.–Dec.		*Oh What A Lovely War* in U.S.A.	

THEATRE ROYAL, STRATFORD

1967
April   8   *MacBird*. Barbara Garson
May   24   *Intrigues and Amours*. Vanbrugh
September   21   *Mrs. Wilson's Diary*. John Wells and Richard Ingrams

CRITERION THEATRE, LONDON

October	24	*Mrs. Wilson's Diary*. John Wells and Richard Ingrams	closed 1 June 1968

THEATRE ROYAL, STRATFORD

November   28   *The Marie Lloyd Story*. Daniel Farson and Harry Moore

1970
October   1   *Forward Up Your End*. Ken Hill
December   6   *The Projector*. John Wells

1972
March   29   *The Londoners*. Stephen Lewis
May   26   *The Hostage*. Brendan Behan
July   21   *The Ffinest Ffamily In The Land*. Henry Livings
October   6   *Costa Packet*. Frank Norman
December   29   *Big Rock Candy Mountain*. Alan Lomax

1973
February   17   *Is Your Doctor Really Necessary?* Ken Hill
May   11   *Sweeney Todd*. C. G. Bond
June   8   *Nuts*. The Company
November   16   *So You Want To Be in Pictures*. Peter Rankin

Theatre Workshop cast list

I have tried to make sure that this list includes everybody who was ever a member of Theatre Workshop but fear that, inevitably, there will be some omissions, and for these I apologise. A note to me, care of the publishers, from anyone whose name is missing will ensure their inclusion in future editions.

H.G.

Delia Abraham
Louis Adams
Peter Agello
Tamba Allen
Donald Allison
Yvonne Ambler
John Armitstead
Peter Armitage
Jan Arnold
Liz Ashwell

Kent Baker
Clive Barker
Roy Barnett
Barbara Barrett
Bryn Bartlett
John Bay
Amelia Bayntun
Ann Beach
Tom Bell
Helen Belov
Edmond Bennett
Gerard Benson
Jo Benson
Jeffrey Bernard
Barry Bethel
Edward Bishop
Carmen Blanck-Sichel
John Blanshard
Jean Boht
Anthony Booth
James Booth
Jill Booty
Ann Bowdler
Richard Bowdler
Harold Bowen

Ronald Bowman
Ruth Brandes
Gloria Bremnor
Peter Bridgemont
Patricia Broderick
Ron Brooker
Barbara Brown
Gaye Brown
James Bunstead
Avis Bunnage
Bernadette Burguin
John Bury
Margaret Bury
David Butler
Malcolm Butterworth

Edward Caddick
Isla Cameron
Susan Cameron
Fanny Carby
Michael Caridea
Sandra Caron
Edna Carson
Lilian Carter
David Case
Stephen Cato
Peter Chalke
Robin Chapman
David Charkham
Tom Chatto
Peter Childs
Angela Christopher
Sonia Chung
Mavis Clavering
Barry Clayton
Peggy Ann Clifford

Tom Cockrell
Frank Coda
Michael Coles
Frank Colley
Patience Collier
Una Collins
Gerry Connolly
Jean Conroy
George Cooper
Fred Cooper
Harry Corbett
Barbara Cording
Judy Cornwell
Terry Coster
Brian Cronin
Carmel Cryan
Frances Cuka
Richard Curnock

Peter Dalton
Maureen Daly
Lyn Darell
James Dark
Larry Dann
Stephen Dartnell
Nigel Davenport
Griffith Davies
Mary Davies
Bill Davidson
Philip Davis
Jean-Christophe Dejey
Shelagh Delaney
Nicholas Denney
Bettina Dickson
Paola Dionisotti
Trudi Van Doorn

Peter Doughty
Keith Dowling
Prudence Drage
Eileen Draycott
Rex Dultin
Davina Dundas
Colin Dunn
Ivor Dykes
Gerard Dynevor
Shirley Dynevor

Wallas Eaton
Glynn Edwards
Frank Elliot
Jack Elliot
Benedict Ellis
Deidre Ellis
George Eugeniov
John Evans

Barbara Ferris
Terence Finlayson
Grace Fisher
Tom Fletcher
Carl Forgione
Carol Ann Ford
Denis Ford
Michael Forrest
Dudley Foster
Francis Fowler
Eric Francis
Brian Freeland
Derek Fuke
Peter Furnell

Turia Gandhi
Kenneth Gardiner
James Garrett
Carol Gibson
George Giles
James Gilhouley
Robert Gillespie
Phyl Gladwyn
Julian Glover
Jeanne Goddard
Renee Goddard
Roy Godfrey
Bernard Goldman
Maurice Good
Rosalind Goodger
Clive Goodwin

Howard Goorney
David Gordon
John Gower
Roger Grainger
John Grange
Bob Grant
Vivien Grant
Harry Green
Teddy Green
Eleanor Griswold
Philip Grout
Bill Grover
Norman Gunn

Ron Hackett
John Hands
Janice Hardiman
Timothy Harley
Richard Harris
George Harvey-Webb
Nigel Hawthorne
John Hayes
Lorna Heilbron
Robert Henderson
Ellis Hill
Ken Hill
Tony Holland
Marie Hopps
Edward Horton
Ray Hoskins
Martine Howard
Jenny Howe
Bryan Hulme
Barry Humphries
Joyce Hutchinson

Clare Isbister
Michael Ivan

Godfrey James
Myvanwy Jenn
Nadine Jennings
Keith Johnson
Rosemary Johnson
Ian Jones
Julia Jones
Ken Jones
Pamela Jones
Shirley Jones
Paddy Joyce
Yootha Joyce

John Junkin
Miriam Karlin
Maurice Kaufmann
David Kelly
Colin Kemball
Will Kemp
Merelina Kendall
Eileen Kennally
John Keogh
Roy Kinnear
Roberta Kirkwood
Alan Kitching
Gertan Klauber
Anna Korwin

Felicity Lam
Diana Langton
Mary Larkin
Marjorie Lawrence
Martin Lawrence
Beverly Lawson
Dilys Laye
Ori Levy
Kristin Lind
Joan Littlewood
Henry Livings
Joe Lloyd
Arnold Locke
Philip Locke
Jenny Logan
Joan Loughnane
Jimmy Lovell
Dick Loveless
David Ludman
George Luscombe
Alfred Lynch
Christine Lynch
Penny Lynch
Sean Lynch
Patricia Lyon
Johnny Lyons

Ewan MacColl
Sylvester McCoy
John McEvoy
Olive MacFarland
Shelia Macintosh
Michael McKevitt
James McLoughlin
Grace MacNeil
John Maitland

Mikki Manuel
Rita Margo
Derek Marlowe
Andreas Markos
Joyce Marshall
Barry Martin
Hilary Mason
Daniel Massey
Isaac Matalon
Stella Maude
Murray Melvin
Robert Mill
Martin Miller
Jimmie Moore
Rick Morgan
Leonard Morris
Bernard Morton
Margery Moyne
Declan Mulholland
Neville Munroe
Brian Murphy
Alex Murray

Clovissa Newcombe
Jean Newlove
Anthony Nicholson
David Nott
Alan Nunn
Brian Nunn

Michael O'Brian
Bernard O'Connell
Kathleen O'Connor
Eric Ogle
Brian O'Higgins
Colette O'Neil
Elizabeth Orion
Bill Ormond
Michael O'Sullivan

Joyce Palin
Kevin Palmer
Toni Palmer
Judith Paris
Clifford Parrish
Wally Patch
Ian Paterson
Rudi Paterson
Jimmy Perry
Joan Pethers
Tom Pounder

Joseph Powell
Mary Preston
Israel Price
Bryan Pringle
Jack Pulman

Gerry Raffles
Ataur Rahman
John Rainer
Peter Rankin
John Rapley
John Reece
Peter Reeves
Malcolm Reid
Bernard Rice
Stella Riley
James Rist
Annette Robertson
Tony Robinson
Tracy Rogers
Jon Rollason
Edward Roscoe
Margaret Russell
Mark Russell

Pam St. Clement
Celia Salkeld
Kathryn Sansom
Jill Sayer
David Scase
Kenneth Scott
Helen Segal
Tony Selby
Nina Baden Semper
George Sewell
Maxwell Shaw
Mary Sheen
Jackie Sheffield
Jean Shepheard
William Sherwood
John Sichel
Pauline Siddall
Milton Sills
George Sloman
Peter Smallwood
Harry Smith
Kevin Smith
Trevor Smith
H. Verity Smith
Jeremy Spenser
Francis Spinetti

Victor Spinetti
Charles Stanley
John Steed
Bob Stevenson
Margherita Stone
Sheila Storri
Dudley Sutton
Gordon Sutton
Maureen Sweeney

Oscar Tapper
Harry Tardios
Laurie Taylor
Eirlys Thomas
Michael Thompson
Royston Tickner
Alan Townsend
Jenny Townsend
Derek Toyne
Alan Travell
Sally Travers
Patrick Tull
Charles Turner
Pearl Turner
Meir Tzelniker

Ernst Ullman

Gaby Varley
Peter Varley

John Wallbank
Bill Wallis
Valerie Walsh
Doreen Warburton
Rita Webb
Veronica Wells
John Wells
Billie Whitelaw
Nicholas Whitfield
Josephine Wilkinson
Clifford Williams
Glen Williams
Rosalie Williams
Donald Wilson
Barbara Windsor
Jimmy Winston
Karl Woods
Joan Worth

Barbara Young

Finances

Arts Council Grants

'And so Joan had a lifetime of patching and stitching together bits and pieces and making do, and inside I always felt that her heart yearned for something better. We had to do the Molière without ballet shoes, without proper costumes, so all we had were tights with bits of ribbons tied round, and the critics made such a song and dance about how brilliant this was. This must have galled her – she must have wanted to say "I would have put bloody costumes on if we could have afforded the sodding things".'

Harry Corbett

FINANCIAL YEAR	THEATRE WORKSHOP	ENGLISH STAGE COMPANY	
1954/55	£150		
1955/56	£500		
1956/57	£500		
1957/58	£1,000		
1958/59	£1,000	£5,500	
1959/60	£1,000	£5,000	
1960/61	£2,000	£8,000	
1961/62	£2,000	£8,000	
1962/63	£3,000	£20,000	
1963/64	£3,000	£20,000	(plus £15,000 capital expenses)
1964/65	nil	£32,500	
1965/66	nil	£50,555	
1966/67	nil	£88,650	
1967/68	nil	£100,000	
1968/69	nil	£98,300	
1969/70	nil	£98,050	
1970/71	nil	£99,596	
1971/72	£10,000	£105,400	
1972/73	£41,000	£120,771	
1973/74	£46,900	£137,730	
1974/75	£60,500	£181,927	
1975/76	£80,500	£196,738	
1976/77	£87,000	£241,200	
1977/78	£89,645	£250,510	
1978/79	£108,765	£305,000	

The English Stage Company at the Royal Court Theatre were, of course, performing a different function from that of Theatre Workshop. Listing their grants, however, serves to indicate the money that was being made available over the period to a Company whose needs were certainly no greater than Theatre Workshop's. A quote from Irving Wardle's book *The Theatres of George Devine* is revealing:

> Their grant did go up from £20,000 to £32,500 in 1965. 'The shoe string we started with' Devine told the Press 'has turned into a bootlace. With Wilson's assistance may it blossom into a small rope.'

I wonder how Devine would have described Theatre Workshop's £3,000 withering to nothing that same year.

Local Authority Grants

	1957/58	1958/59	1959/60	1960/61	1961/62	1962/63	1963/64
Barking	£137/10/-	£250	£250	£250	£250	£250	£250
Bethnal Green	£87/10/-	£100	£100	£100	£100	£100	£100
East Ham	–	£100	£100	£100	£100	–	–
Hackney	£137/10/-	£300	£300	£300	£300	£300	£450
Leyton	£137/10/-	£150	£150	£150	£150	£150	£250
Poplar	£50	£50	£100	£100	£50	£200	£200
Shoreditch	£137/10/-	£200	£200	£200	£200	£200	£200
Stoke Newington	–	–	–	–	£50	£100	£100
Stepney	–	£150	£150	£150	£150	£300	£150
Walthamstow	£137/10/-	–	–	–	–	–	–
West Ham	£137/10/-	£150	£150	£150	£150	£200	£150
L.C.C. (London County Council)	–	–	–	£1,500	£1,500	£1,500	£1,500

Financial Situation: January 1964

An extract from the minutes of the Annual General Meeting of the Theatre Royal Advisory Council, the body set up by Local Authorities in the area, held on 22 January 1964:

Is there a Future for the Theatre Royal?
Mr. Raffles told the meeting that after going through the accounts the inescapable conclusion he had reached was that it was no longer possible financially to run the Theatre Royal.

Since its formation (three financial years) Theatre Workshop (Stratford) Ltd. had made a profit of £50,696 from activities outside the Theatre Royal. The intention was always that one half of any profits should be used for the maintenance of the Theatre Royal and the other half should form a reserve to use for the furtherance of the Theatre Workshop idea in other places.

However, the Theatre Royal had cost so much to keep in operation that more than £36,000 had had to be paid over to settle the overdraft of Pioneer Theatres Ltd., the company running the Theatre Royal.

At present Pioneer Theatres Ltd. had a current overdraft of about £14,500 and the total bank balance of Theatre Workshop (Stratford) Ltd. was about £16,000.

This meant that even taking into account the grants likely to be received from the Local Authorities, the London County Council and the Arts Council, it was very unlikely that there would be anything left at all in either company's account at the end of the current financial year.

With productions costing approximately £4,000 each to mount it was not feasible to face future activities without any reserve or financial security. As an example, during the previous four weeks, the running loss on the shows totalled £517.6.od. – in addition to maintenance costs during that period of £110 per week.

In the circumstances *A Kayf Up West* which would open at the Theatre Royal on 10 March would be the last Theatre Workshop presentation at the theatre. For so long as it was possible to let the theatre to outside managements, the Theatre Royal would be kept open and after that it would be closed. No grants would be applied for in 1964/65 as £30,000 was needed to run the theatre for a year, and it was not possible to do it on any less.

Financial Situation: January 1974

In January 1974, Gerry Raffles made what was to be his last plea on behalf of the Theatre Royal:

The Theatre Royal, Stratford, by its location and reputation is the regional dramatic centre of a densely populated area which has no other professional theatre.

It is also immediately surrounded by a new development scheme of shops and offices.

We have been here for twenty-one years, but we think that it is not worth keeping the theatre alive any longer without four things:

(1) A subsidy adequate to enable a permanent company of actors and technicians to be formed and kept. Having to keep recruiting ad hoc companies makes it impossible to keep up the standards we have set in the past.

(2) Storage for the sets and costumes. Because our stores have been demolished by the redevelopment we have to destroy or give away very expensive sets and costumes at the end of each production because we have nowhere to keep them.

(3) The area immediately outside the theatre needs to be cleaned up and made attractive enough for an audience to cross. The Council would not let the new shops in the precinct until their pavements were decent. Why should the theatre be treated worse?

(4) The provision of more leisure facilities adjacent to the theatre. The huge office blocks which surround us have hidden the theatre from passers-by. Unless there are other attractions close to us the only local people who will know the Theatre Royal will be those who were born before the redevelopment.

If the nine local boroughs whose population we serve and the Arts Council consider that the cost of having a Theatre in East London to be more than they can afford, then from the new financial year, on April 1st, we will find some other place or some other way to continue our work and will leave the Theatre Royal to be a historically preserved wreck of a once beautiful theatre.

Company Meetings

The following sets of minutes, taken down in long hand by Gerard Dynevor, came to light while I was collecting material for this book. Printed here without alteration, they give a fair picture of the nature of the items discussed at meetings which took place at intervals during the first five years or so at Stratford.

H.G.

31 March 1955

AGENDA
1. Constitution and function of members of Group. (Joan)
2. Future.
3. Paris.
4. End of Season.
5. Bideford.
6. Warsaw.
7. Next season.
8. Appeal.
9. Equity.

FINANCIAL REPORT

GERRY   Not possible to give full financial report on *Volpone*.
£50 of Yardley income spent before Christmas.
£110 L.C.C. *Androcles* booking paid last season's rent.
There is a fairly constant debt of £400.
Other Animals left us with £1,000 debt (owed to brewers – printers – Nat. Ins. etc.) Now largely back to normal.
Of the £390 rent due between Christmas and June this year £95 has been paid.
John B. raised query about *Volpone* wages. Gerry read following figures:

1st week	Income at doors	£210 (inc. Yardley)
	Gross income	£358
	Wages to Company	£85.10.0d.

Theatre running expenses are approx. £140.

2nd week	Income doors	£228
	Gross	£315
	Wages to Company	£99.15.0d.
3rd week	Income doors	£270
	Gross	£370
	Wages to Company	£125
4th week	Income doors	£339 (including £10 *Androcles*)
	Gross	£405
	Wages to Company	£115

Howard pointed out that the £140 running expenses should not include rent since this has not been paid.

GERRY.	There are more people in the theatre for the *Midwife* than can be paid a living wage.
HARRY C.	Thought £3 minimum wage inadequate. Suggested £4 would be more realistic.
GERRY.	Yardley's paid £25 per night and extras. Company has received £96 from the Arts Council for advertising. Six weeks trial. Future of grant uncertain.
JOAN.	Suggested that it is time to take another 'census' of the audience.
GERRY.	It had been suggested to him that he had a 'boss complex' and asked the Company to voice its opinions. Gerard said he felt uninformed about Company affairs – perhaps because the previous Company meeting had been held so long before. Joan considered that there was disunity in the Company. She said that criticism should be public and that often decisions made by the Company are arbitrarily overruled by Gerry. She said that there seemed to be two, often antagonistic, blocs – the Management and the Company and that we must find a democratic way of working. Howard considered that a vital subject was being discussed flippantly and the important issue obscured.
JOAN.	The differences between the Art Directors was not ready for group discussion. She asked what were the rights of the Company and said that any criticisms of 'ways and means' should be made in Public. Company decisions are binding.
CAMEL.	Suggested that newcomers should receive their wages in an envelope. The Company didn't feel any loss of dignity in queueing for wages. Joan raised Gerry's allocation of money to various departments – Gerry and Camel felt it a matter for production meeting.
MAX.	Criticised Gerry's attitude when giving complimentary tickets. Everyone to be allowed two a week except Saturdays. He said that he had been trying to find another company with which to exchange on a monthly basis but that at the moment it was impractical. There was a chance of certain London managements co-operating with us.
PARIS.	Financial terms: Pay our expenses, take all the takings. The Company will be asked to sign a document saying that they have been paid in advance to avoid having to place a deposit with Equity.
BIDEFORD.	Doubt about the rights of *Mère Courage*. Gerry to report at next Company meeting. If we do play *M.C.* it will probably transfer to West End.
WARSAW.	Polish Youth offered us accommodation. World Federation of Democratic Youth offered to pay expenses except for £15 a head. We would only be called upon for six performances and would take a new Ballad Opera by Ewan and a classic. There would be opportunities to tour from Warsaw. George Luscombe and Howard asked to manage Warsaw. Howard wanted to examine situation before accepting. Camel suggested special meeting to deal with Warsaw.
DOMESTIC ISSUES.	1. Harry S. to fix light outside lavatory by costume room. 2. Lavatory O.P. disgraceful state – cleaners to leave toilet paper.

3. Company asked not to leave bottle tops in shower. Dierdre appointed to look after it.

4. S.M. to be firmer with backstage visitors.

5. Friends at photo-calls sit at back of auditorium.

Gerry undertook to stop the turning out of emergency lights in the auditorium during the last act.

A man should be posted to the gallery to deal with occasional rowdiness.

Harry C. was appointed as liaison with costumes for Paris.

F.O.H. needed more efficient signposting.

A more efficient method of re-seating audiences after intervals was necessary.

Because of the enormous amount of work to do for Paris, Camel was given authority to ask for work when he needed it with the proviso that the 24 April (A.G.M.) was left free.

Read and passed. Chairman –
(signed) George Cooper

21 April '55

21 April 1955

George C. in the chair.

BIDEFORD. Rights *Mother Courage* still doubtful – situation re *Mother C.* and Bideford fluid.

WARSAW. Howard had had discussion with Ewan. Suggestion that Company doesn't go as 'Theatre Workshop' but as individuals.

F.O.H. Impractical to post man in gallery. F.O.H. still needs signposting. Israel to look after shower.

FINANCE. Week ending 19 April:

Gross doors	£149.17.11d.
Staff Wages	£53
Company Wages	£88.10.0d.

Situation this week grim with 24 on books.

PHOTOS. Harry C. suggested Company gives J. Spinner present at end of season as some return for his free work.

HABEN [*The Midwife*] Howard thought financial problem could have been ameliorated by audience organisation. Gerry stated that there were more party bookings for this play than any other season.

APPEAL. Gerry thought Appeal Fund would have to be used to subsidise wage. There would only be 30/- to £2 per person this week. Howard and Joby were violently opposed this proposition and said that Gerry had been opposed to the appeal from the start and seemed to do everything in his power to oppose it. Howard submitted that the fund was administered by a committee subject to the Company and completely independent of the Management of the Theatre. There was a fracas over putting out the collecting boxes on the first night of *Haben*. Gerry said that it was tactless to ask our first night audience containing so many Press to contribute to the appeal fund. Howard maintained that he was attempting to carry out a Company decision. Gerry said that he was reconciled to the appeal continuing for the remainder of the season.

HOWARD.	The appeal is a welfare fund. It will just last this season and start off next. The emergency was too big for the appeal to help it without being used up. He added that there was a basic problem to solve and it was stupid to go on plugging holes.
HARRY.	A vote should not be taken on using the appeal until the root of the problem had been dug up.

A decision was taken to accept wages and to call a meeting on Monday or Tuesday.

DENTIST.	Camel suggested that in view of the level of wages dental bills should be paid by appeal fund.
GERRY.	Elastic consciences!

Decision was made that people with bills dating from *Richard II* could ask for a grant.

DOMESTIC ISSUES.	Harry C. appointed liaison with wardrobe.
HARRY.	Eddie was a man brought into a position of authority (S.M.) in the Company whose attitude cut right across the usual unregimented way in which we worked.
GERRY.	Would raise matter with Camel.
GERRY.	Noise backstage appalling.
COMPANY.	Very dangerous stairs Prompt side – highly polished, badly lit.
SHIRLEY.	Complained at the continual lateness of audiences and said that by holding the curtain for them we encouraged their lateness. Said that doors between lavatories and auditorium (P. side circle) should be kept shut. Programme girls should not be dressing in W. wing.
CAMEL.	Requested that the pigeon that had built a nest in a fire bucket should be respected.
GERRY.	Electric light being wasted backstage.
JOBY.	Star billing on Paris programmes was contrary to Company policy.
COMPANY DECISIONS.	Gerry did not answer Joan's question as to whether Company decisions were binding on him.
MAY DAY.	Gerry opposed to the Group taking part in direct political activity.
JOAN.	Suggested that in view of the state of the world the Company should discuss its attitude to taking part in political demonstrations; and then withdrew the proposal as being premature.
WARSAW.	Idea of taking two shows abandoned. Ewan would use as many actors as were able to go.

Meeting adjourned for lunch 1.30 – 2.30.

* * * * *

Meeting resumed 2.35.

TIME OFF.	Because of the pressure of work there would be no complete days off

for the Company as a whole. Rehearsals would be staggered to ensure as much free time for individuals as possible.

There were two extraordinary meetings held: one on first night of *Haben*, the second after D.R. of *Arden* to authorise Howard to pay £2 per head from the appeal fund to supplement wages.

Tuesday 31 May 1955

Barry in the chair.

(Camel, Joan, George C., Shirley, John B. Absent.)

AGENDA.	Paris; Pepito; Immediate Future; Devon; Warsaw; Summer Break.
GERRY.	Paris has done immeasurable amount of good to the prestige of the Company throughout the world.
	Financially expenses about £620 (200 fare, 400 wages). We left with £750. Last two performances paid the expenses of the two extra days in Paris. These two days enabled us to make further valuable contacts.
	Hébertot holds 500. Our receipts were per performance: £49; £180; £160; £180; £25; £25.
	A newspaper strike at the crucial moment prevented publicity for the two extra performances.
	Company invited to return to next year's Festival. We now have an agency in Paris for all foreign tours.
GEORGE L.	Criticised apparent lack of arrangements for Company's arrival in Paris and our being left in a strange city to find our way to our hotel.
SPANISH FIESTA.	Excise refused to waive entertainment tax. *Spanish Fiesta* were on a guaranteed minimum of £50 per week. They did not take this sum and we should have to find it. How much exactly Gerry did not know.
PEPITO.	The first week's wages would have to come out of Friday's and Saturday's performances. Arts Council has offered £100 guarantee against loss.
BANKRUPTCY.	Theatre Workshop Ltd. now wound up. At the moment Company technically employed by a committee of the four directors. Future Company will be called Theatre Workshop Drama Group Ltd. Made bankrupt by Mavis Clavering — ex member of Group. Present trading debt about £1,000.
IMMEDIATE FUTURE.	
GERRY.	Joan labouring under the three-fold strain of adapting, producing and playing *Mother Courage*. Company should strive to be doubly co-operative.
GEORGE L.	Submitted that she was in a ridiculous situation.
GERRY.	Agreed, but said much of the strain was due to external pressures. e.g. bringing forward of Paris date and Bideford insisting on *Richard II* as well as *Mother Courage*. Bideford has a £500 guarantee for us.
WARSAW.	Howard engaged in trying to raise money and finding a place to run in the play. Leave for Warsaw about 25 July. Festival ends 11 August.
SUMMER BREAK.	Date for next season's opening vague. Possibly early September. Whole of future season depends on many possible happenings.
EQUITY.	Next season everyone must be on contract and two weeks wages deposited.

Index